THE POLITICS OF DECISION-MAKING

Volume 34, Sage Library of Social Research

SAGE LIBRARY OF SOCIAL RESEARCH

The Politics of Decision-Making

Strategy, Cooperation, and Conflict

ALLAN W. LERNER

Introduction by MARTIN LANDAU

Foreword by HARMON ZEIGLER

Volume 34
SAGE LIBRARY OF
SOCIAL RESEARCH

 SAGE PUBLICATIONS   Beverly Hills   London

Copyright © 1976 by Sage Publications, Inc.

For information address:

SAGE PUBLICATIONS, INC.
275 South Beverly Drive
Beverly Hills, California 90212

SAGE PUBLICATIONS LTD
St George's House / 44 Hatton Garden
London EC1N 8ER

Printed in the United States of America

Library of Congress Cataloging in Publication Data

Lerner, Allan W
   The politics of decision-making.

   (Sage library of social research; v. 34)
   Bibliography: p.
   1. Decision-making in public administration. 2. Government
consultants. I. Title.
JF1525.D4L47   350   76-22632
ISBN 0-8039-0694-3
ISBN 0-8039-0695-1 pbk.

FIRST PRINTING

TO
LAURIE

CONTENTS

ACKNOWLEDGMENT

I would like to thank the following people for allowing me to stand on their shoulders, so that I might get a clearer view of the important issues and how they might be treated, for their readiness to catch me when I lost my balance, and for their encouragement: Laurie Lerner, Tom Hovet, Joe Allman, Brent Rutherford, Dick Hill, Judy Merkle, Art Hanhardt, L. A. Wilson, Harlan Strauss, Gus Alef, Marty Landau, and Harmon Zeigler. Of course, they are blameless for what I misperceived or failed to see.

Thanks also to Craig Miller and Mike Shimoda for serving as the "confederates" of Chapter 2, and to the University of Georgia Press for cooperating in my use here of a portion of my contribution to R.T. Galembiewski (ed.), *Two Decades of Small Group Research in Political Science* (Athens, Georgia: University of Georgia Press, 1976) in Chapter 2.

And special thanks to Rhoda Blecker for helping to turn a pile of papers into a book.

INTRODUCTION

It is now commonplace to observe that ninety percent of all scientists who ever lived are alive now. It is now cliche to state that ours is an age of expertise. Nor is it a surprise to record that our problems—education, health, transportation, production, and distribution—require the utilization of knowledge far beyond the grasp of the ordinary person. Such properties of contemporary society have given rise to fears that expertise threatens to displace politics, that our visions are those of the expert, and that a technical-administrative state will subvert systems of democratic values by the sheer force of technology. Whatever the merit of such claims, it seems clear that expert and politician are now locked into an interdependence that has become a critical feature of our public decision process.

This is the problem domain that Professor Lerner addresses, and he does so with a graceful sophistication. Defining decision-making as a collective, political process based on the interaction of politician and expert, Lerner proceeds to provide an analysis of the dynamics of organizational decision-making—i.e., of bureaucratic politics. Informed by a firm grasp of interdisciplinary factors which bear on the problem, Lerner has produced a powerful and enlightening work. A lot of knowledge has gone into this book—of social psychology, political science, public administration, and organization and decision theory—and it has been constructed in a controlled and sustained manner, supported by a methodological diversity that renders his arguments all the more powerful. At a time when so many mistake recapitulations for thought and jargon for analysis, Lerner's book is a refreshing experience.

Students of public administration will find that Lerner's treatment of the collective decision process in bureaucracy is invaluable in the consideration of such problems as line and staff, the role of the expert, specialist-generalist cross-pressures, the interface of authority and power, and the concepts of administration as science and as politics. While students of politics will find much to learn from his descriptions of the dynamics of public policy-making and the parametric factors which bind it.

It needs also to be said that Lerner succeeds in combing a rigorous format with an elegance of expression that is as felicitous as it is clear.

Martin Landau

FOREWORD

The political influence of technological elites has captured the imaginations of social scientists, and for good reason. In a technological age, especially one in which the conservation of scarce resources replaces the distribution of abundant resources as a focus of policy, elected officials are required to deal with issues containing components too sophisticated for them to comprehend. Thus they turn to experts for information, and the experts' knowledge is easily transformed into a political resource for the acquisition of influence. Recognition of the growing importance of experts has caused social scientists to re-evaluate their empirical and normative models of public policy formation.

Traditional democratic theory holds that political influence follows—and ought to follow—lines of legal authority. The public elects a representative legislative body (Congress, city council, school board) to make policy; an executive body, whose senior officials are elected or appointed, is employed to administer policy; administrators follow the instructions of legislators, who follow the instructions of their constituents. The major source of power is popular electoral support, and the norm of policy decision-making is responsiveness to public desires and preferences. The newer model, what might be called the technological model, sees the implementation of information systems and management science techniques causing a fundamental change in the governing process. Problems and policy alternatives are now too complex for the public and its representatives to evaluate. Legislators solicit and follow the recommendations of professional administrators. The major source of power is information; the new norm of policy decision-making is deference to expertise.

It is to this developing source of political influence that Professor Lerner's book draws our attention. The merits of the book are conspicuous. Clearly, it is "timely." However, timely books have a way of losing their significance as events prove them obsolete. There is no danger of obsolescence here. Polemics against the power of experts are less important than systematic theorizing. One of the most intriguing aspects of Professor Lerner's theory is his modification of the traditional dispute between elitist and pluralistic explanations of American politics. He believes there are *two* elite centers: One political, the other technological. Alliances between the two are required in most policy settings.

In view of the recent "anti-Washington" slogans offered by most presidential candidates, such a theory requires us to be more realistic. How likely is it that the next group of elected officials can match resources with experts?

Harmon Zeigler

Chapter 1

THE PROBLEM IN PERSPECTIVE

This book is about a very troublesome problem in the study of politics: That of understanding the impact of nominally apolitical experts in decision-making politics. Decision-making may be viewed as a political process whose actors we will call experts and politicos. In one sense the problem is only now beginning to take clear form in post-industrial societies; in another sense it is as old as the first tribal chieftian who found that his medicine man could more easily predict tribal victory on a full stomach. While the problem may have special interest for the political scientist, its manifestations dot the whole spectrum of social activity.

One form of the problem appears when policemen's victims "expire at 0400" instead of dying at 4 o'clock, or when warplanes launch "protective reaction strikes" instead of attacking the enemy. Another form of the problem appears when a consumer must decide whether to permit a mechanic to replace in his car parts he has never heard of. A variant of the problem also troubles the Congressman who must decide whether the nation should pay for weapons he can sometimes only remember by their initials.

Understanding the impact of experts in basic decision-making situations involving nonexperts (often nonexperts with final authority) is difficult because aspects of the problem are timeless, and because the problem, when construed in broadest social terms, takes many forms. For these reasons alone, the first task of simply defining the dimensions of the phenomenon is exceedingly difficult. This book is concerned with how experts influence *political* decision-making, but yet in a fundamental sense the sources of expert influence on political decision-making are not distinct from the sources of their influence in other spheres of social activity besides politics.

If only by virtue of their mere presence in decision circles ranging from community politics to international relations, experts affect policy decisions in one way or another. When the county must decide whether to renovate the local jail or seek funds for replacing it, architects are asked to predict the costs of either alternative, and their recommendations must be weighed against the advice of consulting penologists from the university. When the big city contemplates expansion of its mass-transit system, mass-transit experts are invited to submit designs. Urban planners are asked to predict the likely effects on downtown centers. The brain trust of the comptroller's office predicts that expansion will require at least a minimum fare increase. Opposition politicians wave studies before the press to prove that minimum-wage workers will be impoverished if their transportation costs are raised. In the political controversy, facts and figures become important, and so then do facts and figures people.[1]

In 1962 President Kennedy had to decide how to deal with Russian missiles in Cuba. Early discussions within the ad hoc White House committee on the crisis produced interest in a preemptive "surgical" air strike before the missiles were fully operational. The option had to be abandoned when the generals warned that only saturation bombing could remove the missile threat with any certainty.[2]

In 1958 when the superpowers attempted to negotiate a test-ban treaty, the question of inspection procedures arose. Soviet diplomats worked with their scientists to prepare a case for the adequacy of electronic detection devices. American diplomats and scientists prepared technical arguments for the necessity of on-site inspection teams. As compromise proposals were offered, counterproposals had to be prepared. Diplomats and scientists conferred within delegations to formulate proposals that would be both politically and technologically viable. Within each delegation, diplomats were eager to avoid technical pitfalls when negotiating with the opposition. Some scientists felt pressured to find technological arguments for upholding politically advantageous positions. Proposals issued by each state represented accommodations between scientists and diplomats, or sometimes, to their later chagrin, the failure to reach such accommodations.

At one point in the superpower negotiations, an experts' conference was convened. Scientists within the United States debated whether recent theoretical discoveries made the technical assumptions of the American position obsolete. A number of American politicians opposed to a test-ban treaty publicized the scientific controversy.[3]

No doubt political scientists, historians, and sociologists concerned with real-world policy-making could easily construct long lists of anecdotes concerning the involvement of experts in policy-making and implementation. But anecdotes per se are not enough. Their essence must be extracted. The clues that anecdotal fragments offer about experts in politics must somehow be integrated by the analyst if he is ever to grasp adequately the dimensions of the phenomenon.

Some writers who recount incidents of experts involved in policy-making do offer evaluative statements, of course. But often such statements are not the analytic reconstructions of the phenomenon one would like. Usually (but not always) evaluative commentary on experts in politics consists of assertions that experts are good or bad for politics, being pawns or dictators in the policy process, this sometimes being fortunate, sometimes unfortunate for society generally. The trouble is that often the leap from discussing isolated incidents to offering summary judgments is synaptic.[4] The path of inference is not clear. Few systematic discussions are available on *how* the expert acts in his political relationships to make the impact attributed to him. Few would dispute that the role of experts in politics is an important question, but the fact remains that the question has not yet been subjected to a sustained frontal assault by our disciplines. This is the condition that prompted the writing of this book.

In coming to grips with a pervasive and yet evasive social phenomenon, the first and inescapable difficulty is that of controlling the power of everyday words to distort an idea by suggesting unintended connotations. The richness of language which enables a few words to take many meanings serves well in daily conversation and literature. But the flexibility that enables nuance in conversation can make for hopeless ambiguity in attempts at systematic theorizing. The social scientist struggling to express concepts with words that carry an excess of meaning must rely on a license to define away the pliability of casual speech. The perfectly clear meaning of words used in conversational tone evaporates in discussions aimed at scientific-like command of problems.

So we are faced at the outset with the distressing task of clarifying what an expert is (though the term is intuitively clear if not scientifically precise), what the phrases "policy-making" and "decision-making" are supposed to imply, and by extension, what *political* policy-making is, and what it means to be nominally apolitical while deeply involved in politics. Dealing with these questions is like scratching an insect bite; we are led to ask, in turn, how relations between politicians and experts in politics should be conceptualized, and what in their relationship is presumed to constitute a problem to be analyzed—as far as we can specify what analyzing should mean in this context. Enter the conceptual framework.

The aim of this book is to develop a conceptual framework for analyzing the factors that determine the behavior of experts in decision-making groups composed of experts and politicos. The task seems worth the effort because, as we have already implied, experts are an increasingly important class of political actors. Their apparently unique standing in decision bodies per se and in society generally would suggest that they do not conduct themselves with politicians simply as other politicians might. If we can understand the factors that determine how experts behave in political settings, we will have a picture of contemporary politics that is more complete than that provided by current analyses which neglect the expert as a distinguishable actor in the decision process.

Who is an Expert? Who is Not?

It is difficult to specify the properties that define an expert because ultimately the definition, for our purposes, is contextual. In principle an expert is someone who is better informed or more skilled than others. But that judgment must be made by someone and accepted by those with whom the would-be expert will be dealing. In developing a definition of an expert, we are not interested in experts-without-portfolio—in prophets without honor in their own land.

Focus on the unacknowledged expert might be important in a study of why some decision bodies solve their problems and others don't, but this is not our main interest. This book is concerned with how the behavior of experts in a political decision-making body affects the interpersonal processes within that body. Our interest is in how the frictions, alignments, compromises, patterns of argumentation, strategizing, and psychological warfare in a group are affected by the presence of members with the acknowledged status of expertise. This is the setting that characterizes so much of the modern polity.

Hindsight applied to specific real-world cases might indicate that there were unappreciated wise men functioning in political decision bodies, but their plight is fundamental to the human condition. They constitute a class of political actors that is no more useful to the political scientist than would be a dichotomy of smart and stupid people. The dilemma of the uniquely informed individual may be interesting to the political scientist only when his acknowledged status as such becomes a political trump card, or encourages a unique behavior pattern in the expert, or special problems for those who must deal with him. All these considerations would of course affect the way the group as a whole conducts its business.

The object of analysis, then, is the individual in a political decision body who perceives himself and is perceived by others to be expert on the substantive issue at hand, with both expert and nonexpert being aware of each other's perceptions. Naturally such perceptions are based on some fairly uniform criteria. Experts are generally perceived to be so because they possess superior skill, information, or experience. They may simply be preceded by a reputation as an expert, they may carry credentials that grant them the title, or they may be personally known to other members who affirm their expert status. Some experts may gain their status on the basis of skills or performance shown after joining the group. Still others may gain expert status by claiming a unique experience considered indispensable for fully comprehending problem parameters, or sufficient to resolve otherwise inconclusive debates over subissues. Therefore a welfare mother may become an expert for a day during congressional hearings on the emotional toll taken by ADC regulations. The sole survivor of a catastrophe may be the only person whose personal recollections could resolve a dispute over the adequacy of instrument-controlled emergency devices.

The expert, whatever the source of his expertise, is the person who can most nearly speak with the final word on a substantive issue that has become the interest of some problem-solving group of which he is a member. Emphasizing the importance of pretensions to that final word, our definition of an expert requires that he must be perceived as an expert by his fellow decision-makers, and he must know that he is so perceived. Our definition of an expert is contextual because only the group members can give meaning to the title.

As for these nonexpert group members, we are concerned with situations in which they are politicos. It is extremely difficult to define a politico in the formal sense of specifying a finite set of properties that would be common to all intended referents and unique to them as well. We have yet to define politics. But because we study politics and talk about politicos, definition problems notwithstanding, it is fair to expect the analyst to articulate as far as possible, albeit in stylized form, the sense in which he uses his terms. The eclectic offerings that are inevitable when searching for definitions on the order of politics and politicos will always make for troublesome problems of application at the margin. But boundary problems are never fully eradicable and we emphasize a contextual definition in any event. Therefore we should convey here some basic image (if not formal definition) of the politico. Again, the crucial component of the definition is the context of the individual's relationship with the group.

The Politico

The politico is the person who deals in the handshake and the knowing in-group nod. He or she is the person who works to cultivate a sense of a dynamic in human relationships. In personal dealings he tries to attune his conduct to a sympathetic vibration with the personal styles of those around him to anticipate how best to deal with those people in order to get what he wants. If he works only for selfish ends, we call him a political hack; if his conduct seems tempered by moral principles and aimed toward some worthy goal, we call him a statesman.

The politico may be elected or appointed, holding a visible office or commanding a unit in some bureaucracy. His profession rewards the accumulation of power and influence, and experience in his profession improves his ability to deal with people to this end. The deliberative-persuasive setting is his element; he develops a facility in it much as one may with practice become skilled in parlor games; a sense of structure emerges and knowledge of the nuances of the game evokes confidence and perhaps even a love of the game for its own sake. This then is the image of the politico—the person with an institutional position of authority in a system that leads him to consciously manipulate human relationships in order to achieve goals. There is no need to make a value judgment as to whether such manipulation of relationships is opportunism and demagoguery, or persuasiveness, commitment, and charisma. The point is that, for good or ill, the politico's ware is strategic interpersonal behavior.

For us the definition of a politico is threefold. A politico deserves his title not only because he has made a vocation of strategic interpersonal behavior; he or she must also occupy some position of authority in government, in a government-related institution, or in the government-related branch of some multipurpose institution.[5] Additionally, the politico must be perceived as a politico by his fellow decision-body members. And he must know that he is so perceived. This last condition is a product of our interest in politicos and experts as they interact in the group setting. We must assume the mutual recognition of these roles in order to avoid a discussion of interactions based on misapprehensions of fellow group members.

So the type of decision body we are concerned with is one composed of experts and politicos where the group members perceive the group's composition in these terms. In this sense the definitions of a politico and an expert are contextual; they would apply to members of a decision group where the group recognized these role distinctions in the context of its own activity. We are concerned with groups engaged in political decision-making. It is easiest to explain what *political* decision-making means by first discussing the notion of decision-making per se.

Decision-making

The common denominator of most decision-making analyses is the notion that decision-making is the act (or the process depending on one's academic niche) of choosing among competing alternatives. The alternatives are usually different strategies for solving a problem (or again, depending on variations in terminology, achieving a goal). The fundamental concept is that decision-making is a process of selection according to some criterion adopted by the selector, and the selector (decision-maker) may be an individual or a group. The criterion for making the appropriate selection may be the extent to which an alternative offers the greatest potential value to the selector, the least potential damage, the least investment of time and effort in its discovery or execution, or the greatest reward in terms of some side payment extraneous to the original problem or condition. The point is that the basic concept in the various treatments of decision-making is that of selecting from competing options according to some criterion which, if the decision-making is rational, generally involves a statement of each option's net cost-effectiveness given the goals of the decision-maker(s).

Where decision-making is done by a group, the group may exhibit any of a variety of organizational structures. The group may be organized hierarchically. The final decision is made by the leader, often with options articulated and investigated, facts collected, and suggestions for final decisions percolating up through a sequence of substructures.

Or the decision may be made by a leader under whom all other group members stand equal among themselves but clearly subordinate to the final decision-maker. While such a charismatic decision format is usually associated with bygone societies, it still is a possible format for small groups.

In another organizational form, group decisions may be reached as a result of autonomous action being taken by individual cells working on subissues. Here the group "decision" becomes the cumulative consequence of action by individual units which may in turn have their own formats of organizational structure. Such a cell scheme is suitable only for certain types of problems which must be handled in a hostile atmosphere.

Another organizational format for decision-making groups is the collegial format whereby decisions emerge from the relatively unstructured deliberations of persons in a round-table setting. Here too such an "open forum" as a pure form of organizational structure for a decision group would be appropriate only to groups of limited size facing only certain kinds of problems.

There is no need here to presume some formal typology of organizational formats for decision groups. The point is simply that the decision-making, or selection process, can be carried on by groups in a variety of organizational settings based on mixes and adaptations of many basic formats, including types not mentioned here. The one constant in the organizational scheme, which we will posit for all decision-making groups, is the partial intrusion of the collegial format in every organizational mode otherwise adopted by a decision-making group.

Inevitable Collegiality

Any group that is to maintain its viability as a problem-solving organization must turn its best efforts to evaluating the merits of competing solution strategies. And if the problem at hand for an organization shows any initial resistance to immediate resolution, without appearing hopeless at the same time, it is usually because the problem is ambiguous in some respect. This ambiguity may appear in articulating the problem itself (in specifying its boundaries) or in estimating the consequences of various alternative solutions. To resolve the ambiguity (which the organization must do if it is to function as a problem-solving unit), each serious option or interpretation of the problem must be entitled to an initial, sympathetic advocacy. That is, the climate must be created whereby every point of view is entitled to expression *at least once*, without inhibition, in some unit of the organization.[6] To do this, authority relationships must be loosened implicitly while a partisan view is presented.[7] Organizations that cannot do this reduce sharply their ability to adapt.

The collegial format intrudes on the existing organizational scheme, in one way, to the extent that organizational norms allow for authority relationships to be implicitly relaxed in order to give all serious views their best first presentation.

A second way that the collegial format intrudes on all organizational schemes where it is not the explicit structure itself, occurs in cases where a sophisticated group's system of divided labor cannot operate on the problem until the problem components are recognized to the group's satisfaction. If the sophisticated group is pressed to begin action before these components are recognized, then it must function initially in a more undifferentiated form, mulling over the problem content if only to decide how action on it can be compartmentalized. A collegial atmosphere then intrudes insofar as personnel divisions are temporarily blurred.[8]

Sometimes such a group tries to press an undescribed problem through a differentiated group structure. If the parameters of the problem are somewhat unique to group experience, persons who normally function separately within the group will find themselves colliding over the problem. In such cases authority relationships are unclear and again ambiguity will foster an element of collegiality—of presumed equality in problem solving—if only until organizational directives can resolve the ambiguous relationship of strange bedfellows.[9] The operation of a collegial format in an organization is always a question of degree, but the point here is that it is always present to some extent.

The collegial decision format is of interest here because it is in the collegial setting that members from perhaps diverse parts of an organization, or with diverse roles, competing interests or unrelated skills, come together in a deliberative-persuasive, cooperative, and yet often competitive, setting. Usually the task facing such a group with members of mixed interests, convictions, preferences, backgrounds, or styles, is to reach some consensus if a decision is to be possible. Imagine the plight of a group working to forge consensus from among different views and interests concerned with an important matter in a collegial setting. The irresistible image is that of group-member encounters characterized by cajoling, coaxing, pressuring, and negotiating. There is the sense of a battlefield of psychological warfare. Depending on the size of the organization, the battles may be fought by administrative units or individuals, and probably both.

Regardless of the size of the units engaged and the lines of cleavage along which competing views emerge, the contention is that to some degree every problem-solving organization does a significant portion of its work on an interpersonal level. The problem-solving mode on this level places a premium on proselytization, on co-opting, on in-group strategizing, on persuasive argumentation. For all groups faced with significant ambiguous problems, there is always a significant degree of intragroup negotiation. Therefore we will treat internal relationships in collegial decision-making situations as implicitly negotiating relationships. Thus to look at expert-politico relationships in decision-making bodies is to look at a negotiating relationship. Indeed we will begin from the additional premise that a negotiating relationship between fellow decision-group members faced with an ambiguous problem in a somewhat collegial setting is a political relationship. Our preference for this terminology stems from the presumption that negotiation is the stuff of politics. Some attention to this point will clarify the general perspective from which this book is written, as well as why the promised emphasis in analyzing expert-politico relations is to be on *political* decision-making, as opposed to simply decision-making.

Decisions, Politics, and Negotiation

There still exists a troubling lack of consensus on a proper definition of politics,[10] but scholars seem to prefer those definitions having to do with the allocation of resources. Resources may be values or things that are valued;[11] and allocation may be by market processes,[12] by cliques who alternate the right to make allocations,[13] by nongovernmental monoliths who manipulate masses,[14] or as a consequence of the sociopolitical configuration of the community (in which case allocation becomes a manifestation of some systemic movement toward equilibrium.) [15] This distribution, or allocation, of resources presumably takes place under conditions of scarcity, which means simply that everyone cannot get everything he wants, given the diverse things people want and the amounts in which people want them. Hence decisions have to be made about who gets what. (We know of course that one may add when and how—or even why.)

This emphasis on the structure of interpersonal relationships in political situations leads to the question of how one can best describe the character of interpersonal relationships engendered by the task of people having to make decisions about who gets his way in situations where everyone cannot. In positing some constraints on normally acceptable behaviors in the resource allocation process, the usual assumptions are that the use of brute force and the resort to some random selection process are unacceptable.

When resort to lottery and brutality is thus excluded, an individual vying with others for some valued resource must rely on some form of persuasion. In basic terms, human relationships in which people interact for the purpose of trying to persuade each other are negotiating relationships. If people are to resolve the question of how something of value will be distributed between (among) them, in circumstances where there isn't enough to please everyone with his ideal allocation, where ideal allocations may themselves be inherently incompatible, where flipping coins or killing each other are no-no's, each must try to persuade the other to accept something less than his original ideal. Thus if allocation is the guts of politics, then negotiations—bargaining, persuasion, call it what you will—is the gut political process between people.[16]

It may help to clarify how this perspective on political relationships affects the view of what goes on in a decision-making group. Our concern is with decision groups whose decision rules require some degree of consensus on an option before it can become the group's final decision. In dealing with ambiguous problems, group members will (at least initially) make different evaluations of the problem and the variety and merits of available options.

If the group needs some kind of meeting-of-minds to act on its problem, somebody must persuade somebody else to see things his way. So at the outset begins the process of discussion, perhaps aimed at understanding, but invariably aimed at crystallizing opinion on the next action. We presume that it becomes more intense, probably more devious, more heated, and in any case protracted, as group attention to the unresolved problem continues. Of course the higher the perceived stakes given the values of participants, the greater the fervor in haggling. For those who want their attempts at persuading a counterpart to have more chance of success than yelling or intriguing alone might allow, the prospect of making concessions is always available. Thus haggling, pressing, persuading relationships are also bargaining relationships in principle. From the perspective of interpersonal relationships, the group decision-making process is a negotiating process, and those who participate in decision-making groups of the category described here thereby commit themselves to negotiating relationships. The group can be understood on the interpersonal level as a network of such negotiating relationships.

The Object of Negotiation

Just what is being negotiated? In one sense, of course, everything and anything is, given that there seems in principle to be nothing which a group could not take upon itself to decide. But in another sense one can ascribe some uniformity to the object of intra-decision-group negotiation. Regardless of the problem content considered by any decision group whose decision rule approaches consensus, negotiations among members are aimed at securing each other's votes. The "vote" of a decision-group member need not be interpreted in the literal sense of an actual ballot. Where there are no explicit voting procedures, a member's vote is simply his own contribution to the consensus. Expressed in these terms, one's object in intra-decision-group negotiations is always to secure another's advocacy of the option that one would himself like to see become the consensus of the group. On the interpersonal level, intragroup negotiations are implicitly proxy fights.

We can also express in definitional terms this perspective on interpersonal behavior in decision-making groups: Intra-decision-group negotiation is the process that determines to whom individuals allocate their measure of partial influence in determining the group consensus; the medium of the process is personal interaction. The criterion for making allocations is the individual's estimate of the likely consequences of ceding his piece of the potential consensus (the resource at his disposal) according to the particular arrangements proposed. Such cost-benefit estimates by the individual allocating his "resource" are presumably based on some rational value calculus. This calculus can include items ranging from judgments about the likely solution of the problem to estimates of where the individual's own best political interests lie.

This expression of the resource allocation process might be described as a micro view, [18] in that it begins by positing resources diffused throughout a group, and "politics" entering as individuals allocate their own parcels in ways that determine the profile of the total action unit. The usual macro view first posits an undifferentiated mass of resources proper to an action unit as a total entity; "politics" enters as the resources must be dispersed to its component actors. [19]

The upshot of this view is that all political activity—as it involves people—can be seen as merely the accumulated manifestations of a basic interpersonal relationship pattern. From this micro view, these diverse manifestations of "politics" are related as recurring metaphors of the negotiating relationship. In this sense the negotiating process becomes the essence—the gut process—of politics.

Pursuing this notion that political phenomena are basically related metaphorical representations of a continuing common decision process, we can clarify the relationship presumed here between a decision-making group and a decision-making organization. Admittedly, group and organization have been used interchangeably here; this practice is intentional, but requires some explanation because usually much is made about the differences between the "group" format for personal interaction and the "organization."[20]

Decision-making, Group, and Organization

Usually the distinction between a group and an organization is based on asserted differences in complexity, and formality of structure. The term "organization" is reserved for those groups having some membership hierarchy which cedes varying degrees of formal authority to members, and the notion of a comprehensive system of formal relationships implies complexity. Organizations are also assumed to be more complex than groups in general because they are usually larger bodies than those that the term "group" denotes in casual discourse.[21]

However, there is no specific definitive property that scholars consistently point to in distinguishing a decision-making group from a decision-making organization. Generally, they are compared in terms of a continuum, with the group at one end, the organization at the other, and the point of metamorphosis unspecified but somewhere in the middle. There is no formal distinction on the order of a definition, in the sense that one would have trouble explaining the difference between a casually run organization and a formally run group.

The problem of defending any clear distinction between decision-making groups and decision-making organizations is compounded when students of administrative behavior and organization theory stress the existence in organizations of an informal structure that belies the formal superstructure.[22] In the same vein, so-called "small group" studies often stress the implicit hierarchies and communication patterns that develop in small groups charged with various types of tasks.[23]

Nor is size as a distinguishing characteristic satisfactory since one cannot specify how small is small. Sometimes it is suggested that decision-making organizations are different from decision-making groups because organizations function continuously. That is, while a decision group may develop to solve a single specific problem and then dissolve, organizations do not find their raison d'etre so narrowly defined. Generally an organization's longevity is presumed to exceed the experience of any specific problem; its roots go deeper than any set of temporally limited issues. But here, too, candidates develop campaign organizations which exist only to elect them and then disband. President Nixon assembled a Washington Special Action Group (WSAG) which met presumably for any foreign-policy problem he found especially serious. WSAG members could not know beforehand what would become a crisis, the round-table format of the group and its size would further make one hesitant to call it an organization, yet its existence would transcend the lifespan of any single issue.

The point of this discussion about decision-making groups and decision-making organizations is not to suggest that the distinction is meaningless. Certainly one would not say it is a matter of indifference whether ITT is called a decision-making group or three men adrift in a rowboat built for two are called an organization. The distinction between a decision-making group and a decision-making organization is perhaps more nebulous than some other distinctions in social science, but it serves well for analysts bent on stressing particular perspectives in their work—perspectives such as those cited above regarding complexity, longevity, formality, and so on. What *is* being said is that from the perspective on politics presented here (the interpersonal emphasis, negotiation as the basic process, etc.) we can dismiss the question of whether what we shall say applies to decision-making bodies as organizations or groups. Unless otherwise specified, what we shall say can apply to both.

We will have occasion to discuss aspects of organizational constraints as they affect interpersonal processes connected with decision-making, so we will be raising considerations linked to what is conventionally called the organization and not the group. However, this is simply saying that certain factors affect processes only under specified circumstances. The differences between situations in which such factors operate from situations in which they do not will be merely differences of degree—empirical questions but not confoundings. Whenever the term "organizations" is used in the conventional sense as distinct from groups, this will be made explicit. Such usage should subsequently be seen as a shorthand to dispense with an adjective string that would otherwise have to precede the generic term "group." More frequently in these pages, decision-making group and organization may be read as interchangeable, and again, this stems from the assumptions of our micro perspective on politics and the decision process outlined earlier.

"Political" Decision-making

Having dealt with the distinction (or lack of it) between a decision-making group and a decision-making organization it may be appropriate to further hone terminology by explaining the distinctions intended here between political decision-making (a phrase used earlier) and decision-making. Some clarification seems necessary, given the view that all group decision-making is political to some degree because all decision-group formats are collegial to some degree, thereby allowing for people-to-people haggling and persuasion, and so on. From this perspective, then, the term "political decision-making" might appear redundant. In a sense it is. The "political" in decision-making stands mostly as a reminder—as a convenient way of stressing the bias of these pages. However, the adjective political also serves to an extent to exclude some types of decision-making that groups may engage in but which are outside our interest.

Political decision-making, with its implied stress on the interpersonal give-and-take of the decision process, excludes the hypothetical case of decision-making that is either entirely programmed or dictated. In the case of programmed decision-making, the group is merely playing out the consequences of a previous decision or set of decisions. In the case of dictated decisions, the group is really not doing the deciding. Emphasizing political decision-making also keeps the frame of reference related to government activity. While the ideas in this book are not presented with the idea that they are limited to government-related activity alone, such activity is the central referent from which the range of intended referents fan out, as it were. So to clue the reader on the focus of action as quickly as possible, and to stress the exclusion of perfectly programmed or dictated decisions, the "political" in decision-making was presented literally.

Summarizing So Far

Before proceeding, it may be useful to summarize the main ideas that have been presented. Sometimes the best way to present ideas for a first hearing is not the most convenient form for summary, so dispensing with the particular thread of argument woven into the previous pages, the basic premises underlying this book may be explained this way:

Politics is a process of allocation. Allocating necessitates decision-making. We will deal with decision-making done by groups with certain characteristics. Specifically, we will limit ourselves to groups whose decision rules require some degree of consensus such that there will have to be some meeting of minds within the groups before they can come to their decisions.

Each group member within an individual group commands a portion of the potential consensus to allocate as his "vote" in the group deliberations preceding the group decision. We presume that the diversity of views held initially by members is broad enough to preclude at the outset the consensus that authoritative group decisions require. We also presume that inevitably some degree of collegiality will characterize the atmosphere of interpersonal relations in which members must accomplish this meeting of minds. Collegiality allows for intragroup negotiation aimed at such a consensus; members negotiate for each other's "votes." In the group context, a member's vote constitutes his political resources. From a perspective that focuses on interpersonal relations, this intragroup negotiation is thus the process by which such resources are allocated. In this sense, negotiation is the basic political process on the group level—at least for the type of decision-making groups we are dealing with.

We take the term "decision-making process" to be a synonym for the policy process. Policies are projected plans of action on a problem or long-range sequence of problems. Where a group makes policy it is making decisions, so we will use policy process and decision-making process interchangeably. This overview clarifies how nominally apolitical experts can be seen to be deeply involved in political processes regardless of the external trappings of their role. An expert who is a member of a decision-making group of the type we have described has his portion of the consensus to allocate as do all other members of the group. This is true regardless of the constraints placed on his formal role in the organization, by virtue of our assumption of an inevitable intrusion of collegiality in the organizational setting.

The Strategy Outlined

Now that we have packed our conceptual baggage for this trip, we should specify where we are going. We want to understand the factors that influence the expert-politico relationship in this decision-group setting. To do this, we will look over the expert's shoulder as he plays out his cards with the politico. We want to see what the expert has in the hand he is dealt, and what constitutes a trump card for him in some situations and a lost trick in others. The expert will be the focus of attention.

However, the value of the cards he holds is partly determined by what the politico can match them with in a given round of play. In this sense we will be drawn to the politico as well, albeit in a secondary, derivative way. The concern thus becomes the expert-politico dyad from the view of the expert. The game is the negotiating relationship between expert and politico in the decision-group setting we have described. The goal is to identify the factors that account for the behavior of experts in these expert-politico negotiations; the end product is a conceptual framework. Factors we will be looking for would be understood as variables in a full-blown, formal theory.

Factors Conceptualized by Level

We will begin with the assumption that the factors mentioned above can be found on many levels. Indeed, we will posit five such levels. These "levels" may be understood as analytically distinct categories from which separate clusters of factors such as we are looking for may be gleaned. These levels (we use this term for lack of a better word) do not constitute a hard and fast typology, in the sense that many variations on them might provide the same results. I cannot offer any elegant formulation to show why the problem ought to be attacked in the way I have chosen, except to note that the size of the slices we will take appears roughly to follow conventional boundaries in social science. In any event, the utility of this technique for segmenting the problem must ultimately be judged by the quality of what it yields. Two implications of this view are immediately apparent: First, that the reader will have to make his own judgment of these pages based on what he takes away from this book; and second, by derivation, that we might as well get started.

To envision an expert negotiating a problem in a group setting is to implicitly invoke concepts on several levels. The expert is an individual, identified by a role concept, operating in an organizational setting, cast in some larger social milieu, addressing a problem which presumably has its own generic properties. If the attempt is to specify factors which affect the negotiating behavior of such experts as a class, factors must be drawn from knowledge about patterns of an individual's dyadic style, patterns of role behavior, the constraints of problem parameters relevant in such a context, the constraints of organizational peculiarities so far as they may impinge on expert-politico interaction, and the influence of selected societal values that color expert and politico perceptions of themselves, their task, and their relationship.

Thus the search for factors becomes a process of asking questions on several levels: What negotiating behaviors displayed by experts (in their dealings with politicos) are traceable to their role status as experts per se? To what extent would any such unique expert negotiating style be cross-cut by a typology of individual dyadic styles applicable to all citizens? How might expert negotiating behavior be expected to vary with changes in certain generic problem parameters? How would expert negotiating behavior be affected by differences in the relative positions of expert and politico within the decision-making organization? What in the folklore of post-industrial America regarding values attached to technical skill, expertise, politics, prestigage of occupation, and so on, might have a direct effect on expert-politico interaction?

In short, what factors on the level of role variables, individual personality variables, problem content variables, organizational variables, and societal variables, affect the negotiating behavior of experts vis-à-vis politicos?

We will examine all of these questions—albeit one at a time—in the coming chapters.

NOTES

1. For an interesting example of controversy engendered by the mere hiring of experts in purely consultant capacity on the local level, recall the recent controversy in New York City over the hiring of foreign mass-transit analysts to review the local subway system. *The New York Times,* August 19, 1970: 1:7; August 26, 1970: 82:1; November 14, 1970: 1:2; November 19, 1970: 94:4. The reported cost of this venture ($100,000), as well as partisan politics, gave impetus to proposals for legislation to govern the hiring of experts in consultant capacity. In a memorandum concerning such legislation, the city comptroller, Abraham Beame, wrote: "This bill would provide an opportunity for officials, journalists, educators and the public to consider the vast number (and terribly expensive—$67 million annually) of consultant contracts issued by the City Administration. . . . Unfortunately, one man's professional consultant may be another man's political patronage." *New York State Legislative Annual 1971,* pp. 226-7. In this book we suggest that one man's consultant may be not only another man's political patronage, but also another man's political adversary in the decision-group setting. For remarks on the role of experts in settings of a somewhat similar type, see Edward C. Banfield, *Political Influence* (New York: The Free Press, 1961).

2. The story has been recounted in many places, but for a brief account see Arthur M. Schlesinger, Jr., *A Thousand Days* (Greenwich, Connecticut: Fawcett Publications, 1967) p. 735.

3. The literature on nuclear scientists and nuclear policy is voluminous but for accounts of the 1958 Disarmament Conference specifically see: E. H. Voss, *Nuclear Ambush; the Test-Ban Trap* (Chicago: Regenery, 1963); H. Jacobson, E. Stein, *Diplomats, Scientists, and Politicians; The United States and the Nuclear Test-Ban Negotiations* (Ann Arbor: University of Michigan Press, 1964); Robert Gilpin, *American Scientists and Nuclear Weapons Policy,* (Princeton, New Jersey: Princeton University Press, 1962). For a brief comparison of the 1958 talks with SALT, see Johan H. Holst, "Strategic Arms Control and Stability: A Retrospective Look," in Johan Holst, William Schneider, Jr., (eds.), *Why ABM: Policy Issues in the Missile Defense Controversy* (New York: Pergamon Press, 1969).

4. This is often true of even the best works related to the role of experts in policy-making. See the conclusions of C. P. Snow, *Science and Government* (Cambridge: Harvard University Press, 1961). Two more instances of moving from anecdotes to conclusions are: Morton Halperin, "The Gaither Committee and the policy process," *World Politics,* XIII, No. 3, pp. 360-84; Townsend Hoops, *The Limits of Intervention* (New York: McKay Co., 1969). Notable exceptions are Victor A. Thompson, *Modern Organization* (New York: Knopf, 1961); Amitai Etzioni, "Authority structure and organizational effectiveness," *Administrative Science Quarterly,* 4, 1960, pp. 43-67; Gary D. Brewer, *Politicians, Bureaucrats and the Consultant* (New York: Basic Books, 1973).

5. This second condition distinguishes our referent from those who are simply "social operators" or "manipulators."

6. Again, see Schlesinger's account of the ground rules for ExCom deliberations during the Cuban Crisis. Schlesinger, *A Thousand Days,* op. cit. Also, on the nature of collegial groups, see F. G. Bailey, "Decisions by Consensus in Councils and Committees: with special Reference to Village and Local Government in India," in *Political Systems and the Distribution of Power,* Association of Social Anthropologists of the Commonwealth Monographs 2 (New York: Praeger, 1965) pp. 1-21.

7. Of course, in many organizations there may be substantial costs for the subordinate who speaks out of turn and is *wrong.*

8. This type of situation always reminds me of interdisciplinary seminars. However, there are less uncomfortable analogies. Anselm Strauss, "The Hospital and its Negotiated Order," in Eliot Freidson (ed.), *The Hospital in Modern Society* (New York: Free Press, 1963).

9. This is often the case when field units with diverse organizational roots find that unanticipated field conditions compel ad hoc arrangements for integration. In another vein, the missile technology estate in the United States immediately following Sputnik seems to have reflected this kind of patchquilt of work orders which we presume here to foster collegiality within individual decision cells. As used here, collegiality merely implies the vague, or informal, character of authority relationships. Notice that it does not necessarily predict hostility, which is a measure on a different dimension. See Herbert F. York, *Race to Oblivion; A Participant's View of the Arms Race* (New York: Simon and Schuster, 1970).

10. We do not find the lack of a definition troubling in any deep philosophical sense—inconvenient probably is the word.

11. This is an ambiguity I have never been able to resolve in Easton, David Easton, *The Political System* (New York: Alfred Knopf, 1967).

12. I have in mind, of course, the "new political economy." See William C. Mitchell, "The Shape of Political Theory to Come: From Political Sociology to Political Economy," paper delivered at the 1967 meeting of the American Political Science Association, Chicago, Illinois.

13. David B. Truman, *The Governmental Process; Political Interests and Public Opinion* (New York: Alfred Knopf, 1951); G. David Garson, "On the origins of interest-group theory: A critique of a process," *American Political Science Review,* 68, 4 (December 1974) pp. 1505-19.

14. See any of a variety of pieces ranging from J. K. Galbraith, *The New Industrial State* (Boston: Houghton Mifflin, 1967) to C. C. Walton, F. W. Cleveland, Jr., *Corporations on Trial: The Electric Cases* (Belmont, California.: Wadsworth Co., 1964).

15. See any of the systems literature, e.g., Easton, *The Political System,* op. cit.; Karl Deutsch, *The Nerves of Government* (New York: The Free Press, 1966).

16. Purists may prefer the term "tacit negotiation," but for our part the burden of adjectives might just as well fall on those who use "negotiation" in the *narrower* sense. This view as we have formulated it (hopefully) covers the powerful perspectives on calculating actors' interaction suggested by exchange theory and the broad underpinnings of game theory. I have in mind particularly: John W. Thibaut and Harold H. Kelley, *The Social Psychology of Groups* (New York: Wiley, 1959); Peter M. Blau, *Exchange and Power in Social Life* (New York: Wiley, 1964); Thomas C. Schelling, *The Strategy of Conflict* (Cambridge: Harvard University Press, 1960). This view is also compatible with Schattschneider's broad view of the process of drawing and redrawing the dimensions of political conflict. E. E. Schattschneider, *The Semi-Sovereign People* (New York: Holt, Rinehart, & Winston, 1960).

17. The discussion so far has emphasized the group context, so negotiation between members becomes *intra*group negotiation. But this does not mean that the line of thought pursued here could not apply to intergroup negotiations. For, any set of opponents who coordinate their decision-making activity, even if it is to destroy each other, can constitute a "dyad," and in these terms, then, a decision-making group. In this sense, the reader may substitute "intradyad (triad, etc.) negotiation" for "intragroup negotiation." The ready equivalence of intradyad and interpersonal negotiations should resolve any questions about the generalizability of this approach, especially noting successful generalizing by Thibaut and Kelley from a "dyadic" base. This approach also meshes nicely with communications concepts of intra-unit behavior. See John T. Dorsey, Jr., "A communication model for administration," *Administrative Science Quarterly,* 2 1957, pp. 307-324.

18. We are aware that the macro/micro jargon has been used with many different meanings in mind, but we think its use is clear here, given the context. Economists have perhaps made the most of this distinction though even they have their dissenters who question the usefulness of the distinction in certain instances. In this regard see Abba P. Lerner, "Consumer's surplus and micro-macro," *Journal of Political Economy,* vol. 71, 1963, pp. 76-81. Action within small groups seems generally considered "micro" subject matter. But small groups can, of course, be treated in macro, or "systems," terms—indeed, so may be (and are) individuals treated. See F. K. Berrien, "A general systems approach to human groups," and Jonas A. Schloss-

berger, "The individual as a complex open system," in Milton D. Rubin (ed.), *Man in Systems* (New York: Gordon and Breach, 1971).

19. Of course, one could collapse such a distinction by positing a simple cycle of disbursement and aggregation, but I think the emphasis is different at either starting point, and this emphasis should not be lost.

20. See for example Amitai Etzioni, *Modern Organizations* (Englewood Cliffs, New Jersey: Prentice-Hall, 1964) esp. pp. 3. Also see Talcott Parsons, *Structure and Process in Modern Societies* (Glencoe, Illinois: The Free Press, 1960). Etzioni cites Parsons in this context. Certainly much of this is well-taken given the intentions of some types of analyses. But our emphasis on *decision-making* groups and organizations, plus the direction of our inquiry and level of analysis, make this careful separation of group and organization more harmful than useful. On this issue generally, see Robert T. Golembiewski, "Small Groups and Large Organizations," in James G. March (ed.), *Handbook of Organizations* (Chicago: Rand McNally, 1965).

21. It has also been suggested that groups and organizations differ in that organizations have goals. This distinction evaporates if we talk about decision-making groups and organizations. See Etzioni, *Modern Organizations*, op. cit.

22. This area is nicely treated by Nicos P. Mouzelis, *Organization and Bureaucracy; An Analysis of Modern Theories* (Chicago: Aldine Co., 1968). Specific works on organizations emphasizing the informal dimension include: Melville Dalton, *Men Who Manage* (New York: Wiley, 1950); Peter M. Blau, *The Dynamics of Bureaucracy* (Chicago: University of Chicago Press, 1963); Victor A. Thompson, *Bureaucracy and the Modern World* (Morristown, New Jersey: General Learning Press, 1976) Chapter 1.

23. Indeed, were it not for the assumption of some essential group processes, all small-group research would lose any pretension to generalizability.

Chapter 2

EXPERT QUA EXPERT: ISOLATING THE EFFECTS OF
ROLE STATUS ON EXPERTS' NEGOTIATING BEHAVIOR

The very act of suggesting that experts as a class may conduct political relationships in a way unique to them, despite the fact that experts may be masters of different subjects in different organizational settings, and different kinds of people, implies that the role status of expertise per se can exert a uniform effect on negotiating behavior. To test this assumption and isolate any such behaviors traceable to the status of expertise, volunteer subjects were put through an analogue, laboratory study designed to exhibit the properties of expert-politico encounter as described earlier.[2]

By monitoring negotiations in this setting, specific negotiating behaviors were indeed found to be uniquely a function of adopting the title of expert, per se. From this research, a tentative picture emerges of how the expert, simply by virtue of his role status, behaves differently than he otherwise would in the collegial, decision-making, negotiating setting with politicos. Comprehending the behavior of the expert in this light will be a first step in understanding the dynamics of his participation in politics, or—as we have phrased it—his interaction with politicos. We can pursue this area most conveniently by reconstructing in general terms the research undertaken on this dimension.[3]

Essentials of the Analogue

The first step in constructing a laboratory analogue of any type of real-world situation is to select those few out of the many aspects of the real-world situation which ought to be modeled in the laboratory, given the analyst's interests. The rest of the contextual detail of the real-world referent is discarded. The perspective on our subject described earlier dictates our choices in this regard.

The essential properties of the expert-politico relationship include encounters in a decision-making group, a collegial setting, mutual role recognition, greatest individual rewards for group success, initial disagreement on best solutions, insufficient power of individuals to invoke their own preferred solution without group acquiescence, a group decision rule approximating consensus, a problem amenable in principle to expertise, and of course opportunity to communicate in an attempt to co-opt—by bargaining, compelling logic, trickery, or whatever. To reflect these conditions, expert-politico encounters in the laboratory were structured in the following fashion:

Method

Fifty male, undergraduate, volunteer subjects were randomly assigned to either a test group (henceforth experts) or control group (henceforth laymen).

Subjects selected for the test group were led to view themselves as experts as a result of exposure to a preconditioning procedure administered prior to the actual test condition. This preconditioning procedure was designed to convince the subjects that they possessed a specified inborn skill. The strategy of the experiment was to mix such "experts" with presumed politicos to form triads charged with negotiating a problem within the province of the preconditioned subjects' expertise. The negotiating behavior of such expert subjects in this context would be compared to the behavior of control group nonexperts (laymen) exposed to the identical triad experience.

A total of fifty triads were run.[4] In twenty-five triads (the "expert" triads) an expert negotiated with the two politico-confederates. In the twenty-five layman triads, a layman negotiated with the same two politico-confederates. The use of confederate politicos is described below. Significant differences in behavior between the two groups would be attributed to the effects of internalizing the expert role in negotiation with politicos.

Preconditioning Procedure for Experts

Experts were produced by assembling all subjects assigned to this category for a slide show. Such subjects were informed that the purpose of this assembly was to isolate individuals from the population at large who possessed what research on blindness has shown to be an inborn or infancy-acquired visual cognition skill. The skill was supposedly manifest in the ability to comprehend the array of simple objects on a blank two-dimensional field with a rapidity and accuracy in excess of the normal individual. Subjects were told that, to isolate individuals with this skill, all would be exposed to five slides depicting an abstract pattern of black dots on a blank background. The dots would be flashed too briefly for anyone to actually count them. The task was to estimate the exact number of dots on each slide and record the answer in the interval between each slide and the next.

The experimenter was to score the answer sheets according to a preestablished sliding scale of accuracy which would yield percentile ratings for all participants. Participants falling within a previously determined expert-percentile range would be notified and used in what experts now took to be a second phase of the experiment. This phase was described as involving negotiation in a group format on a visual problem identical to those presently to be used to identify natural experts. In fact, *all* subjects who completed this bogus expert-discovering procedure were notified that they were experts. (Scores in this initial procedure were actually never evaluated and the experimenter was himself unaware of the number of dots on any slide.) Thus experts were recruited for participation in negotiating triads involving politicos, and a dot problem identical to the type used to establish "expertise."[5]

Control-group subjects, or laymen, were simply volunteers recruited for what was described as an experiment in group problem-solving involving persons paired to yield groups with various combinations of skills. Both expert and layman subjects were assigned to triads whose two other members were described to the subject as established politicos. Subjects were told that politicos were so labeled because they met two conditions.

First, they were supposedly recommended to the experimenter by local political groups who were asked to name people who had participated extensively in the recent electoral campaigns. Second, in addition to being so recommended, a battery of psychological tests supposedly administered to them indicated that they conformed to the test profile of the "political personality type."

The politicos were in fact confederates, with the same confederates employed in all triads. Both experts and laymen were told that they would be working with these politicos on a problem involving estimation of dots flashed too quickly to be counted.[6] Experts were told this was a type of problem identical to that for which they showed expertise.

All subjects were told that the purpose of the experiment was to see how effectively groups composed of members with different combinations of skills could work on a given problem. Experts were told that their politico-counterparts for the triad session did not possess the skill enjoyed by experts, were aware of the subjects' knowledge of their politico status, and were aware that all participants had such information about each other.

Laymen were given similar information indicating in their case that

(1) All triad members were aware that none possessed special skill regarding the problem (this being quite natural given its esoteric nature);

(2) All triad members were aware that the two politicos were appropriately so titled;

(3) All triad members were aware that the subject possessed no special political ability or experience beyond that likely to have been had by the average person.

Information given to subjects about the nature of the experiment and the character of participants was provided privately in an anteroom briefing prior to meeting politicos.

Instructions on the rules of triad interaction were given in the presence of politicos and subjects. With all other information given to subjects beforehand, politico-confederates were blind to subject test status. In addition, confederates were told that pilot studies had indicated that both experts and laymen would feign expertise and/or inability regardless of actual self-perceptions, in attempts to gain strategic advantages. This was designed to blind confederates regardless of subject disclosure of his expert or layman status during triad negotiations.[7]

Rules of Triad Encounter

The task for the triad was to offer a single accurate-as-possible estimate of the number of dots on a slide flashed before the participants. In addition to a standard payment of $2 to all participants, $25 would be paid to each member of the triad whose estimate was more accurate than that offered by any other triad. Participants were separated by partitions which obscured vision of each other during the test interval, with communication confined to written messages but otherwise unrestricted. Message slips were coded beforehand to allow reconstruction of the sequence, identification of the source, and the content of all messages sent in the triad.

Participants were permitted to communicate freely for ten minutes and then cease on experimenter signal. If no agreement was reached (a certainty as a result of instructions to confederates as described below) communication would continue for approximately one minute, according to a set of prepared instructions designed to facilitate closure. Any participant was free during the ten-minute period, to withdraw from ("opt out of") the group at any time, if he felt that the group effort "was no longer productive." In this event, the experimenter would poll the group for individual estimates, and any winning individual answer would earn its owner $15 instead of the $25 payable for winning group answers. By promising that the option to opt out would be available in the eleventh minute as well, the game was so structured to make actual opting during the free-exchange period irrational, while allowing reference to the rule for strategic purposes. This insured a standard time of exposure to test situation for all subjects.

Instructions to Confederates for Behavior During Triad Sessions

Confederates were previously instructed to avoid making any number-estimate offers until the subject sent one to either confederate. Confederates then responded with counterestimates that were 50 percent higher and 50 percent lower respectively, than the subject's first estimate. Confederates were allowed free rein in negotiation beyond this point, with the condition that they not reach agreement. At the end of the ten-minute free-exchange period, the experimenter ascertained that there was no agreement, and then instructed each participant to send a single, identical final offer to each of his counterparts. Confederates stalled until receiving the subject's final offer and then returned identical confederate final offers which were 20 percent higher than the subject's.

Triad Procedure After the Exchange of Final Offers

After this exchange of final offers, the experimenter ascertained that one participant (invariably the subject) was a group holdout. The subject was then instructed to select one from the following options: Agree with counterparts, earning each participant $25 if the now unanimous answer were indeed a winning one; stick to his own final offer earning any participants $15 if their answers were winning ones; offer a new number different from the joint counterpart offer and different from the subject's own final offer, again for $15. With the subject response the experiment was concluded. This procedure for closure and the opting rule were designed simply to allow for later measures of several from among many negotiating behaviors and do not reflect any hypotheses of special concern in the design.

The Reasons for Using Confederate Politicos

The use of confederate politicos allowed for avoiding the problem of having to condition a set of subjects to believe they were politicos. This seemed an impossible task for two reasons.

First the state of the art does not allow for a definition that would be comprehensive and specific enough to indicate how the true politico would behave with respect to our dependent variables (described below) or any other list of variables at such an operational level. This means that there would be no way for the experimenter to determine if the "politicos" he conditioned were in fact behaving as real politicos would.

Second, subjects conditioned to believe they were politicos would have a real-world reference group to compare themselves to in assessing whether or not the label assigned to them was accurate. In creating experts it was possible to describe an esoteric form of expertise for which there was no real-world reference group and so the problem of subjects' testing the credibility of their title by comparison with real-world figures could be avoided. This would not be possible with ersatz politicos. While our experts could also accept that they were experts though they had no previous experience in their area of expertise (given that it was described as inborn) it was assumed that no one would believe he was a politico without having had professional political experience. Real politicos could not be obtained for participation in a laboratory experiment. With politicos being confederates in this experiment, it was also possible to program their behavior concerning the establishment of initial levels of disagreement and final offer procedures which allowed for taking several measures of interest here under standardized conditions.

Given our primary focus on the expert-politico dyad from the view of the *expert* and our concern on this level only with the relationship between accepting the expert role and expert behavior, there seemed little harm when taking a first cut, in constricting the analogue by making it a study of expert behavior with *perceived* politicos. Of course, future research with real politicos or experts, or with proven reliable conditioning procedures for creating their functional equivalents would be, shall we say, vastly preferable. However, as long as the limitations of our findings are kept in mind, useful inferences can certainly still be drawn. The confederate politicos performed all of their assigned tasks (described earlier involving synchronized initial offers and final offers, and the timing of offers) without error. Additionally, no subjects indicated skepticism about the accuracy of labels given confederates *or* the subjects themselves. Opportunity for voicing any doubts was provided at the end of the experiment when subjects were invited to comment about any phase of the experiment.

Dependent Variables

In a sense, the dependent variable was negotiating behavior in the presence of perceived politicos, hypothesized to be a function of internalizing the expert role. Operationally, negotiating behavior was defined as scores on a collection of forty-two separate measures applied to communications recorded for the triad. Table 2.1 lists the forty-two dependent variables.

Unfortunately, the state of the art is such that in any research on the actual "how" of interpersonal negotiation, variables must be selected without the benefit of a rigorous model linking all facets of negotiating behavior.[8] Consequently, the selection of negotiating behaviors for operationalization as variables in experimental research must proceed on a somewhat intuitive level.

This does not mean we cannot be specific in describing negotiating behaviors to be monitored in the laboratory. It does mean that it will be difficult to specify the logic that *links* the variables—for if we could do this

Table 2.1   List of All Variables Measured in the Laboratory

Variable No.	Description
1	Number of messages subject received
2	Number of messages subject sent
3	Number of threats to opt out
4	Number of messages against desirability of opting
5	Number of positive references to own role
6	Number of negative references to own role
7	Number of positive references to politico role
8	Number of negative references to politico role
9	Number of subject requests for specific numbers
10	Number of offers of specific numbers on request
11	Number of offers of specific numbers without immediately preceding request
12	Number of references to group condition
13	Number of references to group progress
14	Number of references to own tactics
15	Number of references to counterpart tactics
16	Number of initiations of open coalitions
17	Number of initiations of secret coalitions
18	Number of passive responses, open coalition
19	Number of passive responses, secret
20	Number of rejections of coalitions, all types
21	Number of personal insults received
22	Number of challenging responses to insult
23	Number of low-key responses to insult
24	Number of insults initiated
25	Number of uses of deception
26	Number of positive references to own ability
27	Number of negative references to own ability
28	Number of positive references to counterpart ability
29	Number of negative references, counterpart ability
30	Number of explicit mediator remarks
31	Number of implicit mediator remarks
32	Number of technical messages sent
33	Number of positive references to grand coalition initiated
34	Number of passive, positive responses to grand coalition references

35	Number of negative references to grand coalition, subject init.
36	Number of negative responses to grand coalition references
37	Number of instructional messages
38	Number of identical messages
39	Number of requests for report on other dyad
40	Score on independence scale of final game answer
41	Number of concessions made
42	Net concession value of final offer

we would have arrived at a systemic model of negotiation (or at least part of one). Because the unavailability of a comprehensive and operational formal model of interpersonal negotiation prevents us only from systematically relating variables but not from citing them, we can indeed describe variables worth measuring in empirical research. At the same time, however, if the state of the art does not preclude precision, it does necessitate the appearance of eclecticism. We can partially compensate for this difficulty by abstracting the intuitive reasons for why given variables seem worth investigation.

In the several pages that follow, the list of forty-two variables used to compare experts and laymen is presented and explained. This collection of forty-two measures actually represents a somewhat smaller number of facets of negotiating behavior observed in the laboratory. However, exploring these facets usually required taking several separate but conceptually related measures.

The admitted disadvantage of discussing a list of forty-two measures seems outweighed by two advantages. First, the reader will be able to better grasp the nature of significant variables by understanding their genesis. Second, we shall have occasion to discuss the manifestation of distinct expert negotiating postures, or "styles" as it were, revealed through factor analysis of all except six dependent variables. (Six variables were excluded from the factor analysis because they had means of zero for at least one of the two groups. This point will be elaborated when the factor analysis is presented.) Thus variables not individually discriminating do figure prominently in our analysis. Familiarity with the full list of measures will therefore prove useful. In the several pages that follow, the forty-two variables are listed according to which experts and laymen were compared. Arguments for deeming them significant facets of negotiating behavior are suggested, and their operationalizations are explained.

Variables 1 and 2: Amount of Negotiator Interaction Before Negotiations are Ended

Conventional wisdom generally values negotiation as a problem-solving format partly because it is believed ideally to provide an opportunity for thoroughly "thrashing out" a problem. That is, one socially desirable aspect of negotiation seems to be that its format facilitates the gradual convergence (or at least partial convergence) of views as a result of the scrutiny to which each advocate's view is subjected by the other. The assumption is that if there is actually a shared desire for agreement, the intense give-and-take which negotiation encourages will make it likely that common points of agreement will be reworked to form either a mutually acceptable compromise (in the case of negotiations involving a dispute), or a mutually promising strategy (in the case of negotiations involving a common problem).[9]

Implicit in this assumption is the notion that extended interaction, extended communication, between negotiators may serve to clarify disagreements on the problem at hand. Also assumed is the idea that such interaction will help assure that any solution reached will be more likely to embody the well-considered views of both sides. Such a thoroughly thrashed out agreement, especially when the negotiation is between adversaries, is presumably likely to endure without repudiation after second thoughts. When the negotiation is between people faced with seeking the best solution to a common problem, such a thoroughly thrashed-out agreement is presumed likely to be the best that accurate knowledge of the problem area could produce.

Of course, in some cases too much interaction could prove as harmful to the progress or outcome of negotiations as too little.[10] In any case, a frequently considered factor in analyzing negotiations is the amount of negotiation that preceded the group's reaching its final view.

It seems unwise to generalize for all negotiation settings that there is in fact either a positive or negative relationship between the amount of deliberation that precedes the closure of negotiations, and the desirability of the outcome of the negotiations. But in any case, when studying the way any given negotiations proceed under varying conditions (here expert as opposed to layman participation with politicos), certainly it is worth examining whether there is any difference between the *amount* of communication that is exchanged in one negotiation situation prior to its closure, as compared to the other. In the research described here, these first variables measured the amount of communication between the subject and other participants. The operational question is whether negotiations are more active in layman or expert groups. Either group may conceivably involve much member maneuvering and discussion, or little such activity prior to closure. This seems worth measuring because intensity of communication in real-world negotiation may indicate the "health" of the negotiations at any particular time. (That is, whether they are proceeding in a manner likely to produce what the observer would deem the most desirable outcome.) Thus variable 1 measured the number of messages received by a subject; variable 2 measured the number of messages a subject sent.

Variables 3 and 4: Tendency to Opt Out of the Group

It seems reasonable to expect that, in principle, negotiators will continue their participation in negotiations as long as they feel that negotiation as a method of solving the problem at hand offers better prospects for attaining their goals than do alternative methods available to them.[11] It would certainly seem inevitable that we all, in every consciously undertaken social process, must at some time (if not continually) assess whether the game is worth the candle (especially when there are other games we could be playing).

In a sense, then, we can specify a rational component of the decision whether or not to continue one's commitment to a negotiating situation. On the other hand, students of organization have frequently noted a phenomenon of "goal displacement" whereby a group organized to achieve an objective gradually begins to value the survival of the group for its own sake as a secondary objective.[12] The question is whether ad hoc negotiating groups may not also to some extent develop a desire to maintain the negotiating group as an end in itself.

One facet of behavior involved in negotiation is the implicit act of consenting to maintain the negotiations themselves despite the turns they may take. Assuming the threshold of individual negotiator tolerance of the format varies from person to person, it may be helpful to students of negotiation to know whether such "tolerance levels" vary in some relation to social/behavioral stereotypes of given negotiators. It is with this question in mind that the experimental design was constructed to allow the negotiators the chance to opt out in favor of the individual decision rule.[13] Variable 3 measured the number of threats to opt out. Variable 4 measured the number of messages against the desirability of opting out.

Variables 5 and 6: Consciousness of One's Own Role

The emphasis in analyzing the negotiation process in the experiment reported here was to stress the possible impact of perceptions of social role on the way negotiations are played out. Variables 5 and 6 operationalized the question of whether or not subjects themselves sensed any such role dimension in the social interaction of negotiation with politicos. It appeared that negotiator references to his role status could have served, theoretically, [14] to further several purposes in negotiation.

Conceivably experts (or any holders of role status) could employ their status to gain advantage in confrontation. Also, acclimating to a given role (with some accompanying status) could result in a certain snobbery when dealing with outsiders. On the other hand, identification with a status-evoking role theoretically might also result in a feeling of inferiority in various negotiating relationships. Assuming that these possible attitudes could affect negotiating behavior, variables 5 and 6 (together with variables 7 and 8 below) were designed to measure the extent to which subjects articulated references to the role distinction between negotiators and so explicitly interject considerations of negotiator role distinctions into the actual proceedings.

Variables 5 and 6 were concerned with the extent to which subjects made explicit mention of their own role status. Such references might possibly be self-inflating, in which case we might hypothesize the existence of expert role snobbery in the observed situation. Or such references may be self-deprecatory, in which case we might wish to hypothesize the operation of role inferiority. We shall refer to self-inflating communications as positive, and refer to self-deprecatory references as negative. Variable 5 measured the number of subject positive references to his own role; variable 6 measured the number of negative references.

Variables 7 and 8: Consciousness of Counterparts' Roles

These variables measured the extent to which subjects made positive (variable 7) or negative (variable 8) references to the politicos' role. Our perspective regarding variables 7 and 8 is identical to that governing the view of variables 5 and 6. While the latter measured subject references to his own role, variables 7 and 8 completed the notion of role references generally by measuring a subject's references to his counterparts' role. The distinction between variables 5 and 6 and variables 7 and 8 was maintained to avoid a data yield that might blur what might have turned out to be two distinct categories of role-influenced behavior.

Variables 9, 10 and 11: Eliciting or Offering Specific Proposals

These variables reflect a simple concept relevant to negotiation, but one that seems to tap a fundamental facet of negotiating behavior. These variables were designed as an operational expression of the degree of specificity, of directness, with which each subject approached the negotiating problem.[15]

In our everyday academic discussions we recognize the distinction between "concrete" treatments of a problem, and more abstract, analytical approaches. Indeed, most individuals can often type the "reasoning styles" as it were of their daily contacts regarding their conformity with one or the other of these two approaches. It seemed useful, then, to examine expert negotiating behavior on this plane.

Such a measure seemed additionally important when one considered that the timing with which the discussion of specifics or abstractions is undertaken in political negotiations can often determine whether the negotiations take a fortunate or disastrous turn. While there was no attempt to systematically chart subjects' *timing* of specific or abstract communications, the *frequency* of specific—concrete—communications was charted. This measure was deemed useful on the assumption that, all things being equal, any peculiar expert tendencies to encourage or shun specific proposals concerning the negotiating problem might correspondingly suggest that the expert negotiating style militates for or against the progress of negotiation at certain stages. We will leave it to tacticians of negotiation to determine just what these stages may be during which the introduction of specifics is useful or detrimental to given negotiator purposes. For our purposes here, it will be interesting to note simply whether the expert negotiating style indeed showed any such affinity or aversion to such a level of problem treatment (i.e., the stressing of specifics). To this end, variable 9 measured the number of subject requests for specific numbers from politicos. The number of subject offers of specific numbers on politico request was measured by variable 10. Variable 11 measured the number of subject offers of specific numbers without an immediately preceding request for a specific number by the receiving politico.

Variables 12, 13, 14, and 15: Tendency to Adopt a "Meta-Perspective"

These variables were an operationalization of a facet of behavior akin to that measured by variables 5-8. And, like variables 9-11, these variables also reflected the degree to which subjects were conscious of the character of negotiation as a social relationship in which participants may attempt to manipulate each other.

For us, negotiation can be analyzed on one dimension: As interaction between phenotypes representing different social roles. In this sense it can be seen as a social process in which style of behavior could determine the way the process operates each time it is undertaken. Variables 12-15 examined negotiator behavior for evidence of an awareness of this latter dimension of negotiation on the part of the negotiator himself. They measured the extent to which negotiators themselves showed a recognition of negotiation as a social, partly competitive, process which therefore encourages participant behavior based on strategic and tactical manipulation. In a sense, these variables monitored that aspect of negotiator behavior in which negotiators may exhibit a kind of overview-awareness of the manipulative, socially competitive, character of the negotiation, simultaneous with their playing it out. To emphasize that variables 12-15 tapped this level of overview-awareness, I have described them as measures of participant's *Meta-perspective.*

These meta-perspective variables were designed as measures of the frequency with which subjects self-consciously:

Referred to the group's condition—its dilemma of having to mix contradictory views of differently skilled individuals into a single answer (measured by variable 12);
Noted the progress of negotiations (variable 13);
Articulated their own tactics (variable 14);
Articulated counterpart tactics (variable 15).

These were measures of the ability to see negotiations in the abstract, as a strategic process. They tapped the ability of subjects to step out of their particular group memberships and adopt a larger perspective on their own and their counterparts' behavior.

These variables seemed significant for many reasons. For example, it might be that the greater the ability to adopt a meta-perspective, the greater the ability to negotiate according to generalized maxims of good negotiating behavior. There may be a relationship between tendencies toward meta-perspectives and the ability to exploit negotiating situations as social relationships susceptible to domination, redirection, and so on. While we cannot know a priori whether there are grounds for positing any of these relationships, the measure of meta-perspective tendencies seemed one possible way to uncover another plane of negotiating behavior on which experts might function uniquely. Conversely, it was thought capable as well of reflecting the ability of negotiators to sense that certain *counterpart* communications were part of counterpart tactical maneuvers and were therefore to be resisted in given instances.

Variables 16, 17, 18, 19, 20: Coalition Behavior

This is a familiar concept.[16] It can be subdivided in ways that may have important bearing on the way negotiations proceed and so, ultimately, on their outcome. Subjects may be active or passive coalition members. That is, they may initiate coalitions, or simply acquiesce to the coalescing overtures of their counterparts. In addition to being active or passive coalition members, subjects may show a preference for open or secret coalitions; a secret coalition would be one whose existence is not revealed to a third party. Again, it was hoped that analysis of the record of communication would reveal the frequency with which coalitions were suggested, acceded to, refused, and so on. Variable 16 measured the frequency with which subjects attempted to initiate open coalitions (coalitions revealed to the third party); the frequency with which subjects initiated secret coalitions was measured by variable 17. Variable 18 measured the frequency with which subjects acceded to open coalition offers; variable 19 measured accession to secret coalition offers, and variable 20 measured the number of rejections by the subject of all types of coalitions.

Variables 21, 22, 23, 24: Communications Concerned with Personal Attacks

It seemed prudent for two reasons to measure the amount of negotiator interaction concerned with personal confrontation. One generically important aspect of any negotiations is repartee. In principle it is difficult to operationalize the measure of impact of the "bon mot" per se, if only because its definition is contextual. However, one type of communication which may be included under the general rubric of repartee, and which can be isolated more easily than witty remarks per se, is the personal attack— the sarcastic personal reference, the cutting comment.

Such personal attacks are akin to the kind of sarcastic wit more frequently denoted by the term repartee in that, like repartee generally, personal attack takes its effect in negotiation not by speaking specifically to negotiation developments or problem parameters, but by affecting the personality undercurrents in negotiations. We take remarks concerned with personal attack as our one measure on this plane because messages dealing with personal attacks can be more easily and objectively identified.

A second reason for measuring communications concerned with personal attack, aside from its relation to the realm of repartee, is that such measures may reveal much of the negotiator's attitude toward his counterparts and the negotiations. We may expect that measuring the use of and responses to personal attack can lend insight into the hostility levels of players and the extent to which they value the collegial tone assumed to characterize triad negotiations of the type established here. Hence variable 21 measured the number of personal attacks a subject received; variable 22 indicated the number of challenging responses he offered to personal attacks; the number of low-key or nonchallenging responses he offered was measured by variable 23; and variable 24 measured the number of personal attacks the subject initiated.

Variable 25: The Use of Deception

Deception is a basic concept in all negotiations. Devising some a priori argument for its value as a measure in assessing negotiating style seems artificial. It was included because not even an exploratory study of negotiating style would seem complete without it.

Variables 26, 27, 28, 29: References to
Own or Counterpart Ability

The view of these variables is similar to that governing variables 5-8, concerned with role references. References to ability were distinguished from references to role by holding that remarks about own or counterpart qualifications might not be tied to the role stereotype associated with the participant who is the object of the reference. Ability references were thus references to player qualifications that did not include the words expert, politico, or some synonym. It was expected that ability remarks would usually pertain more to substantive skill regarding the problem itself than would remarks about player qualifications that included specific role

references. The nomenclature used in defining variables 26-29 follows that
for variables 5-8. Thus variable 26 measured the number of subject positive
references to his own ability. Variable 27 measured the number of negative
references to his own ability. Variable 28 measured positive references to
counterpart ability, and variable 29 measured negative references to counterpart ability.

Variables 30, 31: Volume of Mediator Remarks

Daily experience in personal encounters suggests that some individuals
tend to adopt the role of conciliator in social interaction. Of course, some
negotiation formats make this role explicit by introducing titled mediators
who may or may not have a stake in the outcome of negotiations.[17] It
seemed worthwhile to inquire whether de facto mediators arose in multiparty negotiations where no mediator per se was present, and whether any
such phenomenon was related to the participation of experts.

Literature speculating on the impact of mediators is legion,[18] but the
presence of such "natural mediators" would seem well worth examining. Any patterned relationship between the rise of such mediators and the
status of expertise would certainly be important in specifying the uniqueness of expert negotiating style in the presence of politicos.

I assumed that any such mediators may identify themselves with
varying degrees of explicitness, so I tried to measure such mediator
behavior by distinguishing explicit mediator remarks from implicit
mediator remarks. Included in the latter were mediating references that
did not include the words mediator, mediating, or some synonym. Again
the identification of such remarks was contextual, but generally the rule
was to isolate remarks that expressed an interest in, or functioned to
conciliate disputes between, counterparts. Thus variable 30 measured the
number of subjects' explicit mediator remarks, and variable 31 measured
the number of implicit mediator remarks.

Variable 32: Volume of Technological Messages

In monitoring negotiations involving a topic amenable to expertise we
expected some amount of discussion to deal with problem parameters
per se. It seemed useful to know how much of a negotiator's communication dwelled on problem technology, as there may be a relationship
between the amount of substantive discussion and the evolution of expert-
politico negotiations. In any event, we wanted to know if conferring

expertise affected the amount of technological discussion an individual undertook. In our problem, technological discussion included assertions of some formula for computing the number of dots, some symbolic logic for handling the problem, some borrowed algorithm, some computation involving calibrations provided in the margins of the dot picture, and so on. Thus variable 32 measured the number of technological messages sent by the subject.

Variables 33, 34, 35, 36: References to the Grand Coalition

Consummating the grand coalition was akin to reaching agreement in this problem, and references to it became important because they were, in a sense, references to the object of the game. Of course, they were also references to the cooperative element in the game, to considerations that would override those governing two-person coalitions in the short run. The grand-coalition notion is generic to negotiations of this type that reward unanimity, so their measurement needs no justification here. They were distinguished from two-person coalition references because the grand coalition reference lacked the strategic quality of two-person coalitions in this game. The nomenclature for categorizing grand coalition references paralleled that for two-person coalitions. Hence variable 33 measured the number of positive references to the grand coalition initiated by the subject; variable 34 indicated acquiescence regarding grand coalition references by politicos; variable 35 revealed negative references initiated by the subject; and variable 36 measured negative responses to grand coalition references initiated by the politicos.

Variable 37: Instructional Messages

The frequency of instructional messages (i.e., directives, messages that gave orders) was an easy operationalization of behavior concerned with structuring counterpart behavior. It seemed important to know whether a negotiator attempts to control the course of negotiations by influencing the specific content of counterpart communications to come. In multiparty negotiations this may be seen as an attempt to structure proceedings by directly manipulating counterparts and also as making demands on counterparts. It is assumed that giving instructions implies the expecta-

tion that they will be followed, and so may constitute making demands in some contexts. Issuing directives can be considered as
aggressive but not necessarily hostile behavior. It seemed useful to
establish whether such attempts at control varied with expert status in
the presence of perceived politicos. Variable 37 measured the number
of such directives issued by subjects.

Variable 38: Identical Messages

This variable measured behavior akin to sending directives in that it
measured what we may take as subject attempts to structure the group.
Identical messages were messages of the same content sent to both
counterparts simultaneously. Content per se was irrelevant in labeling
identical messages, so this variable differed from the measure of directives
in that there was no inherent interest in assertiveness. It seemed useful to
establish whether expertise varied with a "me-them" view of counterparts,
as a high score on this variable would have suggested. The effect of sending
identical messages would seem to have been that of indicating an attempt
to transform the triad into a single dyad. We should not conclude that
such an attempt at group structuring reflects assertiveness of itself, any
more than insecurity creating the need for simplification. But given that
this variable was to be interpreted in the light of behaviors that might have
co-occurred with it, inferences about subject views of the group may have
been made that much easier, and the aim was to learn whether such views
were affected by the status of expertise.

Variable 39: Requests for Reports on Other Dyad

This variable's importance can be inferred from the treatments of
variables 37 and 38 above. It was marked as a distinct behavior on the
assumption that the elements of behavior implicit in variables 37 and 38
might have taken two forms that could not have been detected given the
phrasing of the preceding variables. Additionally, this variable contained
an element of implied subject concern with the behavior of other counterparts individually, in contrast to the emphasis of variables 37 and 38 on
the unity of counterparts. Thus incorporating variable 39 in our list of
measures not only supplemented the two preceding variables, but provided
data for possible use in inferring the level of subject concern with being
left out—with missing something.

Variable 40: Impact of Group
Experience on Final Decision

Variable 40 scaled the degree of independence from the influence of the group experience that subjects showed in giving their final answer to the game. This measure was important because of its ability to indicate the extent to which experts' views on a problem were influenced by politicos in negotiation.

As indicated earlier, in an eleventh minute following ten minutes of free exchange, the subject and politicos were each directed to make a final offer. Politico-confederates withheld on a prearranged signal, until the subject sent his final offer to each. The confederates then responded jointly with identical final offers that were 20 percent higher than the subject's. The subject then was given essentially four options: To answer in agreement with the 20 percent higher offer, to stick to his final offer, to give a final answer lower than his final offer, or to give a final answer between his final offer and the politico 20 percent plus figure.

We reasoned that the subject's agreeing with the politicos would indicate a susceptibility to group influence, i.e., the proceedings would have had an effect on his initial judgment. Sticking to one's final offer would have represented a somewhat greater independence from the group, but still the influence of the proceedings would be apparent in that the subject would have adopted an answer which initially reflected his own best offer of compromise. Opting out with a number between his own final offer and the politico figure would have indicated a lesser influence of the proceedings, in that there would have been no reluctance to disavow his promised best offer and now inject a totally new figure. Greatest independence from the group proceedings would have been shown by answering with a new low number, to the extent that the proceedings would be disavowed and the number given would not be in the range of that covered by the final offers. Thus in tabulating the subject's game answer, we scored 0, on a scale of independence, for group agreement, 1 for sticking to the final offer, 2 for offering a new number within the subject offer-politico offer range, and 3 for a new number outside the subject-politico final-offer range.

Variable 41: Number of Concessions Made

The importance of measuring concession behavior in a negotiation study needs no elaboration. In an exploratory study it seemed best to employ broad and simple measures of concession behavior.[19] Hence variable 41 counted the simple number of concessions by the subject in the ten-minute round. Concessions were defined as any change in number position regardless of direction. This decision reflects the assumption that the subject would be the middle person on the number scale given confederate instructions, so direction would not be an indication of flexibility.

Variable 42: Net Concession Value of Final Offer

This was the second concession measure; it was designed to reflect the magnitude of concession represented by the subject's final offer to politicos. Magnitude seemed here best interpreted as the difference between the first offer and the final offer. The formula used to compute a subject's score on this variable was designed to adjust for differences in the size of dot estimates and for differences in the direction of concessions.[20] This concludes the presentation of dependent variables.

Results

Data were obtained by coding all subject messages for content reflecting behavior measured by any of the forty-two dependent variables, and then arriving at a score for each subject on each variable. Except for variables 40 and 42, these were frequency scores. Variable 40 was scored with a scale ranging from 0 to 3. Variable 42 involved essentially a percentage rating for the final offer. (See the variable descriptions above.) A multiple-coding system was used whereby a given message could be coded for scores on more than one variable if the coder judged this to be appropriate in light of the message content.

Coder reliability was calculated at 90 percent. One coder scored all messages and then a second coder scored 50 percent of all messages, selected randomly. The reliability figure represents the percent of coder agreement on both items and frequency. Coders were blind to subjects' test status. Table 2.2 reports the means and standard deviations for experts and laymen for each of the forty-two variables.

Expert and layman scores on each dependent variable were compared by applying the t-test for significant mean differences and the f-maximum test for significant differences in variance. Orthogonal (verimax) factor analysis was also undertaken for test and control group scores separately, to ascertain differences in the way dependent variables were orchestrated

Table 2.2 Means and Standard Deviations for Experts and Laymen

Variable	Experts		Laymen	
	Mean	Standard Dev.	Mean	Standard Dev.
VAR001	13.6400	2.1579	13.6000	2.1213
VAR002	10.8800	2.5710	11.6800	2.8243
VAR003	0.2000	0.5000	0.1600	0.4726
VAR004	0.2000	0.5000	0.3200	0.6272
VAR005	0.2400	0.4359	0.0800	0.4000
VAR006	0.0400	0.2000	0.0800	0.2769
VAR007	0.0	0.0	0.0400	0.2000
VAR008	0.0800	0.2769	0.0800	0.4000
VAR009	0.8000	0.8165	1.0400	1.5133
VAR010	1.6800	1.3454	1.8000	1.3229
VAR011	3.3200	2.2121	4.3200	2.3402
VAR012	0.5200	0.8718	1.1200	1.0536
VAR013	0.5600	0.9165	0.4800	0.8718
VAR014	0.8800	1.6155	1.1200	1.5362
VAR015	1.2400	1.3000	0.9200	1.2220
VAR016	0.3200	0.6904	0.4000	0.7071
VAR017	0.0	0.0	0.2000	0.4082
VAR018	0.0	0.0	0.1600	0.3742
VAR019	0.0800	0.2769	0.3200	0.6272
VAR020	0.2000	0.5774	0.5200	0.8226
VAR021	1.2400	1.0116	1.4800	1.0847
VAR022	0.3600	0.7572	0.2400	0.5228
VAR023	0.4000	0.6455	0.4800	0.5099
VAR024	0.5200	0.9626	0.4800	1.0456
VAR025	0.0400	0.2000	0.4800	0.9626
VAR026	0.7200	1.1000	0.1600	0.4726
VAR027	0.2800	0.6137	0.2000	0.4082
VAR028	0.0	0.0	0.0400	0.2000
VAR029	0.1200	0.4397	0.0800	0.2769
VAR030	0.0400	0.2000	0.0	0.0
VAR031	0.1600	0.3742	0.3200	0.5568
VAR032	2.2800	1.8376	1.6800	1.9088
VAR033	0.1200	0.3317	0.6000	0.9574
VAR034	0.1200	0.3317	0.2400	0.5228
VAR035	0.0	0.0	0.0400	0.2000
VAR036	0.0400	0.2000	0.0800	0.2769
VAR037	0.6400	1.1504	0.7200	0.8907
VAR038	1.0000	1.0408	1.0000	1.1547
VAR039	0.1600	0.4726	0.2000	0.5000
VAR040	0.7600	0.8794	0.8800	1.0536
VAR041	3.9600	1.8138	4.4000	1.8484
VAR042	15.1480	15.8218	26.5080	26.8199

for each group. We will consider the factor analysis results and implications first, and then the results and implications of the statistical tests.

Factor Analysis Results and Discussion

The strategy of analysis in this vein was first to establish the structure of the total array of behaviors for laymen. Any difference in the way these behaviors were structured for experts could be taken as the effect of expert role status, assuming the experimental design was valid.

In preparing the data for factor analysis, it was necessary to delete six variables. These are the variables for which either experts or laymen had variances of zero. Variables with zero variance must be excluded from a factor analysis because they cannot co-vary with the remaining variables for each group and have vectors of zero length in the n-space. Unless they are excluded the factor structures of the expert and layman groups cannot be compared. The variables excluded from the factor analysis are variables 7, 17, 18, 28, 30, and 35. The comparison of expert and layman factor structures was thus made on the basis of thirty-six variables.

Factor analysis indicated that the data could best be explained by a four (rotated) factor structure for experts and laymen. The factors may be interpreted as distinct patterns of behavior within the given subject group. A pattern in this context is a regular co-occurrence of otherwise separately measured behaviors.

With a total of eight (rotated) factors and forty-nine principle variable components (loading $\geq .5$) it would be tedious to reconstruct the logic of factor identification. For this reason discussion on this point has been relegated to the appendix, where the reader should find an adequate treatment of this issue. Additional data tables are provided there. We will describe the factors only briefly here.

Patterns of Layman Behavior Suggested by Factor Analysis

The four distinct patterns uncovered in layman behavior may be described as tromped-on follower behavior (layman factor 1; Table 2.3); company man behavior (layman factor 2; Table 2.4); cooperative, contributing follower behavior (layman factor 3; Table 2.5); and conditional follower behavior (layman factor 4; Table 2.6).

Table 2.3   Principle Variable Components of First Layman Factor
             Subgrouped to Indicate Conceptual Similarities among
             Specific Components[1]

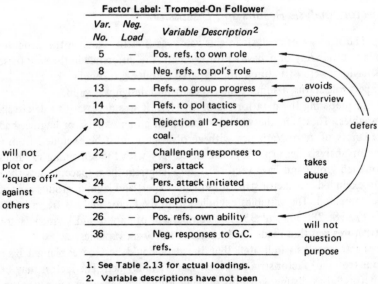

| Factor Label: Tromped-On Follower | | |
Var. No.	Neg. Load	Variable Description[2]
5	—	Pos. refs. to own role
8	—	Neg. refs. to pol's role
13	—	Refs. to group progress
14	—	Refs. to pol tactics
20	—	Rejection all 2-person coal.
22	—	Challenging responses to pers. attack
24	—	Pers. attack initiated
25	—	Deception
26	—	Pos. refs. own ability
36	—	Neg. responses to G.C. refs.

(annotations: avoids overview; defers; will not plot or "square off" against others; takes abuse; will not question purpose)

1. See Table 2.13 for actual loadings.
2. Variable descriptions have not been
   rephrased for negative-loading variables.
   Rephrasing is employed in the text.

Each factor label for laymen (as well as experts to be discussed below) was derived from speculation about the conceptual communality of the factor's principal loading variables.

Tromped-on Follower Behavior (See Table 2.3)

Based on an inspection of the apparent conceptual relationships between the principal loading variables, this first pattern of layman behavior seems to be characterized by reluctance to "square off" against others. Also, it is characterized by a willingness to take abuse on the personal level, to pay deference to others, a reluctance to question purpose, and an avoidance of any overview of the proceedings. To indicate that this first factor for laymen seemed to involve marked subservience (especially compared to other patterns that will be discussed), the tromped-on follower description was assigned. Note again that, as with all

Table 2.4   Principle Variable Components of Second Layman Factor
             Subgrouped to Indicate Conceptual Similarities among
             Specific Components[1]

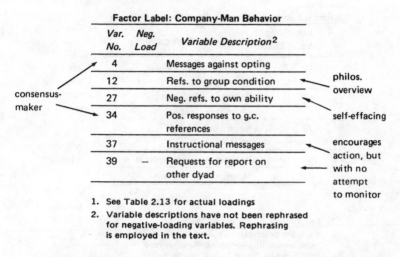

	Var. No.	Neg. Load	Variable Description[2]	
	4		Messages against opting	
	12		Refs. to group condition	philos. overview
consensus- maker	27		Neg. refs. to own ability	
	34		Pos. responses to g.c. references	self-effacing
	37		Instructional messages	encourages action, but
	39	—	Requests for report on other dyad	with no attempt to monitor

Factor Label: Company-Man Behavior

1. See Table 2.13 for actual loadings
2. Variable descriptions have not been rephrased
   for negative-loading variables. Rephrasing
   is employed in the text.

other factors, the inferences involved here in moving from variable descriptions to conceptual similarities among variables and finally to factor labels are provided in the appendix.

Company Man Behavior (See Table 2.4)

This second behavior pattern for laymen is associated with the second layman factor. The behavior involves taking a philosophical overview of the proceedings, and working as a consensus-maker. It also involves encouraging problem action in a vague way that indicates no attempt at monitoring counterpart activity. This pattern also involves self-effacing behavior. The label used in summarizing this pattern is designed to reflect a vacuous yes-man image devoid of real content but supportive of others in tone.

Cooperative, Contributing Follower Behavior (See Table 2.5)

The third layman factor seems to suggest a behavior pattern that indicates flexibility regarding substantive issues. It also suggests a reluctance to disparage the standing of counterparts, along with a willingness to

Table 2.5   **Principle Variable Components of Third Layman Factor**
Subgrouped to Indicate Conceptual Similarities among
Specific Components[1]

Factor Label: Cooperative, Contributing Follower

Var. No.	Neg. Load	Variable Description[2]	
10		Offers specific numbers on request	open to
11		Offers specific numbers without request	and suggests possible solutions
29	—	Negative references to pol's ability	will not
31		Implicit mediator remarks	disparage
41		Number of concessions	
			flexible

conciliating and willing to take responsibility

1. See Table 2.13 for actual loadings.
2. Variable descriptions have not been rephrased for negative-loading variables. Rephrasing is employed in the text.

accept responsibility. The pattern indicates conciliating behavior and an openness to solution suggestions, as well as a willingness to offer suggestions. The pattern is labeled cooperative, contributing follower behavior to indicate that it involves an openness and a constructive approach without any accompanying aggressiveness or difficulty in working with others. Also there is no attempt to "take over," hence the follower characterization.

Conditional Follower Behavior (See Table 2.6)

The fourth layman factor involves behavior that seems to suggest a solution orientation and a willingness to pressure counterparts toward this end. This pattern involves making demands. It involves a willingness to alienate others through participation in secret agreement, and a generally active communications pattern. The pattern is described as conditional follower behavior because, although demands are made, there is no monitoring of the reaction to them, and although there is a willingness to co-align, this pattern does not involve the *initiation* of coalitions. In the absence of leader-like behavior, the follower description seems appropriate. At the same time, following behavior is here not unconditional. According to this pattern, following includes some demands and holds the

Table 2.6 **Principle Variable Components of Fourth Layman Factor Subgrouped to Indicate Conceptual Similarities among Specific Components[1]**

Factor Label: Conditional-Follower Behavior

Var. No.	Neg. Load	Variable Description[2]	
1		Number of messages received	← communi-cative
2		Number of messages sent	←
9		Requests for specific numbers	will follow in intrigue; prepared to alienate
19		Positive responses to "secret coalition two" offers	←
37		Instructional messages	

solution oriented; will pressure for same → (points to 9)

makes demands → (points to 37)

1. See Table 2.13 for actual loadings.
2. Variable descriptions have not been rephrased for negative-loading variables. Rephrasing is employed in text.

possibility of combining with one player against the third. For this reason the follower label is modified and described as conditional.

Patterns of Expert Behavior Suggested by Factor Analysis: Participating Broker Behavior (See Table 2.7)

The first expert factor involves behavior that serves to build consensus. It indicates a solution orientation, a commitment to the group format, and the avoidance of confrontation even when there is provocation. There is noticeable interest in compromising in a situation where unanimity is at stake (the final-offer round). There is clear interest in structuring counterpart behavior taken as a unit and, in this context, an interest in feedback—in monitoring counterpart behavior. This pattern is labeled participating-broker behavior to reflect a pattern of active involvement in group activity coupled with action aimed at forging consensus and adjusting expert behavior to increase the chances of reaching such consensus. In this context, no implication of taking second place—of being a follower—seems to be indicated.

Table 2.7   Principle Variable Componnets of First Expert Factor
             Subgrouped to Indicate Conceptual Similarities among
             Specific Components[1]

	Var. No.	Neg. Load	Variable Description[2]	
	Factor Label: Participating-Broker Behavior			
group commit-ment	3	—	Threats to opt out	builds consensus
	16		Initiates open coal. for two	
avoids confron-tation	23		Low-key responses to personal attack	solution oriented[3]
	32		Technological messages	structures counterpart behavior
	38		Identical messages	
monitors	39		Requests for report on other dyad	
	42		Net concession value of final offer	will compromise for unaminity

1. See Table 2.14 for actual loadings.
2. Variable descriptions have not been rephrased
   for negative-loading variables. Rephrasing
   is employed in the text.
3. Variable 32 seems not to suggest flaunting
   expert ability given that variable 27 (negative
   references to own ability) loads .497.
   See appendix.

Leader (Dictatorial) Behavior (See Table 2.8)

The second expert factor suggests a behavior pattern that includes a
rejection of actions which might create the appearance of subordination. A
kind of overview-awareness exists, but at the same time so does extensive
monitoring of counterparts which may be interpreted (given its components) as making evaluations of counterpart performance. This pattern also
suggests belligerency and appears to involve order-giving and the expectation of feedback in this context. The leader label seems to reflect the total
impression suggested by this array of behaviors. We suggest that this leader
behavior might furthermore be interpreted as a very aggressive, dictatorial
kind of leadership. This stems from the suggestion that the pattern
involves strict controlling and personal aggressiveness, among other things.

Table 2.8   Principle Variable Components of Second Expert Factor
Subgrouped to Indicate Conceptual Similarities among
Specific Components[1]

Factor Label: Leader Behavior

Var. No.	Neg. Load	Variable Description[2]	
13		References to group progress	← takes overview
14		References to pol's tactics	
20		Rejection of all types two-person coalitions	
22		Challenging responses to personal attacks	← fighter behavior
24		Initiates personal attacks	
37		Instructional messages	giving orders; expecting feedback
39		Requests for reports on other dyad	

will not follow; aloof

extensive monitoring; evaluating

1. See Table 2.14 for actual loadings
2. Variable descriptions have not been rephrased
   for negative-loading variables. Rephrasing
   is employed in the text.

Nonhostile, Independent Behavior (See Table 2.9)

The variables associated with this pattern seem to suggest three main
thrusts to this factor. There is a pronounced lack of overview, a commitment to format but noticeable aversion to alignment. There is also the
evidence of independent-mindedness not found in other patterns. The
pattern seems to suggest independent behavior. It is described as nonhostile, to indicate that the detachment is not associated with any hostility. At the same time the context suggests that submission is not involved
here because of a pattern of saying "No" in certain situations. Again, the
logic whereby specific principle variables are linked to broader concepts
that suggest the label is detailed in the appendix.

Insecure Expert Behavior (See Table 2.10)

This factor involves a small number of principle variables. However, a
coherent pattern of behavior is suggested when one considers the variables

Table 2.9 Principle Variable Components of Third Expert Factor Subgrouped to Indicate Conceptual Similarities among Specific Components[1]

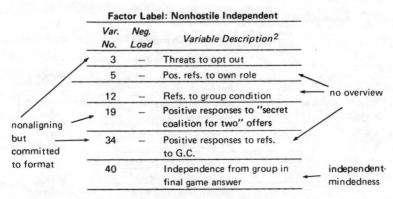

Factor Label: Nonhostile Independent

Var. No.	Neg. Load	Variable Description[2]
3	–	Threats to opt out
5	–	Pos. refs. to own role
12	–	Refs. to group condition
19	–	Positive responses to "secret coalition for two" offers
34	–	Positive responses to refs. to G.C.
40		Independence from group in final game answer

nonaligning but committed to format

no overview

independent-mindedness

1. See Table 2.14 for actual loadings.
2. Variable descriptions have not been rephrased for negative-loading variables. Rephrasing is employed in the text.

Table 2.10 Principle Variable Components of Fourth Expert Factor Subgrouped to Indicate Conceptual Similarities among Specific Components[1]

Factor Label: Insecure-Expert Behavior

Var. No.	Neg. Load	Variable Description[2]
1		Number of messages received
2		Number of messages sent
9		Requests for specific number solutions
11		Offers specific nos. without request[3]
33	–	Initiates pos. refs. to G.C.

task preoccupation; avoiding triad dynamics

much communication

much testing; seeking direction

1. See Table 2.14 for actual loadings.
2. Variable descriptions have not been rephrased for negative-loading variables. Rephrasing is employed in the text.
3. Variables 11 and 33 *approach* principle variable component status (at .479 and –.490 respectively). They are included to facilitate labeling of this factor.

that come close to the .5 level together with the highest loading components.

The pattern suggests expert behavior that involves a pronounced display of intense communicating. (Notice the loadings on variables 1 and 2 detailed in the appendix and Table 2.14). In this context the remaining principle variable can be interpreted as testing behavior—as a preoccupation with seeking direction. The variables approaching the .5 level in this pattern seem to corroborate the view that this pattern involves much testing and direction-seeking. The label, insecure expert behavior, is designed to reflect the image of uncertainty which, coming from the expert and in contrast to other expert patterns, suggests a lack of sure footing in interaction.

Toward an Overview of the Factor Analysis Findings

We have been concerned in the preceding paragraphs with identifying the distinct patterns according to which experts' negotiating behaviors are orchestrated in dealing with presumed politicos. The suggestion is that the distinctiveness of these patterns stems from the fact that they differ from patterns of control-group behavior.

It is important to strive for some overview of *how* the collection of expert factors differs from layman factors. The question is, what is conceptually significant in noting that our laboratory "experts" display behavior patterns that differ from those displayed by the control group?

In examining the labels developed for all out factors, a conceptual common denominator appears to be involved. Stressing the speculative nature of this line of inquiry, labels assigned to factors in both groups all seem to involve the notion of personal assertiveness to some degree.

An "armchair analysis" indicated that by harking to higher levels of abstraction, some logic of shared concepts united the principle variables of each factor and lent themselves to a summary label that sought to capture the underlying theme of these variable relationships. In a similar (but even more speculative) vein, we may be justified in asking whether there is now some underlying theme that indicates a conceptual relationship between the factors themselves which were uncovered within each experimental group. In exploring this issue it is again necessary to retreat to a higher level of abstraction. In other words, we are taking one further step back from the data in an attempt to gain an overview.[21]

As we move away from the data yield itself and sink deeper into the armchair, the caveat inherent in exploratory, speculative study must be stressed even more strongly. But in striving for a first cut at a conceptual framework, and by stressing the tentative character of any resulting judgments, understanding may be improved by the effort.

The Notion of Assertiveness and the Relationships among Factors

If we ask whether there is any concept in interpersonal relations which seems relevant to the collection of factors uncovered ,for each group, the notion of personal assertiveness stands out. Personal assertiveness may be described as the degree to which an individual resists falling into the follower role; it represents the degree to which his is not subordinated by others and, conversely, the degree to which he assumes a high-profile, pivotal role in dealings with others. Assertiveness is reflected in one's insisting on recognition, in maximizing the scope of one's prerogatives. Webster notes that to assert oneself is "to thrust oneself forward."[22] Consider the layman factors in this experiment. (In the following sections, recall that the appendix provides the logic of factor labeling in detail.)

ASSERTIVENESS AND THE LAYMAN FACTORS

Clearly the tromped-on follower pattern can be described in this context as a pattern of extremely submissive (nonassertive) behavior. By our definition the tromped-on follower is deferential; He takes abuse; he will not "square off" or question purpose.

The company-man pattern relates to the notion of assertiveness in that it reflects a supportive, nonaggressive posture in which the attitude toward the group is positive and nonthreatening. The philosophical orientation in this context appears to be consistent if interpreted as retreat to a domain that does not invite disagreement given the more pressing tasks before the group.

The cooperative, contributing follower is also interpretable as a nonaggressive, nonassertive posture. However, the element of subordination here would seem to lack the cowering suggested in the tromped-on follower and, to a lesser extent, in the company man. The cooperative follower does not challenge other members or command a pivotal position in the group; however, his active participation, interest in solutions, and willingness to assume responsibility suggest that submission is not the outstanding characteristic of the pattern. The cooperative, contributing follower is a follower, but also a contributor to the substantive work of the group. This would seem to imply some willingness to defend a position and, presumably, to defend oneself.

The conditional-follower pattern suggests behavior that is more assertive than other layman types. While the conditional follower does not "thrust himself forward" to the point of assuming an outstanding position in the group, his falling into line could not be taken for granted as might be expected for other layman types.

The conditional follower is prepared to alienate others by combining secretly against them and making demands of a sort. He shows a willingness to approach the problem per se and, presumably, to take issue. The label for this pattern was designed to indicate that, although he is a follower, his following cannot be taken for granted; it is not unconditional. He has expectations for counterparts. These qualities suggest that those adopting this pattern would be more likely to assert themselves in interaction than would other laymen.

ASSERTIVENESS AND THE EXPERT FACTORS

It appears that all expert types as well can be related to the concept of assertiveness. The leader pattern for experts (Table 2.8) suggests extremely assertive behavior. As indicated earlier and expanded in the appendix, the leader pattern involves giving orders, initiating personal attacks, remaining aloof, and so on. The pattern was also described at one point as dictatorial.

The participating-broker pattern (Table 2.7) appears to be an assertive pattern of behavior as well. The participating broker monitors behavior, structures counterpart performance, and works actively to build consensus. However, the broker appears to be less assertive than the leader in that the leader's sharp edge is absent. The broker sidesteps confrontation, displays a commitment to the group, and shows he will compromise. The participating broker is an assertive pattern because it involves becoming a pivotal figure; it involves thrusting oneself forward. However, this pattern does not involve attacking others or "strong-arming" others as would more readily seem to be the case with the leader pattern.

The third expert factor, described as the nonhostile independent pattern, can also be related to the concept of personal assertiveness. Someone who is in fact nonhostile and independent might be described as neither controlling nor willing to accept control.[23] Such a behavior pattern could be described as neutral with respect to assertiveness and would be neither a leader nor a follower. Such a person would not conduct his interpersonal relationships in a way that suggested a felt superiority or inferiority regarding counterparts. This does not mean that organizational assignments of leader and follower status could not be made for such people, however; these postures in dealing with others are not sought out. The question of organizational ascription of such roles will be dealt with in later chapters. The point is that, for this third expert pattern, interpersonal cueing alone does not seem to produce a leader or follower preference.

In a group whose other members are perceived politicos, the nonhostile independent appears detached; his orientation to interaction is free of philosophical trappings. He participates but steers clear of involvements. He is not a follower and not a leader, and his independence should be interpreted in these terms.

The fourth expert factor (Table 2.10) is labeled insecure expert behavior. As the label implies, this pattern seems to be the only expert pattern that could be described as submissive behavior, because it seeks direction from others. The insecure expert communicates a great deal but nothing in his profile indicates any attempt to resist persuasion. Including variables which fall just short of principle variable status (variables 11 and 33) the insecure expert appears to be content to offer guestimates, without any resort to pressure or any attempts to monitor others' reactions.

The insecure expert is decidedly unlikely to appeal for support of the common effort. In light of the other behaviors associated with this factor, the latter can be seen as a further reluctance to assume any pivotal role or high profile. In suggesting that the insecure expert pattern can be interpreted as submissive, it should be noted (and will be elaborated later) that submissiveness here is hardly the submissiveness of the tromped-on follower found for laymen. However, if we consider a submissive pattern generally to be one in which there is no "thrusting oneself forward" (while there is also no carefully preserved independence) the label appears justified in relating the fourth expert pattern to the higher-order abstraction of assertive/submissive orientation.

A Qualitative Judgment About the Difference Between Expert and Layman Patterns

The previous discussion suggested that the difference between expert types as a group and laymen types is that experts tend toward behavior patterns that are generally more assertive than layman patterns. The speculative nature of this line of argument should be stressed again. In terms of our strategy of analysis we have already suggested that behavior patterns associated with factors can be interpreted in light of a higher-order concept of assertive/submissive orientation. The assertiveness notion was posited as a conceptual common denominator in the sense that all factors could be related to it in terms of how assertive each behavior pattern appeared to be.

The suggestion at this juncture is that in comparing the collection of expert factors to the collection of layman factors, the expert patterns as a group are generally more assertive than the layman patterns. This is another way of saying that an effect of adopting the expert role in situations approximated by our laboratory setting is an inducement in individuals to strike more assertive poses than they normally would.

Consider the following in support of this view: Two of the four expert patterns merited comparatively assertive labels (the leader and participating broker). One expert pattern was neutral with respect to assertiveness (the nonhostile independent) and only one expert pattern could be judged submissive (the insecure expert).

In contrast, three layman patterns merited submissive labels (the tromped-on follower, company man, and cooperative, contributing follower). Only one layman pattern appeared assertive (the conditional follower).

Moreover, the most assertive expert patterns (leader and participating broker) would appear to involve more aggressive (the leader was even hostile) pivotal, high-profile behavior than the one assertive layman pattern (the conditional follower). The latter was deemed assertive primarily because his following could not be taken for granted. The more assertive expert patterns, in contrast, were so labeled because they involve (as we interpret) deliberate steps to effect a high profile. Similarly, the most submissive layman patterns are far more submissive, it seems, than the submissive expert pattern. Compare the tromped-on follower and company man to the insecure expert.[24]

Keeping in mind the exploratory tone of this work, the factor analysis of our laboratory results suggest the following hypotheses: The effect of adopting the expert role per se in the circumstances we have specified is *to skew behavior toward assertiveness*. Of course this hypothesis must be confirmed in further study before it can be regarded as anything but a cautious guestimate. However, given the state of the art and our larger purpose, discussion in these terms can be useful.

A Further Hypothesis: Generalized Expertise

The discussion of the factor analysis also suggests that experts may have a tendency to generalize their group role. In other words, experts may play active parts in expert-politico groups, not by retaining narrowly defined sovereignty over substantive issues, but by assuming authoritative roles that involve most group processes. If there is a tendency to assertiveness, it seems to be associated with a tendency to broaden the scope of expert activity. The most assertive of the expert patterns posited—the leader and broker patterns—involve assertive behaviors that concern interaction on issues beyond substantive matters.

Confidence in this line of inference is increased by the knowledge that early public administration literature advocated this same view, developed in a somewhat broader context. Gulick wrote in 1937:

> Another trait of the expert is his tendency to assume knowledge and authority in fields in which he has no competence. In this particular, educators, lawyers, priests, admirals, doctors, scientists, engineers, accountants, merchants and bankers are all the same— having achieved technical competence or "success" in one field, they come to think this competence is a general quality detachable from the field and inherent in themselves. They step without embarrass- ment into other areas. They do not remember that the robes of authority of one kingdom confer no sovereignty in another; but that there they are merely a masquerade.[25]

Summarizing the discussion so far in terms of factors affecting expert-politico interaction, we can suggest (with all appropriate caution) the operation of two such factors on the role level:

(1) The tendency of experts qua experts to act personally more assert-ive than they otherwise would as individuals;

(2) The related tendency of experts qua experts to generalize their group roles beyond the narrow province of their expertise.

Statistical Analysis of Laboratory Results and its Relation to Factor Descriptions

In addition to a factor analysis, the t-test for significant mean differ-ences and the f-maximum test for significant differences in variance were

Table 2.11 Behaviors Individually Affected by Expertise: Grouped by
Nature of Effect and Test Used to Isolate

Suppressed Behaviors (t-test, lower expert mean)
Var. 12: References to group condition
Var. 17: Initiating secret coalitions
Var. 18: Accepting open coalitions
Var. 25: Deception
Var. 33: Initiating positive references to grand coalition

Stabilized Behaviors (f-maximum test, less expert variance)
Var. 9: Requests for specific numbers from politicos
Var. 19: Accepting secret coalitions
Var. 25: Deception
Var. 33: Initiating positive references to grand coalition
Var. 34: Positive responses to grand coalition
Var. 42: Net concession value of final offer

Destabilized Behaviors (f-maximum test, more expert variance)
Var. 26: Positive references to own ability
Var. 29: Negative references to politico ability

---

applied to the data. In general terms, the results tend to support inferences drawn from the factor analysis. The variables that scored significantly on these tests involve conceptual relationships which figured prominently in describing the differences between expert and layman factors. The remainder of this chapter describes these tests, reports their results, and suggests how the results may be interpreted in light of the factor-analysis findings.

Recall that Table 2.1 presents the forty-two variables measured in the laboratory; Table 2.2 presents the means and standard deviations for experts and laymen for each variable; Table 2.11 presents the variables that scored significantly at the .05 level or better on either the t-test or f-maximum test. The variables are grouped by the nature of experts' demonstration of them. Inferences in this regard are based on the logic of the tests used, and this will be elaborated shortly.

Before proceeding, however, a few clarifications are in order regarding the use of the t-test and f-maximum test. Tests for levels of significance were two-tailed here. This reflects our judgment in an exploratory study that the directions of any significant effects could not be predicted beforehand. When there was zero variance in a variable for one group, estimation procedures were used in which the standard error of the mean was given by this equation:

$$S_x = \sqrt{\frac{S_1^2}{N-1}}$$

Although the f-maximum test is basically a one-tailed test, it was used according to two-tailed levels of significance here. Also regarding the f-maximum, the algorithm was modified for variables with standard deviations of zero.

According to the t-test, mean scores on each variable for the expert group were compared to mean scores for the layman group. The variables showing significant mean differences are identified on Table 2.11 as behaviors which experts seem to display less often than laymen. This reflects the direction of mean differences that were found; that is, experts had significantly lower means on these variables.

Another way to express this finding is to say that one effect of conferring the status of expertise is to suppress, or inhibit, certain specific negotiating behaviors. The t-test showed that five negotiating behaviors are suppressed by expertise. Before discussing the implications of this finding, it will be convenient to clarify the nature of the f-test findings so that the full set of individually expertise-affected behaviors can be discussed at once.

The f-maximum test involves comparing expert scores to laymen scores on each variable to determine if, for the behavior in question, the variance in scores for experts is significantly different from the variance in scores for laymen. Consider that a significant difference in variance for a given variable indicates that the group showing the greater variance is predictably more erratic regarding display of the behavior that variable represents. Thus referring again to Table 2.11, the results suggest that an effect of conferring expert status on those who negotiate with politicos is to make them more erratic in their manifestations of the behaviors labeled in Table 2.11. Also experts appear to be more stable in their display of those behaviors labeled correspondingly.

Thus, regarding the effects of experts' role status per se on the way they negotiate with politicos (in settings of interest to us), the t- and f-maximum test results suggest the following: Other things being equal, in settings of interest to us, the expert qua expert is inhibited in making references to the group's condition, in initiating secret coalitions, in accepting open coalitions, in undertaking deception, and in initiating positive references to the principle of a grand coalition. The phenotype expert is induced to act more consistently than he otherwise would, in requesting specific alternatives, in accepting secret coalitions, in using deception, in initiating positive references to the grand-coalition principle, in offering positive responses to that principle, and in offering final concessions of uniform value in repeated rounds of negotiation. Also, the expert is induced to act more erratically than he otherwise would in referring positively to his own ability, and in making disparaging references to his politico-counterparts' abilities.

Table 2.12 Behaviors Individually Affected by Expertise: Grouped by Nature of Effect and Conceptual Communality

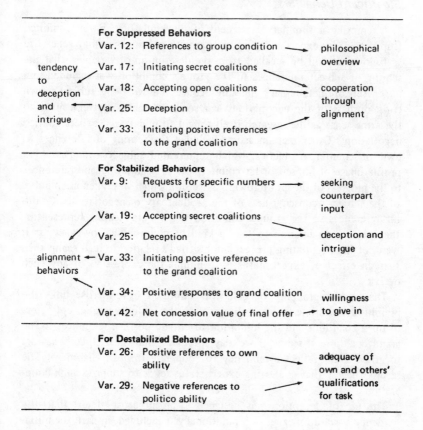

Given our emphasis on exploratory study, some attempt at overview will be useful here. In Table 2.12 these presumed effects of conferring expert status are reproduced as they appeared in Table 2.11. However, in Table 2.12 the behaviors are subgrouped by sets of arrows to indicate behaviors which would seem conceptually to share some relationship. That is, behaviors placed within a subgroup may be identified with a label that reflects a conceptual communality, as it were, for these behaviors. While such orderings are admittedly speculative, or at least subjective, they do seem defensible, and represent an attempt at overview which is important in a first cut.

Toward an Overview of Statistically Significant Behaviors

Attempting a summary statement of the kinds of behavior inhibited (suppressed) by expertise in negotiation with politicos, we may generalize as follows: It will be recalled from the description of variables, that the scoring of subject references to the group's condition was included in a larger set of meta-remark measures concerned with the subject's own consciousness of the negotiations as a social-interaction system, much in the same sense as the research itself sought to understand expert-politico negotiations. Other meta-measures included the scoring of references to own or counterpart tactics, which represented subject awareness of a profile image of himself or his counterparts as negotiators, and references to the progress of the group toward a decision which was taken as an index of the subject's consciousness of the productivity of negotiations. Counting references to the group's condition was a meta-measure representing the subject's inclination to take a kind of philosophical overview, as it were, of the negotiating process and his triad's relation to it. It seems then that an effect of expert status is to inhibit the expression of any such overview.

The second grouping of behaviors inhibited by expertise links the inhibition to initiate secret coalitions with the inhibition to accept offers of open coalitions and the inhibition to initiate positive references to the grand coalition. It seems, if we may speculate, that these three behaviors together could reflect a tendency to cooperate through alignment. The results suggest that conferring expert status tends to suppress such cooperation.

The use of deception was designed as an indicator of just that—the tendency toward intrigue. Computationally it included, in part, the initiation of secret coalitions. This overlap of measures was deliberate because it was assumed that deception is a useful category of itself, and one that, while denoting more than initiating secret agreements, certainly involves this among other things. Thus we can take an overview of the communality of initiating secret coalitions and using deception, taking them together as a measure of the tendency toward deception and intrigue. The results suggest that this behavior may also be inhibited when expert status is internalized.

Overview of Stabilized Behaviors

We can subsume under four categories the behaviors stabilized by conferring expertise. Subject requests for specific number solutions to the problem can be interpreted as an interest in counterpart input. The net concession value of the subject's final offer can be interpreted as a measure of subject willingness to give in.

The significant reduction in expert variance regarding acceptance of secret coalitions and deception seems to suggest, again, stabilization of tendencies toward deception and intrigue. Accepting secret coalitions, initiating positive references to the grand coalition, and positive responses to grand coalition references all involve alignment. The results suggest that such behaviors associated with cooperation through alignment are also stabilized among experts or, again, for the phenotype expert.

Overview of Destabilized Behaviors

For the behaviors made more erratic by conferring expert status, we note a higher-order concept which they too seem to hold in common. Positive references to the expert's own ability and negative references to politico ability may reflect the expert's view on the adequacy of group members for their task. If we choose to attach this higher-order meaning to these two variables, the results suggest that internalizing expertise makes for erratic behavior in communicating on this point. Insofar as communications content reflects attitudes, to confer expertise is to destabilize attitudes about participant qualifications in expert-politico negotiation. This does *not* mean that experts are unpredictable in the way they assess participant abilities relevant to the negotiations at hand. Rather, as we shall see, it simply means that experts may adopt different postures in negotiation with each posture being characterized by one of two extreme views of expert ability relative to politicos. In other words, the phenotype expert is erratic in this regard, or experts differ on this point from one expert to the next.[26]

It should be stressed that we have made several conceptual leaps in moving from statistical test results to this juncture. We suggested that significant differences in means between test and control groups could, given their direction, be interpreted as behaviors suppressed by expertise. It was also posited that significant differences in variance could be taken as evidence of stabilized or destabilized behavior given the direction of differences. These seem to be reasonable and fairly mainstream interpretations. We suggested that the list of significantly scoring variables could be clustered conceptually; the concepts were described as behavioral tendencies. The inference process was similar to that involved in interpreting factor loadings. The statistical tests yield only the untampered list of variables.

The conceptual linkages that we have asserted for variables are not confirmed by any tests. While the inferences seem readily defensible, it should be pointed out that they are armchair extensions of the statistical results proper. Having distinguished again between the results proper and our extrapolations from them, we may continue our speculation while stressing again the tentative, exploratory, first-cut tone of this general line of development.

Statistical Results as Sources of Added Confidence in Factor Interpretation

In discussing the relationship between expert and layman factors, we suggested that expertise produced a general thrust toward assertiveness in relations with fellow participants. Our interpretation of the statistical results can be taken in broad terms, as generally supportive of this suggestion. We posited conceptual communalities for groups of variables that were statistically significant. The reasoning here is that these concepts reflected in the significant variables are related to notions of assertiveness. Also the way that the concepts applied to experts is consistent with our view of how assertiveness related to expertise. In other words, the characteristics that distinguished given factor types from one another seem to be reflected in the statistically significant variables.

Factor Differences and Suppressed Behaviors

Experts "suppressed" references to the group condition; this was described as suppression of philosophical overview. It may be described conversely as a comparatively action-oriented perspective. This could be inferred from the knowledge that the expert types excluded the company man pattern found for laymen. The company man pattern involved an overly philosophical orientation. The suppression of philosophical orientation, or emphasis on action orientation, would also be consistent with a general push toward assertive behavior.

Experts also suppress cooperation through alignment. Except for the expert participating-broker pattern, the leader, nonhostile independent, and insecure expert patterns all involve negative reactions to alignment. (In the insecure-expert pattern, initiating positive references to the grand coalition loads −.49.) This may be compared to the layman patterns which were each described as some form of follower behavior. It might be expected that follower behavior would involve accepting alignment by definition. Thus the ascription of labels seems appropriate at least from this point of view.

Experts also appear to avoid deception and intrigue compared to laymen. This is consistent with the specific principle variables of two out of four expert patterns, and could be taken as consistent with the general tone attributed to all four patterns.

The leader pattern involves rejection of all types of coalitions (including secret ones). The nonhostile independent pattern involves a significantly negative loading on positive responses to secret coalition offers. In more general terms, the leader pattern's aloofness would be consistent with avoiding intrigue. The insecure-expert pattern could be interpreted as involving too much hesitancy to undertake deception. An independent would presumably be reluctant to enter into secret coalitions among others. The participating broker could not maintain credibility with all players if he entered into secret arrangements with one against another. In this sense, the statistical findings concerning deception and intrigue are consistent with the factor interpretations we have offered.

Factor Differences and Stabilized Behaviors

The stabilization of deception and intrigue for experts is consistent with what we have offered above on this point. The assumption is that deception is stabilized at a lower level for experts. Laymen might be expected to vary more in this regard because they include the tromped-on follower pattern characterized by going along with others' lead (which may be into deception of third parties). Also they include task-oriented patterns. They include the conditional follower who is willing to intrigue.

At the same time, laymen include in their patterns the company man, for which the concept of intrigue appears inappropriate given the interest in harmony and the preoccupation with vapid consensus discussion. The layman group also included the cooperative, contributing-follower pattern, which seems more closely related to fair play than to conspiracy. Thus layman patterns as a group might be expected to display more diversity regarding deception than would experts.

The stabilization of alignment behaviors for experts might also be interpreted as stabilization of alignment at a lower level. This could follow from the assumption that assertiveness produces a reluctance to go along with others' lead in the course of thrusting oneself forward. However, there is no reason to assume a priori that laymen will be comparatively erratic regarding alignment since all layman types are followers of one form or another. Two possibilities may be pointed out in this regard, however.

First, it may be that in the experts' suppression of cooperation through alignment (t-test data) scores were so reduced that they tend to show less variance than layman scores. Second, and more likely, the difference in intensity of coalition behavior between the company man and tromped-on follower on the one hand, and the conditional follower and cooperative contributing follower on the other, may be great compared to expert-alignment behavior. The answer cannot be uncovered from the information at hand and requires further study. On this point we must point out that the question of consistency is open between statistical test implications and factor interpretations.

The notion that expert behavior is stabilized regarding willingness to give in and seeking counterpart input is consistent with the factor interpretations we have made if we assume that expert behavior in these areas is stabilized at a lower level than it is for laymen. The hypothesis in this vein would be that the behavior of experts generally clusters around a lower level of concern with these issues while laymen show greater variance within the context of greater concern.

This line of speculation is encouraged by experts having lower mean scores on these variables (though the means are not themselves significant according to the t-test). See Table 2.2 again. Greater layman variance regarding these behaviors could be caused by the extreme sensitivity to counterparts associated with the tromped-on follower compared to the comparatively lesser sensitivity expected for the conditional follower.

Again this is purely speculation and requires extensive testing. The point here is merely that the statistical and factor analysis results are not necessarily at odds.

Regarding destabilized behaviors, we would expect experts as a class to vary more than laymen concerning conceptions of their own and others' task qualifications. This stems from our judgment that experts indicated patterns ranging from insecurity to almost dictatorial behavior while laymen indicated varieties of follower behavior only.

Summary

The previous section suggested that the interpretation offered for our factor analysis was consistent with the results of statistical tests applied to the same data base. However, we are far from any firm conclusions about differences in expert and nonexpert behavioral orientations in specified circumstances.

We have been content with merely trying to indicate the form that further hypothesizing might take and the lines of inference that seem to support them. The two main hypotheses suggested by our treatment of the laboratory results are that experts tend to generalize their expertise and expertise exaggerates assertiveness. To reflect our primary interest and confidence in these two notions (given the stage of our inquiry), we have posited these two notions as factors proper in our conceptual framework of expert-politico interaction.

We have suggested a connection between the subordinate-dominant proclivities of the individual personality and the type of expert a given expert may become. Doing so points again to one of the basic convictions that prompted this book. We see that the expert's relationship with the politico cannot be fully understood unless we undertake an analysis on several levels.

Our treatment of the expert qua expert has suggested that even in a broad, exploratory inquiry into the effects of role, some questions on the role level must remain unanswered until answers are provided on other levels as well. The path we have chosen on the role level leads us next to consider the expert as an individual personality. Specifically, first we must ask what there is to be said about the conditions under which individuals will adopt submissive or assertive postures in deliberative interpersonal settings. Second, we want to know whether other aspects of the individual personality pertinent to the development of interpersonal orientation, may co-vary with the factors that affect assertiveness/submissiveness. If this were so it would suggest that an expert's profile in assertiveness may influence more than the kind of expert he becomes. It may also indicate that experts of a certain kind will likely be group members with a definite interpersonal outlook. And again as with role, any such factors on the level of individual personality will be of interest because they can help us to understand more about the way the expert deals with the politico. We examine these questions in the following chapter.

NOTES

1. There has been a great deal of laboratory experimentation concerned with "negotiation," of course. Some of it has manipulated conditions related to expertise in one way or another, but all of these pieces require substantial translation for use in the sense that interests us here. Even then, these pieces amount to only partial treatments for us, and this seems logical enough because they were designed to answer questions put differently on another plane. Some good examples of what is available in this regard are: D. Cole, " 'Rational argument' and 'prestige-suggestion' as factors influencing judgment," *Sociometry*, 1954, vol. 17, pp. 350-54; B. Mausner, "The effect of one partner's success in a relevant task on the interaction of observer pairs," *Journal of Abnormal and Social Psychology*, 1954, vol. 49, pp. 557-60; R. C. Ziller, "Scales of judgment: A determinant of the accuracy of group decisions," *Human Relations*, 1955, vol. 8, pp. 153-64.

2. Of course every research tool has its weaknesses and the laboratory format is no exception. On the shortcomings of laboratory research see Rosenthal and Rosnow, *Artifact in Behavioral Research* (New York: Academic Press, 1964).

3. The data-collection stage of this research was funded by the National Science Foundation. Needless to say I greatly appreciate their assistance.

4. It may be noted here that three-person groups were used in this experiment, rather than some other group size, in the belief that triads offer the best climate for the manifestation of any tendencies to isolate minority views or form majority coalitions. That is, when coalitions do form, the effects of their presence are most clearly demonstrated in 2 versus 1 situations rather than in say, 3 versus 2. See H. H. Kelly and T. W. Lamb, "Certainty of judgment and resistance to social influence," *Journal of Abnormal and Social Psychology*, 1957, vol. 50, pp. 137-39.

5. Generally the assumption that complex social processes may be reflected through group dealings with trivial problems has received wide acceptance throughout experimental psychology. Examples are legion. Because it also deals with triad problem-solving, see B. H. Raven, and J. I. Shaw, "Interdependence and group problem-solving in the triad," *Journal of Personality and Social Psychology*, 1970, vol. 14, pp. 157-65. In this experiment, a triangular board with turning set screws at each corner and a carpenter's spirit level in its center, was used to approximate conditions·of small-group leadership and their relation to the development of communications patterns.

6. I have elsewhere taken the tack of presenting a sharply truncated view of the experiment retported her to illustrate the potential of laboratory experimentation in treating otherwise resistant research problems in political science. See Lerner's " 'Experts' and 'Politicos' in Negotiating Situations: An Experimental Analog to a Critical Class of Encounter," in Robert T. Golembiewski (ed.), *Two Decades of Small Group Research in Political Science* (Athens, Georgia: University of Georgia Press, 1976). This research and our larger present inquiry emphasize conscious attempts by experts to gain advantage in decision-making interaction; however, the question of *unintended* influencing is another matter. See Lerner's *Experts, Politicians, and Decision-making in the Technological Society* (Morristown, New Jersey: General Learning Press, 1976) in the latter regard.

7. The reason for keeping confederates "blind" was, of course, to prevent them from adjusting their behavior out of some misdirected sympathy for the experimenter.

8. Both experimental research and more general works on negotiation are not much help in this regard. It is certainly true that psychologists have devoted much effort to studying negotiating behavior. However, the technique is usually to investigate relationships between two variables or three at the most. The consequence is a body of literature that for the most part reveals a great deal of information about a multitude of isolated relationships. Characteristically, the hypotheses stem from what are treated conceptually as simple dichotomous or trichotomous phenomena. There is no effort to speak of toward integration. Moreover, many of what pass as studies of negotiation behavior are really studies of auctioning behavior. "Negotiation" in this vein is devoid of any language content. Rather, subjects exchange single number offers according to some bidding scale with the experimenter usually the intermediary. The implied referent is more nearly the auction podium than the negotiating table. In this regard, see as examples: W. H. Starbuck and D. F. Grant, "Bargaining strategies with asymmetric initiation and termination," *Applied Social Psychology*, 1971, vol. 1, pp. 344-63; R. M. Liebert, W. P. Smith, and J. H. Hill, "The effects of information and magnitude of initial offer on interpersonal negotiation," *Journal of Experimental Social Psychology*, 1968, vol. 4, pp. 431-41.

On this kind of problem generally, see Kenneth J. Gergen, "Social psychology as history," *Journal of Personality and Social Psychology*, 1973, 26, 2, pp. 309-320; William J. McGuire, "The Yin and Yang of Progress in Social Psychology," ibid., 26 (3), pp. 446-56.

As far as political science is concerned, the major theoretical treatments of negotiation are not so much models of negotiation as checklists in general terms of what a model should include. (This is not to say that they are not fine works in their own right; it is just that they will not suit our interests here.) Iklé especially comes to mind in this regard–Schelling as well. Other treatments of negotiation familiar to political scientists are too abstract to explain what negotiators really do at a conference table, and still others are so steeped in detailed anecdotes that any attempt at generalization in a closing chapter or two seems strained. We include game theory and the new political economy in the former, and what can only be called "anecdotal works" in the latter, such as: Johan Kaufman, *Conference Diplomacy* (New York: Oceana Press, 1968); Arthur Lall, *Modern International Negotiation* (New York: Columbia University Press, 1966); Charles Thayer, *Diplomat* (New York: Harper Bros., 1959); C. Turner Joy, *How Communists Negotiate* (New York: Macmillan, 1955) and others of this genre, even C. P. Snow, whose work is brilliant in many respects, but not useful here. Schelling sums up the state of the art best in discussing new directions in the study of negotiation. See Thomas Schelling, *The Strategy of Conflict* (Cambridge: Harvard University Press, 1960), especially Chapter 6. Fred Iklé, *How Nations Negotiate* (New York: Harper Row, 1964); C. P. Snow, *Science and Government* (Cambridge: Harvard University Press, 1961).

9. An interesting application of this principle is involved in recent innovations in the field of marital therapy. See R. L. Weiss, "Negotiation Therapy in Marriage," a paper presented at the Western Psychological Association convention in San Francisco, 1971.

10. The common reference to this condition is "talking a problem to death."

11. Of course Clausewitz stressed how wide the continuum of alternatives can be.

12. See Robert Merton, *Social Theory and Social Structure* (New York: Free Press, 1968), pp. 252-54. Merton uses the phrase to describe the phenomenon whereby rules (means) become ends for organization members. I appropriate the term here to describe a kind of secondary implication it has always had for me. That is, I use it here to describe a possible condition whereby, as a result of means-ends transference, not only may rules become ends in themselves, but the perpetuation of the entire group structure (which is itself a means for problem-solving here) may become an end in itself for the group members (our negotiators). Whether we may so extend the sociologists' phrase, or whether the phenomenon may be extended to negotiating groups, is admittedly a moot point, and the use of the phrase is here intended only metaphorically. But in either case, the point is that the phenomenon that may be operating in this vein certainly seems appropriate for examination in this experiment. Variables 3 and 4 are designed for this purpose.

13. Actually the game was constructed to make actual opting before the end of the free-negotiating period irrational. This was accomplished by assuring all participants that they would still have the option to opt out in the eleventh minutes. This insured that all subjects would have equal time exposure to the free-negotiation part of the experiment, while still allowing for the strategic use of opting references.

14. When we say "theoretically" here, we use the term as it is commonly applied, to mean "in principle." The thought is that if we assume players are manipulative, references to role status can be taken as tactical maneuvers consistent with particular strategies that seem readily apparent. Methodologically we are assuming it is useful to measure role references because we have rational players and can therefore retrodict. For some comment on the nature of retrodiction, see Abraham Kaplan, *The Conduct of Inquiry* (San Francisco: Chandler Co., 1964) pp. 349-51. Graham Allison also examines the rationale for this kind of inference process, and quite cogently. See Graham Allison, *Essence of Decision; Explaining the Cuban Missile Crisis* (Boston: Little Brown, 1971).

15. Social psychology has dealt extensively with a group phenomenon whereby some members become "task leaders" and others "socioemotional leaders." We are taking a measure akin to this distinction between leader types. For a brief explanation of this leadership distinction, see A. Paul Hare, *Handbook of Small Group Research* (New York: Free Press, 1962) p. 12.

16. Riker's work on coalitions is of course the outstanding piece. William H. Riker, *The Theory of Political Coalitions* (New Haven, Connecticut: Yale University Press, 1962).

17. O. R. Young analyzes the role of such mediators in important political disputes. O. R. Young, *The Inter-Mediaries* (Princeton, New Jersey.: Princeton University Press, 1967).

18. We don't use the term "speculating" disparagingly. Perhaps a sign of some of our problems is that speculation has come to be considered something improper. It need not be wild guessing any more than imaginative inference. For a good example of how experimental technique can be applied to supposedly ethereal concepts in political science's study of negotiation, see D. G. Pruitt and D. F. Johnson, "Mediation as an aid to face-saving in negotiation," *Journal of Personality and Social Psychology,* 1970, vol. 14.

19. There have been many more elegant, or at least ambitious, treatments of concession behavior. See for example D. G. Pruitt and J. L. Drews, "The effect of time pressure, time elapsed and the opponents' concession rate on behavior in negotiation," *Journal of Experimental Social Psychology,* 1969, vol. 5, pp. 43-60; J. M. Chertkoff and M. Conley, "Opening offer and frequency of concession as bargaining strategies," *Journal of Personality and Social Psychology,* vol. 7, pp. 181-85; R. M. Lieber et al., "The effects of initial offer on interpersonal negotiation," *Journal of Experimental Social Psychology,* 1968, vol. 4, pp. 431-41. Because we are most concerned with the effect of *expertise* on concession behavior, it seems unwise to build on data collected under different circumstances. For this reason we begin simply.

20. The formula used to calculate a subject's score on this variable is as follows:

$$\text{Net concession value of final offer} = \frac{[\text{final offer} - \text{first offer}]}{\text{first offer}}$$

21. For a cogent discussion of the heuristic value of factor analysis, see R. J. Rummel, "Understanding factor analysis," *Journal of Conflict Resolution,* vol. 11, no. 4, pp. 444-80.

22. *Webster's New World Dictionary,* College Edition (New York: World Co., 1968) p. 88.

23. See Schutz, op. cit., p. 165. He refers to this as low control interchange.

24. It may seem appropriate given this line of reasoning to posit a continuum of assertiveness/submissiveness along which all expert and layman patterns could be ranked. However, because the patterns were generated by orthogonal factor analysis, arguments based on notions of a continuum seem inappropriate. We would suggest that given the kind of higher-order concepts involved in positing such a continuum, the approach would in fact be justified. But to avoid the implication that the application of factor analysis per se has here justified these inferences, we have eschewed a line of reasoning which would contend that the orthogonal analysis itself generated any continuum. What we are saying is that it is indifferent to it, given the difference between the level of abstraction on which these notions are developed and the level of abstraction on which the factors themselves were developed. In this context all the factors could in a sense be rotated obliquely in the n-space to a single dimension of "assertiveness" were such measures provided. The discussion here should not, by the same token, be interpreted as a mere verbal presentation of a continuum notion, for the following reason: Judgments about the assertiveness implied in a given pattern are made by inspecting the "conceptual communalities" of

the principle loading variables in each factor. These clusters of communalities can in turn be conceptually linked to notions of high-profile behavior. The implied and rough rankings of factors for their assertive content should be understood not as mathematical relationships or ordinal scales. Rather they are judgments on the extent to which given patterns approximate a pure type implied by "assertive behavior." The appeal in these terms is simply to common sense, and not to claims of mathematical relationships justified by data manipulation. The judgments in this discussion are moreover well-anchored in the independent arguments for using the factor labels that were assigned. See the appendix in this regard.

25. L. H. Gulick, "Notes on the Theory of Organization" in L. H. Gulick and L. Urwick (eds.), *Papers on the Science of Administration* (New York: Institute of Public Administration, 1937).

26. Generally, in predicting stability and instability, predictions concern the phenotype expert. This implies operationally that any given group of experts will show consistent behavior *across* individuals. Thus whenever consistency or inconsistency in expert behavior is predicted, the prediction is for the phenotype expert as an analytical construct. However, positing subtypes (as we shall later) allows for the view that instability in phenotype behavior represents divergence among subtypes.

Chapter 3

THE EXPERT AS INDIVIDUAL: PERSONALITY

PREDILECTIONS AND THE EXPERT MANTLE

The preceding chapter suggested that negotiating behavior is altered by internalizing expert status in dealing with presumed politicos. Four "types" of expert behavior patterns emerged in the laboratory.

To simplify the presentation here, we will assume temporarily that the insecure-expert pattern is not likely to be manifest by real-world career participants in expert-politico interaction. This view is that the normal pattern of expert training is not geared to produce participants in political (governmental) decision-making. The entrance of experts into governmental circles is thus by choice. This would seem so at least in the sense that, though some people may "drift" into such positions, there is always at some point the freedom to decide otherwise.

An expert likely to mirror the insecure-expert pattern of behavior is presumably uncomfortable in the expert-politico setting. The laboratory situation forced people into this setting on a one-shot basis. However, we are primarily concerned with expert-politico interaction in the real world that is not on a one-shot basis. We are concerned with careerists whose relationships develop as part of full-time jobs in an institutionalized format.

Thus while the laboratory may force experts to interact with politicos even though they may be uncomfortable doing so, the real-world market for professionals would presumably allow the insecure to find other arenas for the use of their expertise. This seems true especially when expert training is not geared to politics but rather to physics, law, engineering perhaps, and so on. Even those whose expertise involves areas primarily supported by government (aerospace, for example) could presumably avoid the decision-making interaction with politicos in favor of work in, for example, a technicians-only subunit. (We shall deal with this at length when discussing differences in expert and politico socialization and recruitment patterns in Chapter 5.)

We will assume here that when the insecure expert emerges in expert-politico settings, he is visible only until such time as he recognizes his discomfort or until others recognize that he is unsuited and pressure him to leave, or bypass him for all intents and purposes. The insecure expert, we will assume, may surface in settings of interest to us only when one-shot issues work to bring him in on special projects of limited duration, or when someone has made a poor judgment in career planning. In any case, the view will be that the days of such insecure experts *in settings of interest to us* are numbered.

From the view that the insecure expert's presence is not characteristic of the expert-politico relationship as that relationship has been institutionalized in government, we will posit that the insecure-expert pattern is not a likely pattern for real-world careerists. Again, we will consider the presence of such insecure experts as a special case, and deal with it to a degree, in a later part of this chapter and in Chapter 5.

The implication by separating out this type is that we can dispense with speculation about the relationship between adopting the insecure-expert pattern and individual personality concerns which are the focus of this chapter. From the assumption that the insecure expert's participation is short-lived and governed by issue-specific, noninstitutional considerations, it follows that localized factors will have overriding influence on the course of his relations with politicos. For this reason it seems not only unnecessary but also unwise to posit any set of personality-related factors that could explain his behavior in the politico-populated environment. This chapter, then, will deal primarily with the relationship between individual personality predilections and the manifestation of the leader, participating broker, and nonhostile independent behavior patterns by experts dealing with politicos.

This chapter pursues that question by suggesting certain individual personality needs as reasons for the choice of one or another of the expert postures. In so doing it sketches three distinct interpersonal profiles that would appear to catch the outstanding features of each of our three types of experts. Reasoning along these lines should provide an image not only of what makes experts tick but also an image of the politico postures that would hinder or maximize experts' effectiveness in interaction. The first step in accomplishing the aims of this chapter is to grasp the distinction on a conceptual level between the expert *role* and the *postures* individuals take in playing that role.[1]

Roles and Postures

In describing the expert mantle as a role we mean in common usage a set of norms for proper conduct—a sterotyped manner of, pattern, or style, of behavior.[2] Roles as stereotypes are, to put it simply, well-known, institutionalized (in the sense of being basic to the conventional wisdom) codes.[3]

But stereotypes are never perceived with total uniformity by a population. For one thing, stereotypes are vague, ambiguous. This is necessary because they are to apply to a wide range of particulars through time and space, so to endure they must be flexible. Within that margin of flexibility there is room for a measure of variability in interpretation. If we see such stereotypes as messages which society beams at individuals, we realize that accurate interpretation of the message rests not only on the clarity of the message as it is sent, but on the fidelity of the receiver (the individual).[4]

Stereotypes are manifest with a measure of idiosyncrasy not only because their inherent ambiguity blurs the signal, but also because signals— even when clear—are altered by the receivers.[5] The individual as receiver ingests a signal conveying information of one description from the sender (here the culture) and translates that signal to yield different information for the receiver. Thus roles as stereotypes are manifest with substantial differences by individuals not only because the stereotypes are themselves ambiguous (flexible in behavioral terms) but also because all receivers are, to a degree, imperfectly (nonuniformly) tuned.

In this context, then, the charge to be an expert leaves room for interpretation, and interpretations will vary (hopefully within the limits we have described) insofar as people vary (within the limits we are about to describe). So we can say that the variations of expertness represent individual accommodations to the expert role. To emphasize this distinction between the larger role and individual accommodations to it, we will call the latter *postures*. The outstanding common feature of these postures is that they are voluntarily adopted. In other words, assuming our formulations are correct, experts involved in interpersonal exchange with politicos sought their broker, leader, or independent postures.

Postures, as we are calling them, are thus traceable to differences in individuals' orientations to stereotyped expectations for interpersonal relations.[6] The freedom of individual interpretation is apparently facilitated by the slack in the culture's definition of the stereotype.[7] Thus while the stereotype's vague properties make stylized interpretations of it possible, the variation in individual orientations to cultural cues makes stylized interpretations likely. Because the discernible variations in the execution of the expert role seem limited, the factors militating for variety are mediated by some constants in the way that individuals interpret their marching orders for interpersonal behavior. The next task, then, is to consider possible dimensions for such constants.

Conceptualizing the Universals in Individuals' Interpersonal Orientations

The assumption in these pages will be that the constants we are looking for are related to the perceptions individuals have of their interpersonal environments. In the communications system context, this is analogous to finding the source of variation in a stereotype's portrayal in the idiosyncratic operation of individual receptors.

In the interpersonal context, perceiving the environment means assessing what that environment both offers and requires of the individual in his interpersonal dealings. A necessary operating assumption of this view is that it is possible to specify—on some level of abstraction appropriate to this analysis—a finite number of categories that could encompass the variety of readings people must take in making their assessments of the interpersonal environment.

Explained differently, we are assuming that the elements of the interpersonal environment, which are salient to individuals when learning their interpersonal behavior, can be analytically separated into a small number of categories. In an approach of this sort, an individual's interpersonal behavior may be understood as a function of his perceptions of the interpersonal field, with such perceptions subsumable under one or another of these environment-reading (describing) categories.

The calculus for fitting behavior to perceptions would rest on some maxim of self-interest, or in systems terms, some homeostatic mechanism upon which we will elaborate shortly. But first it is necessary to identify these environment-reading categories.

We should stress again that the underlying interest in this discussion is on considering *why* some experts act as leaders, some as brokers, and others as nonhostile independents. We want to identify the ways that experts of one type conduct their interpersonal dealings differently than experts of another type. We want to understand through a discussion of individuals how and why it is that politicos of a given interpersonal stripe might interact with experts of a given posture in ways that might alternatively facilitate or impede the deliberative process. The discussion so far has suggested that, to this end, we ought to describe—in some way that gives us conceptual control through parsimony—how people orient themselves to an interpersonal environment.

Actually, what we will do is rely on those who have already made some useful findings and suggestions regarding typologies which may explain how people orient themselves interpersonally. The best work in this regard has been by Schutz, Leary, and Bales.[8] Schutz's formulations are best suited to our interests and the following brief reconstruction of this literature's relevant theses emphasizes Schutz's perspective and terminology.

The interpersonal theorists suggest that people orient themselves to their interpersonal surroundings by making what is usually described as a three-fold assessment. For those who would rather not posit an assessing process because of the specter of dealing with whether it is conscious or unconscious (and whether the latter distinction is useful)—for all those people we can say that there are three aspects of the interpersonal environment which are salient in the interpersonal process.

Various theorists use various phrases in labeling these three dimensions of interpersonal orientation. Aside from Schutz, whose phrasing is used here, Bales has his own formulations and Leary prefers a third set of terms. Following Schutz's scheme, we will refer to these dimensions as the *inclusion* dimension, the *control* dimension, and the *affection* dimension. Before going further, a few descriptive words on each will be necessary.

INCLUSION

The inclusion dimension of interpersonal relationships encompasses all those aspects of interpersonal relationships that are perceived to figure in evaluating the proximity of the individual to the group. As the term implies, the inclusion dimension involves the degree to which the individual is included in the group. The aspects of interpersonal relations subsumed under this rubric concern the extent to which a person is an insider, is in the thick of things, is one of the gang. The inclusion dimension subsumes those aspects of social interaction concerned with the *in-ness* of the individual relative to his fellow group members.

CONTROL

The control dimension of interpersonal relations consists of all those relational aspects that concern members' authority within the group. Any aspect of group interaction is presumed to occur on the control dimension if it is concerned with establishing, maintaining, or altering the authority position—the position of dominance or submission—of one member relative to another.

AFFECTION

The affection dimension of interpersonal relations encompasses all those aspects of social interaction concerned with personal warmth—its proffering and acceptance. This dimension is not limited to behavior narrowly concerned with liking. Rather, the intention is to also subsume behavior having to do with congeniality, rapport, pleasantries, and so on. With the affection dimension as well as with inclusion and control, the intended referents are those behaviors that *participants perceive* to involve the factors we have associated with each dimensional construct. As has been stressed earlier in another context, our interest is always with participant perceptions. The range implied by the combined referents of these three categories is presumed to exhaust all possibilities for behavior in social interaction.

These descriptive categories are the constant elements in the interpersonal equation. We have implied that they serve at least two functions.

First, they are the categories with which individuals ingest the stereotyped norms for interpersonal behavior that are associated with whatever roles are foisted upon them.

Second, they are the categories that can be used to analytically order the behaviors that comprise the individual's idiosyncratic interpretations of those roles (i.e., the postures he takes).

In the expert context as we have developed it so far, the charge to be an expert is a vague message to the individual to act on the dimensions of inclusion, affection, and control in the particular way that he generally understands the properly behaving experts to be acting in his society. The posture (leader, broker, or independent for real-world experts) that he adopts in his personalization of that role represents his modification of the stereotype to fit his own style of behavior in interpersonal situations generally—again, expressed in his individual profile on the inclusion, control, and affection dimensions of interpersonal behavior. It will be useful at this point to delineate some reconstructed logic to describe the process by which the individual makes his idiosyncratic modifications. We know the categories according to which he operates; we want to specify the rule he operates by.

The Calculus for Fitting Behavior to Perceptions in Interpersonal Relations

While developing the notion in the previous section of some constants in interpersonal perceptions, it was suggested that the calculus for fitting behavior to perceptions would rest on some maxim of self-interest or, in systems terms, some homeostatic mechanism. This was a general description of the answer to the question we are now asking: When an individual chooses to interpret a stereotyped role with some idiosyncratic posture, why does he choose whatever posture he does?

To this question, theorists committed to a fundamental, all-inclusive typology of interpersonal behavior must posit a decision rule of equal universality. In all works on this order of which we are aware, the tack is to contend that people orient themselves interpersonally by adopting whatever posture satisfies certain "personality needs." The contention is usually that there is a basic human need paralleling each basic dimension of interpersonal relations.

To Schutz, for example, people simply have a need for a certain amount of inclusion, control, and affection in all their interpersonal dealings, and they behave in ways that will allow them to maximize the satisfaction of the corresponding need. People behave differently because the configuration of their needs across the three dimensions varies. The source of these needs is deeply imbedded in their psyches. The needs are fundamental aspects of their personalities—nay, these needs taken together *comprise* their personalities.

Leary substitutes the notion of anxiety for need as the prime force, and suggests that a person displays the interpersonal behavior on a given level that will reduce the anxiety he feels on that level. All of these approaches are fairly interchangeable. One might argue here, for example, that anxiety is the condition before needs are satisfied and anxiety is reduced when needs are met. For all such theorists, these basic human needs, anxieties, drives, and so on, are the primal forces of social interaction; with these concepts we reach the end of the line in asking why.[9] These are the axioms for the interpersonal relations theorist. Further, individual need magnitudes are derived from early-life experiences.[10]

For political scientists it is most useful to speak of these needs corresponding to each dimension of interpersonal behavior as continuous processes of cost-benefit calculation. The individual perceives the social situation, and through his psychic processes he formulates behaviors that maximize his emotional benefits on each dimension. His calculus for behavior-selection is a calculus of self-interest in this sense.[11] Man as a system seeks the relationship with his interpersonal environment that will best maintain his level of anxiety at that balance which will provide both motivation and contentment. Emphasizing the anxiety conception of need, we may say that he seeks a kind of dynamic equilibrium in these terms.

Indeed, the society as a system may be viewed as seeking the same equilibrium in interaction between individuals.[12] In these terms, the culture transmits stereotypes for acceptable social behavior and individuals enact them with variations (postures) that serve to adjust the net balance between collective interpersonal anxiety and satisfaction. This allows for the maintenance of some ratio between productivity and tension in the community.

Postures as Rational Adaptations

Describing the basic axiom for individual motivation as a kind of emotional cost-benefit calculation is preferable given our purposes, because of the term's intimate association with the concept of rationality. We want to stress that the individual adjusts to his interpersonal environment in a way that is rational. What is to be emphasized is that, however mad any individual may be, there is always a method to the madness; he does what makes him feel good. Thus to the extent that he fits means to ends, he is rational in his social interaction. We contend that he does what makes him feel good on the three interpersonal dimensions described above.

More sharply defined, each posture can be interpreted as a three-dimensional profile sketched in behavioral predilections, representing the individual's compromise between how an expert is supposed to act and how he acts as a person. The result is a profile of how he is capable of acting as an expert. The fact that the number of postures we are dealing with is limited to three merely suggests that the rub between role and individuals occurs in a predictable way for all careerists, and this is something the present line of reasoning will eventually lead us to understand in more specific terms. For the time being, the important task is to construct analytically what the posture of broker, leader, or independent consists of in interpersonal terms. That is, we want to identify conceptually the character of interpersonal behavior which is encouraged by taking one of these three postures in a negotiating group.

If postures are rational accommodations to role pressures (which are felt on each of three dimensions), then it should be possible to describe generally the differences between the interpersonal profiles of individuals who choose one posture over another. This is done by asking what each posture requires of the individual on each interpersonal dimension and then making the assumption that individuals will adopt the posture that requires the lesser adjustment in their individual interpersonal predispositions. (Conversely, of course, if an individual *has* adopted a given posture then he must have an interpersonal profile closer to it than to any other posture associated with that role.)

What can we say, then, about the kind of behavior elicited for any one of the three expert postures as opposed to the other two, on each of the three dimensions of social interaction? The answer to this question will take the form of pure types—of idealized profiles of the broker, leader, and nonhostile independent. These idealizations or pure types are attempts to articulate those common images in terms of the three-dimensional format we have adopted. The question is: Given the common image of a broker, how would that image translate in general terms, into a composite picture of behavior with respect to inclusion, affection, and control? How for the leader? How for the nonhostile independent? Our answers in this regard will be facilitated by the knowledge of the specific variables comprising these patterns, and the concepts that were associated with groups of these variables. The speculative nature of this line of inference should be obvious. So, too, should the general line of argument for undertaking this development be familiar by now.

Leader, Broker, Independent, and Control

Both the leader and broker are authoritative group figures. Members look to both to provide direction. They channel discussion; they reinforce the positions of those counterparts whose reasoning is appreciated. Generally leaders and brokers attempt to inhibit those who place obstacles before the group if such individuals are expendable. If they are not expendable the attempt may be to modify their views or argue a totally new approach where there is unusual resistance to persuasion. In any event, universal group norms lead any participants to turn to the leader or brokers when they sense that deliberations have reached any sort of turning point. Leaders and brokers are always what may be called high-profile actors from the perceptions of other group members. They are "heavy people" in anyone's jargon.

The expectation that true brokers and leaders wield substantial intra-group influence makes their positions ones of authority. To be sure, the behaviors associated with such styles of negotiating as discussed in Chapter 2 (and the appendix) suggest that any people who were to select these postures would function as pivotal group members.[13] We posit, then, that the leader and broker postures are ones which satisfy an individual's need to exert a significant degree of control in group interaction. Whenever these postures are voluntarily adopted, it is by people seeking thereby to satisfy a need to act authoritatively in their interpersonal dealings. Whenever an individual feels the need to function in a way that subordinates others to him, the leader and participating broker postures both provide role structures for doing so.

It should be suggested at the same time, however, that while the conventional image of both leader and broker include what we interpret as controlling behavior (subordinating others in the group), there is a stronger implication of assertiveness in the leader than in the broker. This is certainly the case in the kind of leader behavior uncovered in Chapter 2. The leader's control of the group is overt and explicit in his behavior. The broker's is more subtle. The image is one of control through leadership that pulls the group along, in contrast to control through brokerage that channels the group's progress. Therefore, while we interpret both leader and broker postures as role structures that facilitate the need to exert control, we notice that the leader posture is the optimum adaptation for those whose need to exert control is more extreme, other things being equal.

When developing the nonhostile independent label we suggested that the independent was neutral with respect to controlling others and being controlled. The term independent suggests someone apart from others. As such it implies that the independent is not controlled and does not control. We posit, then, that the independent posture is the optimum adaptation for those who are neutral with respect to control.

Leader, Broker, Independent, and Inclusion

The leadership pattern we have identified was described as being somewhat dictatorial. Among other things, it stressed aloofness, giving orders, and belligerency. Presumably, a person who needs the feeling of being one of the gang would not voluntarily adopt a posture that emphasizes these qualities. One who needs the feeling of belonging and in-ness would not be so ready to alienate others or so willing to remain above involvement with others in coalition. Accordingly, we posit that the leader's need for inclusion is low.

Similarly, the independent is, by definition, a loner. His profile is distinctly nonaligning. Moreover, his independent-mindedness would presumably not be compatible with a need to be part of the team.[14] Therefore the independent's need for inclusion would probably also be low.[15]

The picture for the broker is different, however. By definition the broker must be prepared to involve himself closely with the thinking, feelings, and views of others if he is to be able to facilitate mutual appreciation of views as a start in achieving consensus. He must be willing to play the go-between and friend to all parties. He must be prepared to work closely with all members and step in when needed. Such a readiness for close interaction seems to be compatible with comparatively higher scores on the inclusion dimension.

Leader, Broker, Independent, and Affection

If the affection dimension concerns the warmth people require in their interpersonal dealings, we must assume that the leader has less of a need for warmth than the broker does. More specifically, we assume he can tolerate coldness more than the broker can. The leader posture indicated in the laboratory was characterized in part by the initiation of personal attack and challenging responses to personal attacks. These behaviors were not associated with the broker posture.

Describing the leader posture as less dependent on affection than the broker posture seems consistent with the common views of leadership that emphasize the loneliness of command. Command is a lonely position not only because the commander cannot enjoy inclusion, but also because he cannot expect *warmth* in interaction, given the frequency with which he must necessarily frustrate others and reaffirm their submission to him.[16]

On the other hand, for all their presumed superiority, leaders—especially the more dictatorial ones—actually require approval the way vaudevillians need applause. Those who hold this view tend to treat leaders as maladjusted personalities who seek to gain satisfaction through political interactions which would more appropriately be sought in the family setting or some other intimate, more love-emphasizing relationship.[17] From the vantage point we have chosen, the response to this view of leadership behavior and its relation to affection is first to caution against confusing deference with affection, and second, against generalizing from Hitlerian mass-manipulators to self-appointed small-group leaders.

In contrast to the leadership posture for experts, whereby the leader must risk friendliness to maintain control, the broker posture does not set its executor so starkly against his counterparts. Where the leader must respond aggressively to maintain his influence, the broker reaffirms his mastery by displaying the ability to defuse confrontation. Thuse where the leader posture includes challenging responses to personal insult, the broker posture indicates low-key responses to personal attack. Both postures are assertive; both exert control. One does so in a way that requires a preparedness to dispense with friendliness in interaction. The other makes the loss of interpersonal warmth less of a risk.

Recall that from the perspective taken here, postures are role interpretations, or behavior patterns which the individual adopts to satisfy his interpersonal needs for inclusion, control, and affection in the practice of his role. It follows then that, other things being equal, an individual expert who adopts the leader posture has less of a need for affection in interaction than the expert who adopts the broker posture. The latter requires warmth and friendliness in interpersonal relations to a degree that makes the implied risk to affection posed by self-appointed leadership unacceptable.

Regarding the independent and the need for affection, the general tone of self-imposed isolation associated with this pattern suggests little need for affection or, at least, for seeking it out. The assumption, again, is that insofar as postures are voluntarily adopted role interpretations, individuals do not adopt the independent posture unless their need for displays of affection is low.

Summarizing the relationship between expert postures and interpersonal orientations, we have suggested the following: The leader posture maximizes interpersonal satisfactions for individuals who need little inclusion, much control (exerted by them) and little affection. The broker posture maximizes satisfactions for those who need substantial inclusion, somewhat as much control (exerted by them), and much affection. The independent pattern maximizes satisfactions for those who need little inclusion, who are neutral with respect to control, and who need little affection. Notice that these profiles are drawn in comparative terms.

Postures, Individuals, and the Role Stereotype

In the preceding chapter it was suggested that the general encouragement of assertiveness was a result of adopting the expert role. The present hypotheses concerning the interpersonal profile of given role postures seems consistent with this notion. The control dimension figures prominently in two of our three "career" postures. The leader and broker patterns share the need to display control. The need to display control may be taken as a motive for displaying assertive behavior.

True, the profile offered for the independent involves a neutral position on the control dimension; however, neutrality regarding need to control or be controlled still assumes the resistance of subordination (i.e., the assertion of independence). Insofar as third parties would attempt to subordinate the independent, then, we would expect the independent to assert himself in resistance. This is no small consideration in the kind of setting we have posited with its coaxing, in-fighting, and constant interpersonal alignments and realignments with all their attendant pressures.

Assertive behavior was also distinguished in the previous chapter from willingness to play the follower. The follower pattern was characteristic of all nonexpert factor patterns. Given that the independent would not act as follower, the notion that he is neutral with respect to control (rather than low on control) is consistent with the suggestion that the independent may be viewed as comparatively assertive. The implied comparison is here not with other experts, however, but with laymen. It was in comparison with laymen that the notion was presented of an expertise skew towards assertiveness. In short, the idea is that hypothesizing neutrality with respect to control for a given posture is consistent with hypothesizing that the posture is a relatively assertive one, if the comparison is made with follower-like postures.

The independent pattern was also portrayed in the previous chapter as being less assertive than the leader or broker patterns (postures) for experts. This too seems consistent with describing the independent as lower on the control dimension than leaders or brokers. It is also consistent with the view that none of the three postures are low on control.

Having described the posture as an accommodation between the individual's orientation to interpersonal relations and the stereotype's requirement for behavior, we can draw some inferences about the character of the larger stereotype and individuals who have adopted it. We suggest that the leader, broker, and independent postures suggest the least variance conceptually on the control dimension. That is, on the control dimension they range from neutral to high, while on the other dimension, they range from high to low.

Therefore, insofar as there is any common thread in the interpersonal orientations of likely career types, it would be that they fail to suggest any distinct need—readiness, susceptibility—to being controlled in interpersonal relations. The discussion of factors on the role level suggested that expertise exaggerates assertiveness; the discussion of individual personality predilections suggests that perceived role requirements may be interpreted primarily in terms of control. Inclusion and affection considerations are relevant to the extent that they influence the kind of posture that is adopted *within* the general framework of neutral to high controlling behavior.

This line of inference is speculative, of course, concerning the possible relationship between a generalized skew towards assertiveness for all experts and the intensity of control needs associated with given expert subtypes. It suggests a specificity of predictive power which must await further research. However, it is not essential in the development of a basic conceptual tool kit for dealing with the expert-politico relationship.

The main point here is a conceptualization of how individual personality differences cross-cut more general behavioral earmarks of the expert role. In this vein the suggestion is that differences in inclusion control and affection needs traceable to personality idiosyncrasies may determine what *kind* of expert a given expert will be. We have suggested the dimensions of personality that are relevant in this regard, as well as the relationship between differences on these dimensions and the choice among available expert types. In so doing we have also suggested the personality dimension that may be the outstanding component in all expert types (control) as well as the dimensions in contrast, which may influence the choice of one type (posture) or another in broader terms. Expressing these ideas in terms of factors, one factor influencing the development of expert-politico decision groups is the interpersonal profile of the individual (regarding inclusion, control, and affection). This notion has special value in settings of interest to us because we have speculated on the particular relationship between this factor and expert conduct.

In summary, we have undertaken this discussion of the individual personality and interpersonal behavior for several reasons: Fundamentally, it was important to conceptualize how a typology of individual personality variation would enrich the ideas developed on the role level in the preceding chapter. On a narrower level several questions raised on the role level remained unanswerable on that level alone. In this regard the question of what makes an expert tick became pivotal; the answer, we have suggested, is expressed in terms of why an expert will exhibit whatever posture he does.

A second promised dividend of this line of reasoning is an understanding of how the character of expert-politico interaction can be altered by the matching or mismatching of individuals regarding their interpersonal needs. We turn to this now.

The Consequences of Matching and Mismatching Experts and Politicos Interpersonally

The available work on interpersonal behavior says much about the kinds of people who get along together and the consequences of their getting along or not for a given problem they may be trying to solve.[18] We have developed the view that career experts dealing with politicos in the deliberative-group setting will exhibit three types of behavior patterns, each with its own interpersonal profile. We could begin to determine the kinds of politicos who would work well or poorly with experts by identifying the kinds of people who would be compatible with persons displaying one of these profiles. This means identifying the personality profile of an individual who could best get along with a counterpart who was high on inclusion, high on control, and high on affection (expert-as-broker). Also it means identifying the profile of someone who would best get along with a counterpart low on inclusion, high on control, and low on affection (expert-as-leader). Also it means identifying the profile of someone who would best get along with a counterpart low on inclusion, neutral on control, and low on affection (expert-as-independent). The first task in this regard is to specify how the notion of "getting along" is to be understood here.

Getting along implies a "good" relationship according to some criteria. The criterion to be used here is the degree to which a group works at its maximum effectiveness on a problem-solving task. For us, then, two decision-makers get along when they interact in ways that most efficiently marshall group energies for the problem at hand. A substantial sector of the interpersonal literature argues that two people will work at optimum efficiency when their interpersonal needs complement each other.[19] Interpersonal needs complement each other when each partner is led because of his own interpersonal needs to act in ways that invite counterpart behavior satisfying to each one's needs. In such a relationship, each partner gives what he needs to give and gets what he needs to have—both from others and from his view of himself as a participant.

The implicit argument behind this view is that a group functions at optimum efficiency when all its energies are directed toward its problem. In this vein, interpersonal frictions are seen as digressions. If members are preoccupied with power struggles, with placating individuals who feel left out, with fostering cliques, with drowning themselves in inappropriate overfriendliness, and so on, then they are draining energies that should be mobilized for the task at hand. Cast in terms of the previous discussion, such digressive behaviors are undertaken to reduce otherwise poorly satisfied needs in the three interpersonal areas. When these needs persist to degrees that become distracting, it is because individual orientations to interpersonal dealings within the group do not complement each other. In such circumstances members inevitably exhibit behaviors that serve to satisfy these needs or the problems they produce, rather than working on the problem at hand.

It will be useful to see the tension between group focus on interpersonal adjustment and focus on task as a constant process. In the compatible group the distraction of attention to interpersonal dynamics is minimal; in the incompatible group it is maximal, obscuring attention to task. It should be noted here, and it will be elaborated in Chapter 5, that there are strategic possibilities in some members' maximizing the interpersonal friction between others. For example, individuals whose task judgments are deemed incorrect by the manipulative member may be weakened as task opponents by distracting them with interpersonal struggles between them and third parties whose task participation is not essential. Group organizers who are not themselves group participants may also foresee that undesirable task influences will be exerted by some members. Such organizers may therefore attempt to initially distract likely detractors by adding incompatible participants to their work group. In this sense, it is true that group task performance may be made *more* efficient by selectively increasing interpersonal tensions. However, we can acknowledge this possibility without negating the general principle that interpersonal compatibility improves group performance. Chapter 5 (on organizational factors) will probe the strategic implications of this principle in greater detail.

What the general compatibility-productivity idea tells us is that an expert and politico will get along (i.e., work at optimum efficiency) when, other things being equal, their interpersonal orientations are compatible. We have contended that career experts will adopt either the broker, leader, or independent postures. The question then is, what interpersonal postures for a politico would be most compatible with any given one of these expert postures?

The answers flow readily from the compatibility-productivity notion. Both the leader and the independent are low on inclusion. They will get along best with counterparts who can keep their distance interpersonally— who can operate on what is usually called "an impersonal basis" or "professional atmosphere." The broker who, we have theorized, is higher on inclusion, would presumably get along best with counterparts who are comfortable with closer interaction—with an atmosphere where prolonged close and intimate contact is the norm.

Both the leader and broker are high on control. Presumably they would get along best with those who can accept subordination. Such subordinate counterparts would have to be prepared to cede pivotal status to the leader or broker. This is especially true for those leaders who are the most controlling. The independent is neutral with respect to control. Presumably he will get along best with those whose need for control is neither very high nor very low. If primarily subordinate counterparts were involved with the independent we might expect nothing to get done. If dominant types were involved with the independent we would expect that the independent would balk, with the result being intragroup friction.

Both the leader and independent are low on affection needs. They would get along best with counterparts who can function competently in the frost. Notions of a "professional," "impersonal" relationship are implied here as well. The broker needs more warmth in his dealings. He would presumably get along best with those who could display warmth and receive it, and not vary excessively in this regard when disagreements develop.

Other things being equal, then, the politico who can best get along with the leader might be one who defers, who does not need affectionate displays, and who can operate at a distance. The politico who could best get along with the broker might be one who is comfortable with warm personal relationships, close working arrangements, and showing some deference. The politico who might best get along with the independent is one who does not press for superior-subordinate clarification, who can operate at a distance, and without developing warm personal relationships. These descriptions account for the relationship characteristics that politicos must be able to either tolerate in experts or display themselves, if their partnership with the leader, broker, or independent expert is to function at *maximum* efficiency.

With this appreciation of the relationship between individual expert and politico orientations to interpersonal dealings, we have isolated all the factors to be uncovered in this chapter. They can be summarized as:

(1) The interpersonal orientation of the expert expressed in the pos-
    ture he adopts; and
(2) The compatibility of the politico's interpersonal orientation with
    that of the expert(s) with whom he will be dealing.

Hopefully, the previous pages have added depth to the understanding of what is belied by this simple phrasing.

For the remainer of this chapter, and before proceeding to a discussion of organizational and task-related factors, we should specify some unstated assumptions that instructed our development of factors on the interpersonal level. Doing so will not only provide conceptual rigor, but also encourage sensitivity to certain pivotal concepts in later chapters.

Probing Some Implicit Assumptions

DEALING WITH THE DYAD

For the sake of simplicity, we have inferred the character of ideal politico interpersonal orientations within the framework of the dyad. In working through the dyad we gain in analytical simplicity, but certain sources of error are introduced. In the dyadic image, each member is the sole source of his counterpart's interpersonal satisfactions and frustrations with the group experience. We know that most expert-politico decision groups in the real world involve more than two people. This multiperson setting implies that individuals may receive their interpersonal satisfactions and frustrations from several sources. This view alerts us to several possibilities for the likely conduct of relations within the multiperson group. First, other things being equal, individuals should tend to seek group members with whom they are compatible, so the direction of coalition formation, though obviously the product of many forces, will receive its first nudge along the lines of interpersonal compatibility. Second, if we assume that the division of labor in the collegial setting is somewhat fluid, often fluctuating with the agenda, temporary dyads that form may fare better than otherwise expected. This would follow from the assumption that in dyads that are somewhat incompatible, members can bite the bullet if they are receiving satisfaction from other simultaneous relations in the group, and if they believe the mismatched dyad is only temporary.

Of course it could follow that bad relations drive out good ones with dyad members spoiling potentially productive dyads because of spilled-over antagonisms in other group relationships. The critical question here is whether individuals enmeshed in a cluster of overlapping relationships take consolation from the pleasant ones or show irritability traceable to the unpleasant ones.[20]

The question must be answered empirically and the state of the art has not developed sufficiently to yield an answer yet. For our part, we can proceed with constructing our framework along the simple dyadic dimension for analytical purposes. The possible difficulties in extrapolating to the multiperson setting should be noted, however, though at this point the adjustments that might be required would seem primarily to be adjustments of degree.

Clearly no amount of satisfaction in dealing with Mr. X will produce a love affair with Mr. Y, and the upshot of indicating this caution is simply to suggest that the spillover from one relationship to another may affect mood if not manner. We will extract some useful notions from this possibility of spillover in the chapter on organizational variables. There the vagueness of this hypothetical notion will be less offensive because we will cast it in narrowly specified organizational circumstances.

Two more assumptions that we have made in this chapter require clarification. In clarifying them it will be seen that their having remained implicit has not harmed the ultimate product to be developed.

POLITICO POSTURES

We know but have not discussed the possibility that politicos may exhibit postures which have yet to be uncovered by empirical research. If they existed, these postures might modulate individual politico proclivities just as the three expert postures reduced the variety of expert interpersonal proclivities that would otherwise be expected from experts as people.

It might appear at first inspection, then, that our statements about the kinds of politicos who would be most compatible with experts are irrelevant, because politicos might actually adopt postures that would prevent any such ideal politico from ever surfacing. This is true, but not a problem. For even if such a state of affairs were uncovered, it would merely mean that the extent to which politicos were inherently incapable of compatibility with experts was a function of the incompatibility of their postures in certain combinations. The postures could still be described in three-dimensional terms. Postures that were incompatible should still be incompatible because of the same kinds of frictions we have already shown to be possible. Postures that were compatible should still be compatible because of the same kind of complementarities we have already seen to be possible.

The theoretical consequences of the eventual discovery of politico postures, then, amounts to this: Postures may be discovered which make some theoretical combinations we have described very unlikely, or others a far more frequent occurrence than we have any reasons to predict now. But the alterations thereby produced would be alterations in degree, not kind. These issues are not confoundings, but rather unanswered empirical questions dealing with the specification of margins.

NONCAREERIST POSTURES

The last assumptions to be cleared up before summarizing the notions developed in this chapter concern the contention that the leader, broker, and independent postures are the only postures expectable from career experts in the real world, to the exclusion of the insecure-expert posture which was also suggested by the laboratory data. The clarification involves reiterating what we mean by a "career expert."

As indicated earlier, the career expert is someone who works in an environment of politicos on a continuous basis, i.e., as a career, in an institutional setting. This is why it was suggested that the insecure-expert posture could be ignored in fashioning hypotheses about the performance of such careerists. The interpersonal uncomfortableness presumed to accompany this neglected posture was considered a sufficient deterrent to experts making decision-setting confrontations with politicos the substance of their professional activity.

This does not mean that the insecure expert pattern will not appear in expert-politico interaction; it does mean that when this pattern is manifested it will be by experts who are drawn into politico circles by the turn of unforeseen circumstances, with the relationship not long to endure.

Such one-shot dealings that may dredge up such unsuited experts would include the following kinds of situations:

(1) "Experts-for-a-day" who by accidental circumstances hold exclusive information on a single issue of importance to politicos;

(2) Experts recruited for long-term affiliations who are destined to resign but who at the time we encounter them, early in the relationship, have not yet come to that realization;

(3) Experts who were recruited according to job descriptions that were not accurate or whose duties have eventually changed in character because of institutional reorganization or redirection;

(4) Experts who inject themselves into political matters because of ideological motivations and whose attempts to exert influence in decision circles are destined to failure because they can't take the heat that will develop, and so on.

It is important to note the possibility of such unsuited experts' surfacing only because sensitivity to this possibility may help to explain otherwise anomalous anecdotes available in historical accounts of expert-politico interaction. Thus whenever we refer to career experts, the range of referents excludes the people on the scene by accident or only temporarily. They may exhibit the insecure posture of the laboratory, but with this perspective we know how to explain their performance without seeing it as a threat to our basic formulation. With these assumptions clarified, we can summarize the situation so far.

Where We Are

We have posited so far that by virtue of adopting the title of expert careerists will be induced to exhibit certain specific negotiating behaviors traceable to expert status alone. We have posited also that experts as people with their own interpersonal orientations manifest the expert role with one or another postures as a means of accommodating role demands to their individual interpersonal needs.

It was suggested that perhaps the specific negotiating behaviors isolated in the laboratory could be seen as the behavioral earmarks of the postures associated with them. These postures themselves are profiles in interpersonal orientation. We have noted further that each interpersonal profile likely for career experts would seem to be most compatible only with those politicos who display distinct interpersonal qualities. A given interpersonal orientation on the part of a politico will have dissimilar consequences for that politico's compatibility with an expert-as-leader as opposed to a broker or independent. We have specified these differential sources of rub and reinforcement. We know as well that there is a relationship between the degree of interpersonal compatibility between expert and politico, and the quality of their task performance. Lastly, in this regard it was suggested that the nature of this compatibility-performance nexus allowed for the strategic manipulation of counterparts in the expert-politico decision group for the purpose of increasing or decreasing certain members' performance.

However, these formulations can be misleading unless certain other influences on expert-politico negotiation are taken into account. These influences are associated with organizational constraints on the expert politico relationship and aspects of the task they are attending to as well as their perceptions of it.

In the next two chapters we will develop an understanding of just how these forces associated with task parameters and organizational constraints act on the expert-politico unit. We will proceed first with a development of task-related factors because such a development will make the venture into organizational considerations more fruitful. We have dealt with task considerations obliquely in this chapter, portraying group task *performance* as a function of interpersonal compatibility. The next chapter focuses on the relationship between participant ideas about the task itself and the character of participants' interaction.

NOTES

1. Merton's comments on role sets, role status, and multiple roles are relevant here, with some translations which should be clear in context. Robert K. Merton, "Sociological Theories of the Middle Range" in Merton, *Social Theory and Social Structure*, op. cit.

2. Operationally we saw some of its earmarks in the list of individually significant behaviors associated with "expert" performance in Chapter 2.

3. The varieties of phraseology used to define the concept of role are as numerous as textbooks. A typical example is that offered in C. Backman and P. Secord, *Social Psychology* (New York: McGraw-Hill, 1964). Also, see Thibaut and Kelley, op. cit. From the roles as stereotype perspective, see Lippmann on stereotypes and politics. Walter Lippmann, *Public Opinion* (New York: Free Press, 1965).

4. Deutsch has offered one of the most elaborate applications of this image on what we would call the macro level. Karl W. Deutsch, *The Nerves of Government* (New York: Free Press, 1966). For more information on the micro level, see Wendell

Johnson, "The Fateful Process of Mr. A Talking to Mr. B" in Robert T. Golembiewski, et al. (eds.), *Public Administration* (Chicago: Rand McNally, 1972), pp. 248-262.

5. Landau makes good use of this point in Martin Landau, *Political Theory and Political Science* (New York: Macmillan Co., 1972) Chapter 2.

6. See Clyde Kluckhohn, *Mirror for Man* (Greenwich, Connecticut.: Fawcett, 1963) chapter 8.

7. On the functional character of redundancy, see Martin Landau, "Redundancy, rationality, and the problem of duplication and overlap," *Public Administration Review,* vol. XXIX, No. 4, July/August, 1969.

8. Timothy Leary, *Interpersonal Diagnosis of Personality* (New York: Ronald Press, 1957); R. F. Bales, *Interaction Process Analysis* (New York: Addison-Wesley, 1950); W. Schutz, *The Interpersonal Underworld* (Palo Alto, California.; Science & Behavior Books, 1970).

9. Leary has gone as far as contending that anxiety is the psychological expression of the survival drive of evolution. Ibid., p. 14.

10. Here the behaviorists meet the Freudians, though the salient features of the formative years may be described differently by each, being additionally of greater concern to one than to the other. See for instance, S. W. Bijou and D. M. Baer, *Child Development I: A Systematic and Empirical Theory* (New York: Appleton-Century-Crofts, 1961) chapter 3. Compare this with Freud, "Infantile Sexuality," in *Freud: Three Essays on the Theory of Sexuality* (New York: Avon Books, 1962).

11. Of course, we use the concept of rational actors extensively in political theory. The so-called new political economy comes to mind, but so does Morgenthau. See Hans Morgenthau, *Politics Among Nations* (New York: Knopf, 1965) p. 10: "The realist believes that interest is the perennial standard by which political action must be judged."

12. This is an old idea that has appeared in many forms. We don't mean to stretch it to the social Darwinism extreme. Its less harsh manifestations in writings on the functional aspect of anxiety are what we had in mind. See note 9 above. See also Freud, *Civilization and Its Discontents* (New York: Norton, 1962) on the theoretical plane. For empirically based discussion: C. D. Spielberger "The Effects of Anxiety on Complex Learning and Academic Achievement" in Spielberger (ed.), *Anxiety and Behavior* (New York: Academic Press, 1966).

13. Again, the key is volition. We will consider at another point the effects of assigning roles. In the latter regard, see the work of William T. Smesler, "Dominance as a factor in achievement and perception in cooperative problem-solving interactions," *Journal of Abnormal and Social Psychology* LXII, 3, 1961, pp. 535-42. Also Fiedler (and his reference to Mann). Fred E. Fiedler, *Leadership* (Morristown, New Jersey: General Learning Press, 1971).

14. The implicit assumption here is that group members' shared desire for a sense of community ordinarily works to suppress advocacy of minority (unpopular) views. This is consistent with the "group-think" thesis. It has also been the starting assumption for works concerned with the problem of keeping channels of negative feedback open in the executive decision-making process. See for example, A. L. George, "The case for multiple advocacy in making foreign policy," *American Political Science Review* LXVI, No. 3, September 1972, pp. 751-85. Irving L. Janis, *Victims of Groupthink* (Boston: Houghton Mifflin, 1972).

15. Schutz divides each of his dimensions to distinguish between expressed and wanted behavior. We have collapsed the distinction because, given our interests, the dimension itself is what is most important. We will speak of orientations people may exhibit or seek in others when the question arises in specific cases.

16. Abraham Zaleznik of the Harvard Business School has suggested the notion of two types of leaders—minimum man and maximum man. The plane on which differences between them are drawn seems loosely tied to the kinds of formulations suggested here. A. Zaleznick, remarks before the 1971 meeting of the American Psychoanalytic Association, New York.

17. This theme appears to run through Lasswell. See especially H. D. Lasswell, *Power and Personality* (New York: Viking Press, 1962) chapter 3.

18. For example, R. H. Moos and J. C. Speisman, "Group compatibility and productivity," *Journal of Abnormal and Social Psychology*, LXV, 3, pp. 190-196.

19. See Schutz, op. cit. For one of the earliest and basic expositions of the need-complementarity thesis, see R. Winch, "The theory of complementary needs in mate selection: A test of one kind of complementariness," *American Sociological Review*, XX, 1955, pp. 52-56. The theory of complementary needs has sometimes failed to predict behavior according to its critics. It appears, however, that a substantial number of studies suggest the theory has merit. Moreover, shortcomings of the theory may in fact be only shortcomings of the measuring devices used to operationalize the theory. Recent unpublished research using behavioral observation techniques rather than pencil-and-paper tests suggests that the theory has substantial predictive power. For published work in support of the need-complementarity theory, see: G. Becker. "The complementary-need hypothesis: Authoritarianism, dominance, and other Edwards Personality Preference Schedule scores," *Journal of Personality*, 32, 1964, pp. 45-56; A. Kerckhoff and K. Davis, "Value consensus and need complementarity in mate selection," *American Sociological Review*, 27, 1962, pp. 295-303; J. Rychlak, "The similarity, compatibility, or incompatibility of needs in interpersonal selection," *Journal of Personality and Social Psychology* 2, 1965, pp. 334-340; R. Winch, T. Ktsanes, and V. Ktsanes. "The theory of complementary needs in mate selection: An analytic and descriptive study," *American Sociological Review*, 19, 1954, pp. 241-249. For work using behavioral observation see: L. Lerner, "Actual vs. Expected Compatability in the Problem-Solving Dyad," doctoral thesis, Department of Psychology, University of Oregon, 1973, unpublished.

20. This is generally described as the issue of the impact of outside reinforcers. What little empirical work is available is not particularly useful because it does not allow inferences concerning the degree to which such influence can be maximized. The available material is more concerned with establishing what we would take as the unmanipulated base line. R. L. Weiss, unpublished research on outside reinforcers and the dyad, Department of Psychology, University of Oregon.

Chapter 4

TASK-RELATED FACTORS AFFECTING
EXPERT-POLITICO INTERACTION

This chapter will describe four more factors (variables) that would be expected to affect the conduct of expert-politico relations in the kind of decision setting of interest to us. These four factors[1] share a chapter of their own because each can be thought of as relating to perceptions of the problem per se, with which a given expert-politico unit may be dealing. In this sense, we can mark these four variables as a distinct cluster of factors affecting expert-politico relations, separable in turn from the factors grouped on the other levels we have been and will be discussing: Role-related, personality, organization, and society-at-large-related variables. The factors presented in this chapter will be derived from a discussion of group decision-making.

Group Decision-Making

In the group setting that was described in Chapter 1 and posited as the context for examining expert-politico relations, the group task was described as decision-making. The interest at that time was in articulating the character of participant interaction in such a setting. Therefore the stress was on understanding how the decision-making process structured intra-group relations (making them negotiations) rather than on how the decision process mobilized the group as a unit for action on an external stimulus—the problem. Now that we are interested in describing task-related factors in the expert-politico relationship, it will be necessary to clarify briefly assumptions about what a group does *as a unit* when it makes a decision, in the sense of acting on an external stimulus.

Decisions are made with respect to problems. To make a decision on a problem is essentially to choose one strategy from among competing strategies to act on the problem. When a group is faced with a problem we can assume that the group (collectively or as individuals—it doesn't matter at this point) can envision several future states in which the group might find itself, depending on how the problem situation finally works out. We assume that in any given problem situation, the group can roughly rank these possible future states from the most to the least desirable. We assume further that for each future state—for each possible problem outcome—the group can hypothesize an action sequence on its part that would set the appropriate causal forces in motion to produce the corresponding out-come. Thus the intellectual process involved in making a rational decision consists of selecting an action sequence (a strategy) associated with an imagined problem outcome. From this view, to say a group is making a decision is to say that it is both selecting the outcome it wants to bring about, and the action-sequence—the strategy—that it presumes will lead to this outcome.[2]

The preference ranking of imagined possible outcomes is a function of the value systems of the participants. Rankings reflect judgments based primarily on what the judge thinks would be best for himself or the group—or whatever unit he is most interested in protecting.[3] In contrast, the association of strategies with these hypothesized future states or possible outcomes involves problematic statements. Strategies are in a sense empirical statements because they presume a connection between deeds and their consequences. They are hypotheses.[4] We assume that no group is omniscient. Therefore any assumption that a given problem outcome (future state) can be effected by invoking a particular strategy associated with it is a probabilistic statement.

Thus in undertaking the decision process the group undertakes a two-fold analytical process. First, it must have a conception of the relative desirabilities of the possible outcomes associated with the problem. Second, it must have some judgments about the likelihood that a strategy associated with a given outcome would indeed *produce* the outcome if the strategy were executed. The probabilistic element inherent in every option means that no decision can be assured of producing the expected result. The differential value-ranking of possible results means further that not all expected results are equally satisfying.

We will focus on decision groups facing serious problems; a serious problem would be one where significantly undesirable outcomes are possible (if nothing is done, if strategies produce surprising outcomes, or if the wrong people prevail) with a sufficient likelihood to cause anxiety within the group. We will focus on groups facing such problems because they are the groups where interesting things happen, and presumably the groups where important social and political problems are dealt with.

Given that accurate perception of the causal connection between possible future states and their antecedent conditions is problematic, and that certain possible outcomes are undesirable, decision-making is always a dangerous process where serious problems are involved. The danger component in decision-making is usually called risk. The view that we have taken here regarding the sources of danger in decision-making puts us in agreement with theorists who treat risk in terms of so-called expected-value formulations.[5]

In most all treatments, risk is essentially a conceptualization of the disparity between what a plan for action is designed to yield and what it might yield "if things go wrong," taking into consideration the likelihood and costs of failure. Of course, if a plan for action (a strategy) is undertaken and things indeed do not work out, the generated outcome is now different from that which was intended. To cover this scheme, basic expected-value formulations usually posit a strategy S_1 and outcomes, say O_1 and O_2 (O_1 being the desired and O_2 the undesired), each with its own utility value. Separate probability figures P_1 and P_2 are posited for each; that is, the strategy has a probability of success and a probability of failure together totaling certainty. The expected value is a proportional representation of the combination of O_1P_1 and O_2P_2.

We will operate with a slightly different view. When focusing on the politics of haggling over options, it is not wise to use a scheme which posits that the "things don't work out" case is not a set of infinite distinct states with their own O_nP_n possibilities (variously seized upon by disputants as the "real" description of the alternative at hand), or worse yet, a totally undifferentiable fog. Second, given our intention to build on the idea that different participants will dispute the "O's and P's" of the specific alternatives, it is better to describe options as they are seen by each participant, even if this means a given option may carry several different descriptions. Thus we propose the following working language.

Let every strategy, together with all the outcomes disputing participants might associate with it, be called an *option.* Let every particular strategy/outcome combination that one or several (agreeing or disagreeing) participants might conceptualize be called an *option component.* (Thus each association of a strategy with a given outcome would be a different option component.) Let the magnitude of differences between (among) the various option components that may comprise an option be described as the risk associated with the option. If traditional expected-value formulations describe the combined probability-utility products of all possible option components as the expected value of an option, then let the probability-utility product for an individual option component be described as its *worth.* (Thus traditional expected-value calculations would be a measure of net worth.) These modifications consist essentially of the distinction between an option and its option components. We are pleased if the subtleties appear as a small point; indeed it is only a small point that is involved. The distinctions simply avoid later confusion.

Lastly, before picking up the main thread, the more conventional approach taking a dichotomized view of a simple success/failure profile for options is suitable, to the laboratory where all possible outcomes and odds on their occurrence are provided beforehand to players, who then literally pay their monies and take their chances. It is also useful in theorizing about single actors or groups whose actions yield to reconstructions as if a single-will logic for choice were operating. We are dealing, if there is any analogy, with the process of finding that single will, so a conceptualization that makes it easiest to phrase disputes about whether there is an actual (de facto) empirical correspondence between alleged outcome-strategy correspondences is preferable. Our slightly more modified language seems to allow this more easily because it is more sensitive to the separate identities of the alternate scenarios hidden in a single option, offering a summary phrase for their existence (option component) and value (worth of the component).

For any option component then, the interplay between the probability that a given strategy will produce the outcome associated with it, and the value of that outcome, generates the perceived worthiness of the option component. The value of the outcome is, of course, the product of value judgments by the decision-maker(s). The probability associated with the companion strategy is a measure of decision-maker confidence in the accuracy of the hypothesis contending that the strategy and outcome are causally connected.

In the type of decision-making group of interest to us, we will assume that initially at least, individual members assign different values to (and have different value rankings for) the perceived possible problem outcomes. We will assume also that members have different estimates of the probability of success of a given strategy associated with any such outcome. We are positing, then, that members will initially see some decision-options as being superior to others and that there will therefore be disagreement among the members about the worthiness of option components. We will assume further that, other things being equal, the perceived worth of option components is a factor in the individual's decision to lobby for or against an option's being adopted as the group decision.

Harking back to our image of group decision-making as an implicit negotiating process, we would expect that a member will always try to elicit others' support for the option he prefers and which they may be less enthusiastic about. One way to enlist the support of the reluctant for one's own preferred option is to convince him to reappraise his probability and utility calculations of that option's components.

The form that an argument for re-evaluation may take can vary. Depending on the relative positions of lobbyist and reluctant counterpart, the lobbyist for re-evaluation may argue that:

(1) The option he prefers is closer to the counterpart's ideal option than is the counterpart's presently adopted position;
(2) The counterpart's presently advocated position is not in fact what he perceives it to be;
(3) The lobbyist's preferred option is superior to that preferred by some third member conducting his own lobbying act, and so on, always offering redepictions of option components.

Regardless of whose or which option is the focus of re-evaluation, the task for the lobbying member would be to urge the reassessment of option components by suggesting re-evaluation of their worth. Before suggesting how this would have to be done given the context we have described, it is necessary to explore the general character of objections to tentative options that are based on unfavorable evaluations of their components' worth.

If option components are defined in probability and utility terms, then there are two factors in an individual's evaluation of their worth. Either factor may appear in such a way as to make a particular component unattractive or, in the more extreme case, unthinkable. Taking the value factor first, we said that option components can be assessed for the value of the problem outcome they are designed to produce, from the point of view of any given decision-maker. Using a hypothetical utility scale for a decision-maker, imagine a range of values for all perceived possible outcomes from (according to conventional notation) -1.0 to +1.0, with the least valued outcome conceivable scored -1, and the most valuable outcome conceivable scored +1.

The probability factor can be represented (again according to conventional notation) on a scale from 0.0 to 1.0 with 0.0 representing no possibility at all that a strategy would produce the outcome that is (in this case erroneously) associated with it, and 1.0 representing the certainty that the strategy would produce the companion outcome. Juxtaposing these scales, any option component can be mapped for its worth as perceived by a given decision-maker. Our interest at this time is in describing the general character of opposition to options based on unfavorable evaluations of their components' worth.

Presumably a group member will always prefer the option that ranks best compared to all other alternatives. Because we assume that players are rational we would expect that, as far as evaluations of options based on their components' worth are concerned, members will prefer options whose components show attractive net combinations of likelihood of success and desirability of outcome. This would mean, in terms of our scaling, that members would prefer options whose components combined a high positive score on the value scale with a high score on the probability scale—compared to other options before the group.

According to the expected-value argument, probability and value scores are combined to arrive at what we are calling the worth of an option component according to a simple multiplication algorithm. That is, if W = worth, if P = the probability that the strategy associated with a given outcome will indeed produce that outcome, and if U = the value (i.e., utility) of that outcome to the decision-maker, then $W = (P \cdot U)$. Thus for a component where probability of success is .1, and the value of the outcome if produced is .9, the worth of that option component is expressed as (.1) (.9), or .09.

The most interesting implication of this approach is that components may be equally worthy though their probability and value scores differ. Thus a component with a probability of success score of .9 and a value of outcome score of .1 would also have a worth of .09. Using the notion of juxtaposing the probability and value scales to produce a two-dimensional space for locating option components by their worth, the possibility of equal-worth scores for various components means that one could posit "worth-isobars" as it were. These would be lines connecting all the possible permutations that produced a given worth. Given the simple expected-value algorithm, then, these worth-isobars might be viewed as worth-indifference curves. That is, for the pure expected-value decision-maker, all option components on the isobar would be of equal attractiveness.

Earlier we expressed a primary interest in theorizing about decision-making behavior where what we described as "serious" problems were involved. At that time a serious problem was defined as one where significantly undesirable outcomes are possible with a sufficient likelihood to cause anxiety within the group. The reason for focusing on groups facing problems of this type was the view that such problems were:

(1) Generally the most interesting, and
(2) Presumably characteristic of the way important social and political problems (and certainly crises) actually appear in real-world decision circles.

Focusing on this type of decision-making situation means, in the present context, that a substantial proportion of available options would probably have components with extreme value and probability factors. To elaborate within the framework we have developed, the most serious problem situation would be one in which components that scored high for the value of the outcomes associated with them had a low probability score—i.e., where the relatively desirable solutions are hard to come by. Also the outcomes with low-rated value (high negative utilities) would be probable (high probability score). Presumably such components would share the same parent option.

If we concern ourselves with decision-making groups facing this type of serious decision problem, we begin to see that some modifications are advisable concerning our image of the way decision-makers evaluate option components based on their worth. The difficulty lies in the character of the simple expected-value model $(W=PU)$. Specifically the rub is in the algorithm which allows for the possibility of a worth-indifference curve, or worth-isobars as described earlier because, given this formulation, we would expect the decision-maker to be indifferent to distinctions between option components leading to outcomes of little value with great probability and those leading to outcomes of great value with little probability. This would hold according to the simple expected-value formulation as long as the numerical representations of probability and outcome value for each option were reciprocal (and the sign were the same in our notation).

This characteristic of the algorithm is of less importance when the actual numbers involved in describing component value of outcome and probability of success are close on the number scale. Indeed one would expect decision-makers to be indifferent between two option components when one had, for instance, a .4 chance of success and a .5 payoff, with the other having a .5 chance of success and a .4 payoff. In contrast, we would expect the so-called serious problem to exhibit options scored more extremely. Here a choice between one option perhaps with a .1 chance of success and a .9 payoff as opposed to another option with a .9 chance of success and a .1 payoff. We do not want a model of option selection that predicts equivalent decision-maker interest in these two option components.

Why not? Because common sense tells us that there are alternatives people simply will not contemplate when they appear to exceed some subjective limits on acceptable odds or possible consequences. In terms of the probability component, long shots beyond certain limits, no matter how great the associated payoff, are not defensible strategies in high-stakes situations. They are for the reckless and naive (as others perceive them, at any rate).

Similarly, we know that even miniscule probabilities associated with cataclysmic outcomes pose too great a risk to be run by the decision-maker who feels that accepting them is not consistent with his "sense of responsibility," translated as the need to protect himself and his charges from catastrophe. Our conception of serious problems leads us to assume that the available options regarding such problems will often tend to extremes, and that they may therefore often approach these value and probability limits subjectively established by individual members.

Subjective Limits and Objective Worth Evaluation

These subjective limits may be thought of as the limits on an individual's ability to make detached evaluations. These limits define realms within one's "psychic space," as it were, where emotional reactions obscure the ability to view options in cold, analytical (objective, in common parlance) terms. The limits can be understood to operate as trip wires that close off the ability to view options instrumentally. The individual's position on such options tends towards the nonnegotiable. In our framework this means a resistance to reperception based on discussion of the option in question. In conventional terms we would say that the individual in such instances is unable to "keep an open mind."

We will contend that the source of such resistance in this case is the perception that the option's components have probability or utility scores that are nonnegotiable because of their extreme character. Willingness to negotiate implies a preparedness to yield under the right conditions. Options beyond the delimited realm approach being nonnegotiable because the individual finds it so difficult to conceive of yielding his position on them (again, because of perceived extreme component character.) In such circumstances, arguments aimed at persuasion will fail to take their usual effect. They will encounter resistance in excess of what would be the common reaction of the listener in similar cases concerning options that have not crossed these limits. This point will be expanded, but it will be better at this stage to first probe the notion of upper and lower limits.

Lower Limits

We contend that individuals operate with subjectively established lower limits on their ability to evaluate both the probability and outcome value of option components. Recalling the notion of scaled probabilities and outcomes, the lower limit on the *probability* scale would be the point below which no component could be assessed for its worth without a pronounced weighting of its probability (departing from the simple $W = PU$ scheme). We expect this from the view that, for the particular individual making his assessment, the probability that the outcome would be produced in such a component is so low that it cannot be considered in normal terms. Without data, and in our exploratory imprecision, it is unwise to portray this weighting notion as arithmetic, geometric (by a constant, or exponentially), or as a function to be captured by any precise algorithm at this time. Our point is simply to posit that idiosyncratic limits exist on the extent to which low probabilities can be treated as "realistic" probabilities by given individuals.

The reaction to options with such components would depend on the relation of the component to the larger option of which it is a part and to the position of the perceiver in a group considering such an option. If the component is portrayed by some other group member as the preferred eventuality (strong point, or "things-go-right" nexus) the member over whose shoulder we are looking is likely to be strongly opposed to the option (again, in excess of $W = PU$ terms). If the component in question represents the "things-go-wrong" eventuality in another member's proffered option, the perceiver may be excessively supportive (in excess of $W = PU$ calculations) in the sense that the undesirable option component is now hardly a cause for concern. If the component is the "things-go-wrong" eventuality of the perceiver's own proffered option, his enthusiasm for the option would be, to say the least, understandable. Presumably no one would propose an option he himself considered to have as its preferred eventuality a component with so low a probability factor.

When the *utility* facet of an option component is assessed as falling below the perceiver's lower utility limit, it offers highly undesirable outcomes, indeed, catastrophic outcomes. In hard times, components with such perceived utility facets may represent the "things-go-wrong" eventuality of the person's own proffered options. Or they may represent either the sought-after or hopefully avoidable eventuality of other group members' option offerings. Presumably no member himself would propose options whose sought-after eventuality would appear to that member to have such an undesirable utility facet. In any of these circumstances, the point is that components with utility facets scored below the lower utility limit would be so undesirable to the perceiver that they would influence the view of the option component they in part comprise (and the option it in part comprises) in excess of what the simple expected-value scheme would suggest. The implication, which we will soon explore further, is that the negotiability of such components and the options they may comprise becomes an especially difficult matter.

Upper Limits

Just as excessively low probability and utility scores for components may sharply skew their evaluation by perceivers, we assume that excessively high scores may do so. Here we are positing upper limits to the simple expected-value calculation of option components, and hence (albeit indirectly) options per se. The upper probability limit would be the idiosyncratically established point beyond which components were perceived to be a certain eventuality, and hence for all intents and purposes synonomous with the options purported to contain them. For the individual who perceives that an option component has crossed his upper probability limit, that component describes the eventuality produced by that option; no other components exist, practically speaking, in a discussion of that option's merit. Beyond the upper probability limit, probability scores would be treatable essentially as if they were in fact 1.0. In the perceiver's eye, this would be the death knell of an option where such a component had an unacceptable value of outcome, for example. The pattern, in a sense reversed from the preceding section, should be clear by now. Where the scoring of a component was such that the utility facet crossed the upper utility limit, the assumption is that the perceiver inordinately esteems the eventuality portrayed by that option component. Its desirability is, for all practical (negotiating) purposes, unquestionably far in excess of what the simple $W = PU$ scheme would suggest.[6]

The issue of limits to the detached calculation of option component worth was developed here as a convenient context for discussing the problems and strategic implications inherent in trying to persuade a decision-maker to adopt some option other than the one towards which he leans initially. However, before proceeding to such a discussion, it will be useful to graphically summarize developments up to this point. In doing so we can also extract a few additional notions as to how the character of option evaluation may be described as a function of whether or not any particular limits have been exceeded in individual cases. Discussion in these terms will allow us to identify the special problems in successfully persuading (or resisting the persuasive efforts of) experts as opposed to politicos.

Describing Limits

In Table 4.1, the vertical axis represents the notion of an individual's utility index for the outcome facets of components belonging to given options before his decision group. Consistent with conventional notation its values range from -1.0 to $+1.0$. The horizontal axis scores the perceived probability with which the particular strategy associated with an option will indeed bring about the companion outcome ranked on the vertical scale. Again, consistent with conventional notation, these values range from 0.0 to 1.0. The horizontal line labeled U_L represents the individual's lower utility limit as described earlier. It is presumed, as regards all such limits, that the exact positioning of the limit is idiosyncratic. In other words, it differs for each member. Here it is drawn at some point below the zero point on the utility scale to reflect the assumption that, for most individuals, some options with components involving losses may be seriously entertained under certain conditions. Similarly, the lines U_u, P_L, and P_u represent the upper utility limit, the lower probability limit and the upper probability limit respectively.

Table 4.1 is a grid. A point on the grid would represent one option component as perceived by one decision-maker for whom the grid is drawn. The point (component) would be defined by the score of its utility facet measured on the vertical axis, and the score of its probability facet measured on the horizontal axis.

Thus if the decision group were considering, for example, four options defined by two components each, every individual in the group could have a grid constructed for him and each grid would have eight points on it—one per component. However, the eight points might appear at different locations on each person's grid depending on the extent of differences in the perceived worthiness of the components (from the two-fold standpoint of the probability of the strategies' success and the attractiveness of the associated outcomes.)

The particular probability and utility values by which a given decision-maker defined a given component would determine where it appears in his psychic space. As we will discuss, scores of given magnitudes for components for a given decision-maker would position them in any one of the nine cells on the grid. The cells may be considered sectors of the indi-

Table 4.1   The "Psychic Space" of Option-Component Perceptions

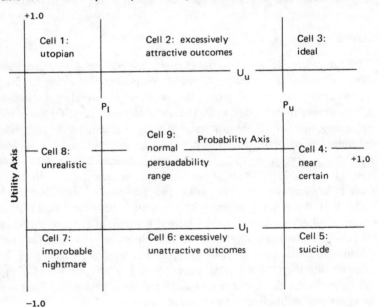

vidual's psychic space in which any option may appear depending on how its components are scaled in the mind of the decision-maker.

By way of further clarification, assume that a group of six people is considering four options of two components each. The total context of group deliberation on these options could be represented by six overlapped grids. Each grid would have eight dots on it; each dot representing the individual's evaluation of one of the eight components. On the overlay, if the points representing a given component clustered together, it would indicate that the group showed a common interpretation of the worth of that component. If the components of an option yielded to such common interpretation, it would indicate agreement on the expected value of the option.

The cells, or sectors, on the single grid for the single individual represent areas of the psychic space of component perception in which different schema for calculating the net worthiness of components obtain. The selection of scheme would be determined by whether the sector a component fell in were defined by any of the upper or lower limits on detached evaluation's having been crossed. In the overlay, group-profile, context this would mean that if a given component were scored in one cell for some players and in another cell for others, the players would not only view its worth differently, but also they would evaluate differently any worthiness-relevant information on it. This suggests that problems in persuading re-evaluation of options will be difficult and different depending on whether the person to be persuaded has relevent option components located in one cell or another. We will develop all of these issues later in this chapter. First it is necessary to explain the nature of each of the cells and what is implied in considering that an individual has construed a component in such a way as to "place" it in that cell.

It was suggested earlier that for components falling beyond any of the limits, worth assessments would not be made in the unweighted manner expected for those scoring short of the delimited areas. For simplicity's sake, we can call the space not governed by upper or lower limits the middle range as opposed to the extreme ranges (on the perimeters). Consistent with the basic expected-value model, we will presume that the worth of components within the middle range is calculated by giving equal emphasis to probability-of-success and value-of-outcome facets. It was further suggested that when a component was perceived to fall in the extreme ranges, the facet that fell beyond the limit associated with it would be weighted in the calculation of worth. Consider the overlapping extremes first: Cells 1, 3, 5, and 7.

For cells 3 and 7, the direction of overlapping extremes is the same. That is, in cell 3 component perception is governed by the upper limits of both probability and value assessment. In cell 7 it is governed by both lower limits.

CELL 3

If an option component is located in cell 3, it is irresistably attractive because it offers an extremely attractive outcome with virtual certainty. While an "objective" (as in unweighted) evaluation of any component in this area of the grid would indicate that we have a desirable component, the point is that if a component in this area has exceeded the limits in question, the individual is taken with it beyond its objective merit. In this case, normally telling arguments that may eventually develop against the relevant option or in favor of only slightly less attractive options would fall on virtually deaf ears.

Where counterparts perceive an option to contain such a component, dissuading them from support of it would be difficult. The best but still weak strategy for the lobbying member would probably be to associate a second component with the parent option which offered a catastrophic outcome. (However, if we assume a scheme where all option component probabilities summed to 1.0, such a component's necessarily low probability score would still make counterpart resistance to the parent option unlikely.) Similarly, lobbying members who could succeed in having counterparts perceive a component of the lobbyist's preferred option falling within the counterpart's cell 3 would enjoy "locked-up" early supporters. Components falling in this cell would merit the label "ideal."

CELL 7

Option components located in cell 7 for a particular decision-maker are extraordinarily distasteful in outcome but also extraordinarily unlikely. They are improbable and nightmarish, as the cell label reflects. As we have begun to indicate through the discussion of cell 3, the strategic issues in dealing with counterparts who perceive an option to contain such a component depend in large part on the sister components of the option and on whether the would-be persuader sponsors another option, the same option with another or this component as its (differently) perceived strong point, and so on. It seems safe to generalize that appropriate tactics would include an emphasis on the axiomatic wisdom, or (if the situation particulars allow for it) the situational desirability, of paying prior attention to practicalities—to focusing on probabilities, a nonmalevolent natural world, a healthy mix of optimism with pragmatism, and the like, and therefore defining the parent option not by focusing too much on any cell 7 components. Successful lobbying for an actual reperception of such components involving any movement in the direction of cell 3 would seem unlikely. The separation of such components from the set of components alleged to define the option or the association of desirable components with the parent option would seem more promising strategies than that of attempting to have the cell 7 component re-evaluated.

Cells 1 and 5 are the ambivalent extremes. Our discussion of limits leads to the view that two contradictory forces operate in each of these cells. The question is whether an unfavorable or favorable reaction should obtain. We can arrive at an answer by verbalizing the conditions depicted in each cell as they should appear to the decision-maker.

CELL 1

Cell 1 describes an option component perceived to have a miniscule chance of producing the outcome associated with it. The outcome itself is extraordinarily attractive. Such components are utopian; they describe a wonderful future state that realistically cannot be attained.

Where counterparts perceive a component which is the alleged "selling point" for an option proffered by a lobbying other, that other must dissociate from the parent option any high probability, comparatively negative, outcome components, to the eye of the counterpart target of persuasion. Alternatively there is the possibility of encouraging riskiness or daring in the counterpart's option preferences. Third parties in such a situation may succeed in drawing to further, third options, the counterpart with cell 1 component perceptions under a lobbying member's possible influence. Our view would lead us to theorize that extremely attractive third-option alternatives in such situations would be those with components which, other things being equal, offered only slightly greater probabilities (but beyond P_L for the target) with not necessarily other than somewhat the same utilities. Because limits have been crossed for cell 1 components, arguing for reassessment of their worth would be exceedingly difficult.

CELL 5

In cell 5, the high and low limits are now reversed. Here evaluation is characterized by the extraordinary unattractiveness of the associated outcome and the extremely impressive certainty that the companion strategy will produce that outcome. Another way to describe the situation is that the parent option, if undertaken, is extremely likely to produce a suicide. Obviously it would be natural in intragroup haggling to try to avoid having one's preferred option perceived to involve any such component and to have one's personally unpreferred options so perceived by others. Only rarely might one actually seek others' views of one's own preferred option in these terms—that is, when any group "lepers," whose support is a liability, might otherwise be difficult to dissociate oneself from directly.

CELLS 4 AND 8

These cells encompass those option components perceived to be characterized by the upper and lower idiosyncratic limits on detached ($W = PU$) probability assessment. Utility assessments here may range to the undesirable and desirable short of extreme forms. All components perceived to fall within cell 8, if not utopian or nightmarish, are impractical as definitive characterizations of the parent option; they are the respectfully nodded-to but hardly dwelt-upon footnotes in the evaluation of options.

Perceptions pertaining to their utility facets are comparatively negotiable but the discussion is academic. Quite the opposite is true in cell 4 where, for (moderately) good or ill, the option component is perceived to represent the near-certain eventuality of the parent option. Members perceiving components in cell 4 are ripe for the most prolonged and serious attention to the parent options as realistic concerns in the decision process. While there is hardly an attention problem in such circumstances, the question of favorable or unfavorable reaction to such parent options as decision candidates is a difficult issue, though again, fanaticism (note U_u and U_L boundaries) would seem avoidable in discussion. This can be a realm of hard, pragmatic bargaining on "relevant" issues if a number of rival options each have such a component, other things being equal.

CELLS 2 AND 6

These cells govern option components characterized by value-of-outcome facets that fall either below (cell 6) or above (cell 2) the utility limits, with the probability facets within the nonextreme range. The evaluation of components in these cells is inferred from earlier discussions of limits. That is, components in cell 2 appear especially worthy and in cell 6 especially unworthy—both in excess of what simple expected-value calculations would indicate.

The general negotiability, or susceptibility to reperception, of option components in these cells (as can be inferred by now from our general approach in this grid metaphor) is minimal as far as movement on the very high (cell 2) or very low (cell 6) evaluation of the outcome facet is concerned. The probability facet is the comparative "negotiable" for such components. Regarding cell 2 perceptions, wise lobbying-member strategies, depending on the direction of difference between lobbyist preference for the perceiver and the perceiver's location of the component, would probably involve attempts to induce reperception tending towards cells 1 or 3. Obviously the choice of direction in this case would be equivalent, other things being equal, to encouraging support for (toward cell 3) or disenchantment with (toward cell 1) the parent option. In each case this could occur without attempting to take issue with the perceiver on the resistant facet of the (for him) option component, i.e., the projected-outcome value.

Similarly, regarding components perceived to fall within cell 6, support for the parent option might be salvageable if perception could be steered toward cell 7 and might be wrecked if steered toward cell 5. It is interesting to note regarding cells 2 and 6 (as well as cells 4 and 8 for that matter) that their descriptions serve as broad rubrics conveying the more specific character of cells defined by additional limits having been crossed, i.e., the corner cells.

CELL 9

Cell 9 represents the range of possible components for which an individual would arrive at worth assessments with subjective detachment. That is, components perceived to be placed in this range have probability-of-success and utility-of-outcome values for the individual that do not exceed any of his idiosyncratic limits. Presumably, then, the individual evaluates a component in this cell without reacting "excessively" to either of its facets. He does not find the component unduly attractive or unattractive because he perceives neither facet to be extreme—as he would for components appearing in any other cell. In cell 9 utility and probability are equally influential in evaluating options. No fellow decision-maker could rightfully accuse the individual in this case of showing some irrational attraction or antipathy to the component in question and hence the parent option. No "red flags" as it were have gone up for the decision-maker considering components in cell 9. He is, from his point of view, comparatively capable of a "detached" dialogue on the merits of components in this range, and so comparatively amenable to or "ripe for" persuasions to reperception in the haggling and cajoling process.

So What?

The point of all this summarized in Table 4.1 is to suggest the kind of things that go on in people's minds when they evaluate a decision option on its merits. Admittedly, this view supposes that when perceptions of task-related parameters *alone* govern option evaluation, the concept of worth assessment—as we have construed it—is broad enough to subsume the mental processes at work. Given our larger interest in isolating the factors that influence expert-politico interaction per se, this discussion of perceived option worth becomes especially important. As we will soon consider, the intragroup persuasion process should be handled more or less successfully by experts as opposed to politicos, depending on whether the sticking point of a given option pertains to its perceived probability of success or value of outcome for components.

Before taking up this application of the discussion to expert-politico issues, it will be useful to clarify how it is that our view can be interpreted to subsume other aspects of option-evaluation which should be associated with evaluation based on merit alone. Pausing to clarify this point will enrich the discussion of how the character of worth perceptions can work for or against the negotiating efforts of experts or politicos.

Options in Broadest Terms

A number of frequently mentioned considerations in option evaluation and selection can be subsumed under our view though they may appear at first glance to merit independent status and so require their own paralleled development in a conceptual framework. By a subtle conceptualization of components it can be seen that this need not necessarily be the case. Taking the trouble to clarify this point allows one to conceptualize the process of option evaluation parsimoniously. Also it permits the strategic considerations in group option selection to be developed from the discussion already provided in this chapter.

A significant degree of uncertainty surrounding a problem presumably reduces the probability that strategies associated with available options will in fact succeed. Decision theorists frequently note that this situation may be remedied by obtaining additional information. Such information must in a sense be purchased, to the extent that resources of one sort or another must be expended to obtain it.[7] Thus we come to the notion of the cost of information and, in subtle treatments, the cost of information discounted by some coefficient representing the probability that the information will actually prove of value in reducing uncertainty. Related to this theme of the cost of information as a factor in option evaluation is the notion of "satisficing," whereby decision-makers select one option that is minimally acceptable rather than searching for an option that is maximally desirable, in order to get on with the task at hand.[8] Similar ideas fuel the disjointed incrementalism principle and the process of muddling through.[9] Now these considerations in reconstructing the option-selection process can be absorbed in our view.

Satisficing may simply be treated as the process of establishing *group* upper limits on utility and probability calculations such that any options exceeding these group upper limits are acceptable as group decisions. Presumably these limits would fall far lower on the utility and probability scales than do the upper limits of objectivity that we have discussed, but all the same they can be treated as idiosyncratic limits were treated here. Thus under the satisficing rule, the first option that scored beyond the established group limit (and which would be so perceived by the deciders) could satisfy as a decision.

The cost of information purchasing can be treated as a component in the assignment of outcome utilities. If the contemplated information purchase involves information about the problem itself, then all outcome values associated with all options can be discounted to reflect the resource expenditure that is the "purchasing price" as it were. If the information purchase concerns information about the properties of a particular option, the cost can be subtracted from the net value of the outcomes associated with that particular option alone. The benefits of the information might also be reflected in an improvement of the probability-of-success estimates for a given option. If the value of the expected information is itself problematic, we simply have a probability-of-probability increment estimate, which can be treated as a second-order measure where the same conditions governing an original determination could obtain.

Disjointed incrementalism can be absorbed by our simple evaluation metaphor by incorporating the satisficing and information-purchasing adjustments with one more idea. Namely, it need simply be further assumed that the individual and group criteria in calculations are flexible, i.e., redrawn from issue to issue, and generally weighted in favor of marginal adjustments.

Thus, with a willingness to interpret probability-of-success calculations and utility-of-outcome calculations broadly, our scheme is sufficient to describe the process of option perception and thereby selection. The one qualification, again, is that option perception must here be construed to be based only on the perceived merit of the option components. That is, we are holding constant, for the moment, considerations such as organizational machinations, interpersonal frictions, and so on.

Expert-Politico Persuasiveness and the Perceived Worth of Option Components

We have described the expert as the person who can most nearly speak with the final word on a substantive issue. It was posited in describing the processes of option perception that the particular probability associated with a component is a measure of decision-maker confidence in the *hypothesis* that strategy and outcome are causally connected. Probability assessments were thus portrayed as hypotheses about empirical relationships in the problem environment, and subject as such to verification in principle. In contrast, the value-of-outcome factor in worth assessment was said to rest, obviously, on value judgments—on hierarchies of preference, on matters of taste, so to speak.

If experts are the masters of substance and if probability judgments in worth ascription are hypothetical, empirical statements, then, other things being equal, experts can speak with persuasiveness about the appropriateness of probability evaluation. They can do so not only because they may know more but also because people believe they know more. This would hold true as long as a modicum of technology is associated with the problem—that is, as long as the presence of experts is appropriate in the first place because there is something to be expert about. We will consider soon the relationship between expert-politico influence and the technological component of problems. At present the point to be stressed is that the expert's preeminence in the empirical domain lends authority to his discussions of empirical considerations in option evaluation. Because probability assessment turns on empirical considerations (the validity of alleged causal connections) experts have an edge when arguing the wisdom of estimations concerning the probability of success of the strategy associated with a given option. Specifically, this edge is the counterparts' perception that the expert is more likely to be factually correct than the politico in his empirical evaluations.

In the purely collegial setting the politico qua politico cannot compensate for expert persuasiveness regarding probability considerations because the politico has no corresponding advantage in discussions of the utility aspects of worth calculation. This is so because individual evaluations of outcome attractiveness are considered value judgments. They are not based on empirical contingencies and so their re-evaluation cannot be argued without arguing that an individual readjust his value scheme. The politico may not be able to make a case in this regard any better than the expert in private intragroup councils to the extent that the politico-as-statesman image is only problematic and not inherent.

Remember at this juncture that the group context is the purely collegial setting and implicitly an autonomous decision group. The latter qualification suggests a group free of any other outside group or individual's power to alter the decision. The question of whether a decision group is or is not predominantly collegial or autonomous is a question of its organizational structure. We shall see that as organizational parameters (as well as others) are altered, the relative advantages in persuasion of the expert and politico change. But organizational considerations will be examined in the next chapter. Suffice it to say here that as far as the operation of perceived task parameters alone on expert-politico interaction is concerned, experts enjoy an advantage traceable to their preeminence in empirical matters bearing on the problem before the group. The consideration of task parameters leads to the conclusion that regarding discussions about the proper assignment of outcome utilities, expert and politico are on equal footing in the persuasion of counterparts.

We can translate this notion of persuasive ability—treated earlier as a discussion of lobbying—into general predictions about the likely direction that reperception of an option would take in the analytical space described by Table 4.1. In this context, we define persuasive ability as the ability to induce a counterpart to re-evaluate a given option component so that it would appear on a new point on Table 4.1. To say that experts enjoy a persuasive edge in discussions concerning the empirical (probability-related) basis of option evaluation is to say then that, other things being equal, experts will be able to induce greater counterpart movement horizontally on Table 4.1.

From this notion we can anticipate that in rebutting the arguments which politicos offers to counterparts for movement on the horizontal plane, experts will have more success than politicos will. Where politicos try to persuade experts to move on the horizontal plane, experts will be better able to resist without appearing unreasonable in the eyes of on-looking members. Whenever politicos have an interest in inducing horizontal movement by counterparts, persuasion would be most effective if it could be conducted by allied experts. Politicos interested in resisting arguments for re-evaluation on the horizontal plane would do well, where possible, to have allied experts make their cases for them. Whenever there is a desire to move a counterpart out of the realm defined by his lower or upper probability limits, the advocacy of experts is *crucial.*

Additional permutations may be spelled out but the point seems clear. However, this notion of an expert edge also leads to a series of general predictions in terms of the specific cells we have developed. Given expert advantage in inducing lateral movement across Table 4.1, it should follow, for instance, that experts will be more efficient than politicos in persuading that options with utopian components should be re-evaluated as especially attractive alternatives. Experts would have no advantage over politicos in arguing that utopian components be re-evaluated as *simply* unrealistic. Experts would have somewhat of an edge in arguing that ideal components should be viewed instrumentally as all other options that escape excessive nonnegotiable categorization (cell 9). The expert edge in resisting persuasion should follow a similar pattern. Regarding these predictions concerning specific cell-to-cell movements, there are again many permutations we could articulate,[10] but the point seems clear.

It is wise to assume that the strategic possibilities that occur to us regarding expert persuasive primacy on empirical questions would also occur to them. So we can expect negotiations associated with option evaluation in expert-politico groups to be substantially influenced by the special status of experts, with respect to empirical matters bearing on component perception.

Some of the tactical possibilities that this special standing allows for have been suggested in the preceding paragraphs primarily for the purpose of illustrating the likely uses to which this notion of an expert persuasive edge can be put by the analyst (and the strategically-minded group member). In the following chapter we shall see that the politico can have an advantage in persuasion traceable to the more common organizational constraints that obtain in given groups. From our understanding of the politico advantage, such as it may be, we can extract politico tactical ploys likely to be effective in group deliberative-persuasive sessions.

Summarizing So Far

From the ideas presented up to this juncture, it appears that the conduct of group deliberations about options—and presumably the outcome of such deliberations—can be strongly influenced by perceptions of specific task-related parameters governing the calculation of option component worth. Recalling the logic of the arguments presented here, the basic task of all decision-making groups is option selection as a result of option evaluation. The process of option evaluation can be thought of as a process of comparative component assessment undertaken first by individual members and then resolved in group deliberation. The aim within the group is to establish the necessary minimum consensus for producing a final group decision represented by a single parent option.

The concept of component evaluation can be treated as the product of two processes, broadly construed to absotb the major constructs associated with group decision-making in general. Introducing the notion of idiosyncratic limits on the detached execution of these processes, one can conceptualize a psychic space, as it were, within which all individual reactions to given components can be located. By doing so, it is possible to develop expectations as to the likely effects of attempts to persuade given individuals to alter the character of their evaluations of (and hence their eagerness or reluctance to support) given options. The character of initial evaluations can thus be described in such a way as to allow predictions about the likely success of attempts to persuade re-evaluation—depending on whether these attempts are made by experts or politicos.

We have seen so far that the relative influence of experts and politicos can be treated as a function of an initial position of the target individual (expert, politico, or unspecified, who is to be persuaded). This line of reasoning leads to the conclusion that, other things being equal, the influence of experts as opposed to politicos in decision-making groups will be a function of the initial position taken by members with respect to a given component—regarding the value of the outcome it is presumed to produce and the probability that the strategy associated with it will in fact produce that outcome. Also the relative influence of experts as opposed to politicos will be a function of the extent to which consent to persuasion would entail re-evaluation of the probability and/or value facets of a given option's components.

Summarizing in terms of specific *factors* influencing expert-politico interaction, this line of reasoning indicates three such factors traceable to task parameters:

(1) The initial component evaluations made by individuals who become the targets of expert or politico persuasion;

(2) The status of such target individuals as experts, politicos, or some unspecified others; and

(3) The nature (in probability and utility terms) of the difference between initial evaluations made by target individuals and the evaluations which expert or politico would advocate in their place.

We have not considered the impact of differing propensities for risk-taking, which may be defined based on our earlier discussion as propensity to choose options with components of disparate worth. This issue has not been examined because of the desire to avoid the assumptions that experts or politicos would have any inherent differences in such matters qua expert and politico, or any persuasion advantages in such matters. Such propensities, if asserted, could be absorbed in our framework as personality-level factors.

Lastly in this chapter we will suggest a fourth factor influencing comparative expert-politico effectiveness in the group setting and hence expert-politico interaction.

Technological Complexity

In describing the persuasive edge enjoyed by experts when dealing with empirical matters, no consideration was given to the content of such empirical matters per se, beyond the caveat that the expert edge would only operate assuming the technology of such matters was sufficiently sophisticated to warrant expert participation in the first place. Our fourth factor comes from a closer consideration of this point.

The degree of technical complexity of a given issue can be conceptualized as a trichotomy. In simplest terms, the technology of an issue can be slightly sophisticated, moderately sophisticated, or extremely sophisticated. Consider moderate technical sophistication to be sophistication beyond the minimum point necessary to justify expert participation in the eyes of counterparts.

It has already been suggested that the expert's persuasive edge in empirical discussions cannot be utilized in empirical discussions that are unsophisticated. The expectation is that the lay status of the politico with respect to the technology governing such empirical questions is sufficient to argue empirical matters convincingly. This is so simply because the parameters of such simple empirical problems can be adequately managed with common sense. The unsophisticated nature of such issues puts the politico (or any nonexpert) on equal footing with the expert. Cogent presentations in such discussions simply do not require technical expertise.

When empirical matters are more complex, however, the expert can utilize his "edge" for reasons already indicated. He begins to outdistance the politico in effectiveness in rational discussions of such matters. The expectation is that the politico is still capable of making a coherent case. However, now he can only make it less effectively. Moreover, as issue complexity is perceived by third parties to be sufficiently sophisticated to warrant expertise, the arguments offered by politicos opposing experts are in principle more suspect with respect to empirical accuracy.

Consider now the most extreme case: Intragroup deliberation on matters of an extremely technical nature. Other things being equal, one would expect that experts can be at their most influential. However, we should consider another possibility. Expert influence may radically decline in mixed expert-politico groups once the technical intricacy of empirical issues exceeds some maximal level. This point would be idiosyncratically established for each nonexpert participant.

The underlying assumption here is that effectiveness in persuasion—influence—presupposes not only a compelling persuader but an amenable "persuadee," or target individual. Without digressing into the presentation of some weighty model of face-saving behavior or human learning, it can be reasonably argued that to allow oneself to be co-opted can threaten not only one's self-esteem but, more assuredly, the image of oneself that is held by counterparts. To be sure, there is a certain psychological resistance to abandoning one's own views to accede to the arguments of another. In the competitive-deliberative setting, the fidelity to the norms of objective analysis can become a face-saving device.[11] Where it is painful to accede to an individual, one may more easily accede to an individual's argument. The ability to adopt the latter posture and thereby retreat gracefully in the eyes of on-lookers requires, however, the capacity to show that the subtlety of argument has been mastered. This requires that the willing convert demonstrate his command of the issues involved; it requires, moreover, the convert's judgment that on-lookers themselves can be convinced of this mastery that has made concession an objective issue and not a test of individuals. It is here that the extremely technical format can work against the lobbying expert seeking option re-evaluation by others. His persuasive edge is a liability if it becomes too glaring; it is difficult for would-be converts to be co-opted if they cannot yield gracefully. If issues are so technologically complex as to rob such willing converts of the ability to engage in cogent discussion, or make it unlikely that such discussion would register with on-lookers, then the expert edge is severely lessened. Indeed, others' awareness of the expert's clear persuasive superiority may even make it a liability as individuals move preemptorily to isolate him.

In a simpler vein, without invoking notions of face and graceful retreat, we can posit a second source of expert difficulty in intragroup lobbying on extremely technical issues. Simply put, the expert who may have a sound position may be at a loss to make his case if appreciation of his argument requires a sophistication that is lacking in his listeners. While it is true that nonexperts may find it easier to yield when they can claim that yielding to experts on technical issues is no disgrace, this is a tactic that would seem easily overused. The object, after all, is to secure support for one's option. Yielding for whatever reason can jeopardize that support. Moreover, from what we know of the dual aspect of option evaluation, one cannot yield on technical issues and still make the best case for one's preferred option—given that all options have empirically related components.

Conclusion

The upshot of this discussion is that we have a fourth factor that may influence behavior in the expert-politico decision group: The degree of technological complexity associated with the empirical content of options under consideration. The treatment here suggests that it operates in curvilinear fashion as it were. According to this view, expert effectiveness in intragroup negotiations would tend to be at its greatest on empirical issues that are moderately sophisticated. Other things being equal, it would tend to decrease as technological complexity approached either extreme for the reasons indicated.

We want to stress that these expectations proceed at this juncture from an analytical framework that holds other factors constant. Later chapters will suggest that the simultaneous operation of additional factors may lead to diverse effects. Indeed, the point of developing a conceptual framework is to separate the complex interaction system into a series of conceptually isolatable inputs—factors as we are calling them—or variables in a formal theory. The next step in this vein regarding our expert-politico problem is to identify several factors related to the organizational setting which affect expert and politico behavior in groups of the type that are of interest here. We shall see that some of these factors exert their effect by coloring the way that factors we have already developed actually operate. Other such factors on the organizational level will be seen to exert their effect more directly. We consider these factors in the following chapter.

NOTES

1. Again, the word "factor" is used here as a synonym for "variable" and should not be confused with factor analysis. We are making the distinction between factors and variables periodically, to stress that there are no pretensions to a formal theory but simply a conceptual framework. The term pretheory is sometimes used as a synonym for the latter.

2. Martin Landau summarized this conception nicely in his definition of rationality. See Martin Landau, "Decision theory and comparative public administration," *Comparative Political Studies*, I, 2, July, 1968.

3. The notion of acting in the interest of extraneous parties raises the question of fiduciary behavior. Admittedly fiduciaries do not always behave as self-representatives do, but what we have to say poses no problem in this regard. For a good treatment of fiduciary behavior, see R. Curry, Jr., and L. Wade, *A Theory of Political Exchange* (Englewood Cliffs, New Jersey: Prentice Hall, 1968) chapter 5.

4. Landau, op. cit.

5. The concept of risk can be presented in various ways, though the expected-value concept is frequently at the core. One interesting formulation is the subjective expected-utility model. See A. Vinokur, "Cognitive and affective processes influencing risk-taking in groups: An expected utility approach," *Journal of Personality and Social Psychology*, 20, 3, 1971, pp. 472-86. Also for a good overview of approaches in this area, see D. Cartwright, "Risk-taking by individuals and groups," ibid., pp. 361-78, and Donald W. Taylor, "Decision-Making and Problem-Solving," in James G. March (ed.), *Handbook of Organizations* (Chicago: Rand McNally, 1965).

6. We have not considered the possibility of "islands" of irrationality located idiosyncratically and erratically over discontinuous ranges, short of the extreme outer ranges of probability and utility assessment. Such islands might be viewed as blindspots developed for some (neurotic?) reason or other. We will avoid this though it probably occurs, because it is by nature nonstandardized and also irrelevant in regard to expert-politico distinctions.

7. See for example Anthony Downs, *An Economic Theory of Democracy* (New York, Harper & Row, 1957). Downs's discussion of the rational argument for being relatively uninformed in one's political behavior is a good example of what we have in mind.

8. James G. March and Herbert Simon with Harold Guetzkow, *Organizations* (New York: Wiley, 1958) pp. 140-41.

9. Charles E. Lindblom, "The science of 'muddling through,'" *Public Administration Review*, 19, spring 1959; David Braybrooke and Charles E. Lindblom, *A Strategy of Decision* (New York: Free Press, 1963).

10. Where a given option or options are viewed differently by two members, and where a third member desires to mediate, experts (other things being equal) would be the most persuasive intermediaries when the differences are along the horizontal plane—where opponents were in cells 4 and 8, for example, and the object of mediation was to bring both into cell 9 where discussion would be more fruitful. Also the present line of reasoning has implications for strategizing where two blocs vie for the swing support of a third party and all three groups support a different option or a

different perception of the same option. Depending on the expert or politico status
of the competing and swing groups, contestants may abandon their initial position in
favor of a new fourth position, which might facilitate lateral movement of the swing
group under influence of experts who lobby for the group that moved.

11. On face-saving in negotiation, see D. Pruitt and D. Johnson, "Mediation as an
aid to face-saving in negotiation," *Journal of Personality and Social Psychology,* 14,
3, March 1970, pp. 239-46.

Chapter 5

ORGANIZATIONAL FACTORS AFFECTING

EXPERT-POLITICO INTERACTION

The first factor to be considered in this chapter concerns the relationship between having formal authority and having an advantage in the persuasive-deliberative setting. The factor itself is identified as the *collegiality-differentiation balance* in the expert-politico decision group. Chapter 1 argued that the type of decision groups of interest to us will always exhibit some degree of collegiality. The question about collegiality in this chapter is how much.[1] The first factor to be developed here is based on the assumption that more or less collegiality will affect the relative influence of experts and politicos in real-world decision groups. To examine this notion it is important to stress that collegiality is the absence of explicit (formal) hierarchies of authority.

The more a group is collegial the less there are explicit, formal, authority distinctions among members. Authority distinctions mean that members are differentiated by official titles and powers which establish de jure superior-subordinate hierarchies. The more that elements of such a system appear in intragroup dealings, the less can members enjoy organizational parity, as equals in an informal relationship network.[2]

Given our current interest in describing the extent to which authority relationships within a decision group are formally prescribed, and given our assumption that all groups are collegial to a degree, it will be best to denote the pervasiveness of formal authority arrangements by referring to a collegiality-formality ratio (or tension in dynamic terms) for all decision-making groups. To emphasize that formality pertains to formality of prescribed differences in authority, and to avoid the implication that some complex scale for measuring authority will be introduced here, this first factor is called the group's collegiality-differentiation balance.

Formal Authority Differentiation and the Intragroup Persuasion Struggle

Consider further the concept of prescribed authority distinctions. Where such divisions are established, members perceive that the group is organized in such a way that some members have the legitimate right to exercise certain prerogatives at others' expense.[3] It is true that authority may be vested in individuals only for specific purposes. Recording secretaries have the authority to take official notes, sergeants-at-arms have the authority to throw people out of meetings after the appropriate procedures have been observed, chairmen have the authority to wield the gavel with all its privileges, and so on. It must be recognized, in other words, that authority is authority to do some but not necessarily all things.

For the time being, consider the character of authority as it appears at or near the top of the group hierarchy. With due respect to the point that the scope of individuals' authority can be limited to particular functions, it is still possible to generalize about the nature of authority at the top. There are universal characteristics of such senior-status positions. They are first of all relatively prestigious positions; that is, holding them is per se a mark of relative distinction—of esteem—other things being equal.[4] They are proof that the individual possesses some qualities valued by the group to a degree that makes him more worthy of the position than other group members who are eligible, but who have not been selected for such a post.

Although we suffer the disadvantage of a lack of empirical studies on the subject, I think it is still fair to say that in the real world, as far as groups of interest to us are concerned, it is politicos more often than experts who occupy the senior positions in established hierarchies. This would seem to be the case especially in large-scale formal organizations. This assumption follows our primary interest in government or govern-

ment-related decision bodies where political types presumably predominate. In any event, even where experts hold the senior group
positions, occupying the top of the formal hierarchy is, other things being
equal, an advantage in the deliberative-persuasive setting. From the discussion so far, we can offer several reasons why this would be likely.

Senior Positions and Control Over Patronage

Occupying the senior position is an advantage in the in-fighting, negotiating setting because one of the features of this setting is the need to
attract supporters for the option one advocates. As described earlier, the
counterpart who is the object of persuasion assesses the merits of competing options before taking a position. The member who occupies a
senior position is in a better position than others to dispense patronage.
Patronage can make a coalition offer more attractive than it might be if it
were evaluated purely on the merits of the option which the coalition
supports.[5]

It is important that patronage not be understood in the narrow sense of
jobs to be allocated, though this is certainly a possibility whenever the
group in question is part of a large-scale formal organization, especially a
government organization. Rather, patronage in the broader sense would
include any perceived benefits which the senior members of the hierarchy
have the ability to dispense among other members in exchange for cooperation.

The term "patronage" implies also that the benefits involve matters
extraneous to the properties of the issue under immediate consideration.
Thus the term in its broadest sense can absorb what are usually described
separately as pork-barrel benefits, bribes, privileged treatment on pro-
cedural and other matters, and so on. In this sense, patronage is a form of
side payment and those at the top of the hierarchy are in the best position
to offer such payments and hence enjoy a negotiating advantage in the
persuasive-deliberative setting.

Maximizing Identification; Intangible Patronage

Another type of benefit which hierarchically senior members are best
able to offer prospective allies, and which thus serves to give senior
members a negotiating advantage, is what may be called maximized identification.[6] In an appointment by merit system, and especially in large-scale
formal organizations, the senior members more than others presumably
personify the ideals of the organization. Additionally, all properly social-

ized members, regardless of rank, espouse the organizational ideals which these senior members best personify.[7] Sympathy with the senior member's position can thus provide the individual with a sense of positive identification with organizational ideals. Insofar as this is perceived to be desirable (i.e., insofar as organizational ideals are esteemed and senior members appear to merit their status) members will seek to align themselves with their seniors in the group, other things being equal. This tendency constitutes an advantage for the senior member and can be seen as a kind of "intangible patronage" which can be of value if dispensed wisely (delicately). The senior member's advantage in using both tangible and intangible patronage as bargaining elements should be seen as a facility not only in providing such benefits, but also in denying them and in diminishing the amounts to which they are already enjoyed.[8]

In sum, advantages in negotiation accrue to decision-group members in senior authority positions when the following conditions are present. First, organizational positions must be perceived to be assigned on merit and accurately so (for intangible benefits through identification to be manipulated); that is, people at the top of the hierarchy are perceived to be there because they have the qualities the organization values in its people. Second, control over tangible patronage must generally follow hierarchical patterns. Third, members must identify with the organization and hence its senior people in their official capacities.[9]

It must be stressed again that we are assuming politicos will occupy the senior organizational positions more frequently than experts in government and government-related decision groups. Where this is the case the bargaining advantage that the superior has will thus accrue to politicos and thereby serve to partially offset the expert's persuasive edge traceable to empirical preeminence on the task dimension. In cases where experts enjoy prescribed hierarchical superiority, their persuasive advantage is of course increased even further. But given our expectation about where formal authority most frequently lies in the real world, we will continue to mark the advantages of formal seniority in the politico's column. For convenience, this negotiating advantage traceable to preeminence in the formal authority hierarchy we shall call the *superior's advantage*.

This "superior's advantage" can be utilized only to the extent that members are amenable to choosing options on some basis other than their intrinsic merits defined in perceived probability of success and utility of outcome terms. The superior's advantage is thus an advantage only in the realm of side payments, of patronage—tangible or intangible. For it to be effective, participants must have their sources of career and personal satisfactions closely linked to their organizational standing. This would make them most vulnerable to manipulation on side-payment issues because they would have fewer outside sources of support, gratification, and career advancement.[10]

What this means is that the superior's advantage is most effective in large-scale formal organizations where the decision group that participants belong to is enmeshed in a series of layered (hierarchically organized) groups where upward movement through the layers is a career ambition and literally a full-time job.[11] Correspondingly, the superior's advantage would be less effective in independent, ad hoc work groups where career affiliations were primarily extraneous to the group.[12]

In sum, the superior's advantage is an advantage on side-payment issues. It can be utilized when the collegiality-differentiation balance is skewed toward differentiation in decision-making groups that are part of larger organizations. It can be utilized when negotiators are amenable to discussion in terms of side payments.

A Politico Advantage Independent of Side-Payment Issues

Where certain organizational characteristics are present, politicos can also enjoy a negotiating advantage in discussions concerning the merits of options per se. That is, under certain conditions politicos can use their organizational position as a base for speaking with final authority about options in a way that parallels the expert's edge on the task dimension. The politico's advantage on the task dimension stems from his ability to speak about value-of-outcome considerations in the way that experts speak about probability of success. The politico's task advantage is developed in this chapter because it is conditional upon the presence of organizational properties which are themselves problematic.

This politico advantage should be considered an advantage on the task dimension that is traceable to a unique position on the organizational dimension. In contrast, the expert's persuasive edge is anchored in task-level considerations proper. It is an advantage inherent in the relation between empirical mastery and the empirical component of option evaluation. This will become clearer as we proceed.

To begin to understand the nature of this politico's task advantage which can be invoked when certain organizational conditions obtain, it will be necessary to explore the notion of means and ends in decision-making.

Means, Ends, and the Large-Scale, Formal Organization

It is by now orthodox in the study of organizations that the empirical and preference components of option evaluation can be likened to considerations of fact and value.[13] Also, fact and value may in many ways be likened to means and ends. In *Administrative Behavior,* Simon suggests that where organizational decision-making is concerned, means and ends ought to be viewed as a chain linked upward through the organizational structure.[14] That is, if we consider the organization as a hierarchy of layered decision-making units, each unit undertakes the decision process when it searches for means appropriate to ends it has in mind. We have treated these ends as conceptualizations of alternative future states in which the group may find itself when the time frame encompassing the problem at hand is completed. Simon tends to view ends as future states which the organization prompts its units to attain on the level of action appropriate to that unit. The latter view is consistent with an emphasis on administration rather than puzzle-working (i.e., problem-solving) but the concepts are compatible here.

The point, then, is that the empirical component of decision-making from the perspective of any single given unit lies in the process of means selection. The value component lies in judgments about the ends for which means should be sought.

The notion of a chain comes from acknowledging the limits of the fact-value dichotomy, which lie precisely in the inadvisability of presuming a clear distinction between facts (means, empirical judgments) and values (ends, goals, preferred outcomes). In suggesting the proper perception of means-ends distinctions, Simon invokes the notion of the means-ends chain: That the definition of means and ends is contextual.

Our next factor comes from this idea of a means-ends chain. The notions developed in this regard apply only to large-scale, formal organizations. For reasons that will be elaborated later, the advantage that accrues to politicos in this regard is thus only one that can be anticipated where the expert-politico unit is immersed in a larger formal structure of hierarchically stratified decision units. The discussion is worth undertaking, however, on the assumption that this is a setting which frequently characterizes expert-politico units in government and large corporations related to government activity.

The Means-Ends Chain

In describing the definition of means and ends as contextual in the large, layered organization, the contention is that decision-making tasks are defined differently for units at different levels in the organizational hierarchy. With the stress here on problem-solving, the operational definition of organizational problems is different for decision-making units who must deal with the problem on different levels within the larger unit. (We are assuming at present that a given problem is felt at all levels within the organization, but this presently simplifying assumption will be modified later.)

In addition to the assumption that a problem will make itself felt in some form throughout the entire organizational hierarchy of decision units, this line of argument further supposes that as one proceeds upward through the hierarchy of units, problems are defined in increasingly broader terms. In other words, the possible *outcomes* associated with the problem are portrayed in more general policy terms. The assumption is that as one moves upward through the organization, a given problem takes a form that is both different at each organizational level and appropriate to that level.

The upper levels perceive the fact that decisions taken on lower levels have the cumulative effect of altering the problem environment. The consequence is that when lower levels take actions within their problem sphere, a re-evaluation of the problem field by the next higher level is required. Such re-evaluation can detect the need for adjustments which might be needed to keep the organization as a whole in the best position vis-à-vis the problem area. In administrative terms, the goals of upper-level units must be re-examined to determine that they are compatible with the best interests of the organization, given the cumulative effect of lower-level actions in the problem area.

What this means is that outcome preferences (value judgments) asserted by lower-level units are viewed *instrumentally* by higher-level units. In other words, from the point of view of upper-level units, it is an empirical question whether the value judgments of lower-level units will facilitate maximization of the broader goals the upper level is concerned with. If lower-level decisions to strive for given ends produce the intended result, the new future state brought about by lower-level action constitutes a new set of givens for the senior unit; for it is the senior unit that must now deal with its related problems in a new empirical environment created in part by the action of groups beneath it.[15]

Therefore outcome preferences which are value judgments for junior-level decision units serve to define the range of means from which senior units must find strategies to attain more broadly defined goals (outcomes concerned with larger issues). In this way, what are *ends* for lower-level decision groups in the organization, because they are viewed instrumentally by higher levels, become *means* for these higher-level units. The question for the higher-level unit is this: Given that lower units bring about new combinations of circumstances vis-à-vis the problems they perceive, what strategies are now appropriate for senior-unit action in an altered environment where problems are defined in broader terms?

What we can say about the means-end chain, then, is this: In the large-scale formal organization characterized by a highly differentiated hierarchy of decision units, whenever higher units deal with problems defined on a progressively broader scale, ends for lower units are means for higher units. That is, future states that lower units strive for would largely contribute to the empirical field from which higher units must fashion strategies to alter their more broadly defined goals. Similarly, means for higher units would be ends for lower units. To cultivate the empirical field that will provide high-probability strategies for achieving its preferred goals, the higher unit sets as an end for the lower unit the attainment of a problem outcome in the latter's sphere of action, which the senior unit deems desirable as a starting point for attaining its own preferred outcomes.

Before suggesting how politicos can gain a negotiating advantage over experts in this situation, we will indicate how some of the more rigid assumptions underlying this line of reasoning may be relaxed without doing violence to the basic notion of means-ends chains and the contextual definition of empirical and outcome-preference judgments.

Relaxing Rigid Assumptions

First, regarding the assumption of a formal hierarchy of decision units within the larger organization, the notion of a means-ends chain is appropriate even where the hierarchical stratification of units is only partial. That is, as long as there are at least two units within the organization which are perceived by members to share a subordinate-immediate superior relationship, the chain concept can apply. The concept would emphasize the contextual character of means-ends perceptions within the two units and the relationship between one's perceived means and the other's perceived ends (goals, outcome rankings).

Second, by way of relaxing rigid assumptions that facilitated presentation, low-level problems do not have to reverberate throughout the entire organizational hierarchy for senior levels to view the ends sought by lower levels instrumentally. Senior levels need only be aware that outcomes sought by lower levels are liable in given instances to have the effect of altering the environment for the organization as a whole. As long as this is perceived, it can safely be argued that senior units have an interest in assessing lower-level decisions for their impact on issues of special interest to senior units. Presumably it is the senior units which have primary responsibility for assuring the continued viability of the organization as a whole with respect to its larger environment.

Inter-Unit Dependency and Decision-Group Autonomy in the Larger Organization

The discussion so far has concerned perceptions of means and ends in the organizational setting. It has dealt with formal organizations as a complex of at least partially layered decision units where problems of progressively broader scope comprise the action spheres of units taken in ascending order.

The problems of all such units are related in that senior units charged with maintaining a viable organization will tend to view the narrower goals of all junior units as perhaps good or bad—but presumably related—to larger organizational interests and hence senior unit concerns. This does not mean that all junior units will be scrupulously instructed; it does mean that if a given level of activity becomes salient to senior levels for any reason, that activity will always be relatable, for good or ill, to senior-level interests proper.

The notion of perceived, linked, larger interests between units suggests that units within a large organization will be viewed as being dependent to a degree on each other. Interdependence here reflects the idea that, in organizations with some degree of authority stratification, all units in the hierarchy can never be assured of complete sovereignty over their problem areas. If any unit perceives that its problem-solving activity will be influenced by the action of another unit, a case can always be made that the secondary unit have some input to assure its ability to perform at optimum efficiency under the broader organizational mandate. We would expect from the discussion so far that arguments in this regard would involve the claim that the means or ends chosen (probability or outcome judgments made) by the unit with immediate jurisdication will weaken the probability and outcome position of the objecting unit in its own problem sphere.[16] The justification for complaint would presumably entail the claim that obstructing the complaining unit would harm the organization more than failure to satisfy the encroaching unit.

The degree of sovereignty which a unit enjoys in its problem area can be called its *decision-making autonomy*. We will assume that autonomy can vary within limits, from issue to issue, and that steps may be taken by encroaching or encroached-upon units to alter the degree of autonomy for a given unit on a given issue. From the discussion so far, the degree of decision-making autonomy enjoyed by a particular decision group within a larger organization can be seen as a function of the degree to which the organization is hierarchically stratified, and the degree to which problems which units encounter involve means and ends (probability and utility choices) which alter each other's problem environments defined as ranges for such choices.[17]

Recalling our expectation that politicos would most frequently occupy senior positions within units that have any degree of authority stratification, we now have all the concepts necessary to explore the second important source of possible politico advantage in intragroup deliberations with experts.

Politico Advantage in the Instrumental View of Outcome Preference

The context is the large, formal organization with at least partially established inter- and intra-unit hierarchies of authority, where politicos tend to occupy the senior intra-unit positions. In terms of earlier phrasing, the setting is one in which intra-unit option evaluation by any unit is related to that of others by a means-ends chain. The collegiality-differentiation balance tends toward differentiation; the organization is hierarchical. Decision-making autonomy is therefore reduced at least to the point of making it reasonable, on given issues, to sometimes consider what the reactions of other units would be if certain options before the group were selected as the group's decision.

Where such an organizational climate prepares members, in principle, to consider the possible reactions of other units to decisions taken by their own unit, politicos may profit by urging such consideration. Before explaining why, we shall indicate how the issue of considering other units would appear to the unit in question (henceforth the prime unit).

Where the prime unit deems it necessary to consider the impact of its decision (any option it may select) on lower units, the question it must ask, given our notions about means and ends, is whether the means associated with the option it selects will be consistent with the goals the lower unit is pledged to maximize in its organizational activities. That is, the prime unit must consider whether it is drawing on options with strategies that presume an empirical field which the lower unit is in fact working to maintain. Presumably, probability judgments concerning strategies considered by the prime unit reflect, among other things, the strategies' availability. Thus the question in this regard becomes one of maintaining unity of larger purpose in the organization as a whole. This becomes an important practical consideration for senior units because if unity of purpose is absent, strategies desired by such units may become unavailable.

This sort of consideration is admittedly more appropriate to decision-making on long-range issues—or what is usually called policy-making. Given our primary interest in decision-making concerned with perceived significant problems which tend to be defined as short-range crises or immediate opportunities, we would expect concern with lower-unit reactions to lack practical import. Rather, whenever prime-unit attention is focused on dealing with an immediate, pressing problem, any concern with likely lower-unit reactions becomes a relatively "altruistic" (for want of a better word) concern.[18]

Given this setting, it is difficult to imagine that consideration of lower units would exert a strong influence on the course of negotiations within the prime unit. This would be especially so where the strategies being considered involved resources the lower units had already secured. Only for the extremtly ideological organization might this be otherwise. Of course, it might be that consideration of lower-unit reaction could weigh heavily for nonideological reasons wherever lower units appealed to higher figures or lower-unit disruption over the long run could result in adverse consequences.

For such considerations to weigh sufficiently, either the loss of long-range productivity by the lower unit or the possible loss because of appeal to higher figures would have to outweigh the expected net loss in moving to the option that appeared less desirable to the prime unit, though more in sympathy with lower-unit needs. Such issues become too localized to specific organizational and problem concerns to be considered here. However, the situation would seem to be unlikely. Therefore we will posit that prime-unit consideration of other units' reactions to option selection will usually flow upward, not downward, where so-called serious problems are concerned.

Option Attractiveness in Light of Expected Upper-Unit Reactions

While the adverse reaction of lower units can lead to arbitration or localized inter-unit disharmony, the adverse reaction of upper units can lead to punishment or, perhaps worse, the disregard of all prime-unit input on the problem at hand. Consider the situation faced by the prime unit whenever upper-unit reaction is an issue in intra-unit negotiations over option selection.

The prime unit seeks some understanding of how the upper unit would react if any of the options the prime unit is seriously considering were to be offered as the prime unit's decision. Thus the prime unit is interested in assessing the future state associated with an option it is considering, for that future state's desirability as an empirical setting for upper-unit decision-making. It is interested in evaluating the desirability of its own goals as means for the upper unit; it looks at its own goals instrumentally— not as ends in themselves but as means to further ends (ends sought by the upper unit).

This means that prime-unit members are now prepared to evaluate their own preferred outcomes on a second basis in addition to the outcomes' compatibility with their own value systems. Judgments on the value component of options are no longer made exclusively according to a value hierarchy, once these organizational issues concerning upper-unit reaction arise. Rather, empirical questions now enter into the evaluation of the value component. Specifically, the new empirical element in assessing value components (goals) associated with options is the probability that they will be viewed favorably by the upper unit. The question is whether these outcomes will be perceived as good "starting points"—good field positions as it were—in the eyes of upper-unit members who have the power to take action in some form against the prime unit.

For a prime unit in this situation, some knowledge of likely upper-unit reactions to options under serious consideration by the prime unit would be exceedingly important. The question for the prime unit in this regard can be expressed in terms of feasibility: Given the organizational interests of prime-unit members, and presumably their desire to see the problem treated, is it feasible to select particular options otherwise acceptable to the prime unit as decisions to be presented to the upper unit? Failure to properly resolve this question once the need to consider it is perceived might result in career setbacks. Also it might result in having meritorious decisions ultimately circumvented. As a result, problems that could have been resolved might now go unsolved or even worsened.[19]

If some knowledge of the upper unit's likely reactions becomes important to the prime unit, an advantage in negotiation accrues to the participant who is perceived to have the best line of communication with the upper unit. A member in communication with the upper unit can provide information about its likely reaction to specific options. This can be done either by conveying specific messages, by sifting interaction in another context for clues as to likely responses, or by offering personal opinions, shaped by general exposure, to the upper unit with a frequency not matched by other members. A member who is perceived by others to be in such contact with the upper unit should enjoy an advantage in negotiation insofar as he can urge the reassessment of option outcomes on a pragmatic, feasibility—appeal to upper-unit perceptions—basis.

Opening Value Discussions to Pragmatic Considerations

We contended earlier that generally participants cannot easily induce others to re-evaluate the desirability of given future states because positions on them stem from value judgments linked to individuals' fundamental value systems. The view in this regard was that, in contrast to judgments about the probability facet of option components, value judgments by their nature resist incremental changes for the sake of compromise because they yield less to intersubjective evaluation and segmenting.

Once there is an interest in viewing such value judgments about goals as means from the perspective of the upper unit, then calculations about their desirability become negotiable, i.e., more susceptible to incremental adjustments. This becomes possible because a new dimension of feasibility—of political propriety, of instrumentality, we might say—has been introduced. True, it is still not the desirability of the associated outcome itself that is negotiable. Rather it is the probability that the upper unit will view the outcome's desirability in the same way that its advocates in the prime unit do. This becomes an empirical question. As such, individual positions on it are subject to incremental adjustment in reaction to the negotiating-deliberative exchange.

We suggest that in circumstances such as this, where interest in upper-unit reaction has introduced an empirical element into value-of-outcome considerations, a negotiating advantage accrues to participants who can best speak with pretensions to the final word about likely upper-unit reactions to prime-unit decisions. The organizational setting that we have posited as the context of this discussion leads to the conclusion that in such circumstances this bargaining advantage accrues to the politico. Let us reiterate the key assumptions in this regard.

The context is the intragroup setting that tends toward formal authority differentiation in a government or government-related organization. It is assumed that in the real world politicos tend to occupy the senior formal-authority positions. The group is immersed in a larger organization that tends toward a hierarchical organization of decision units. Hierarchical stratification of authority relationships implies explicit superior-subordinate lines of communication.

The contention here is that the politico, not the expert, has clearest access to the upper decision unit whose reactions are now of interest to the prime unit making a decision. This view is merited by the assumption that the politico, as senior organizational member of the prime unit, is the prime-unit member whose immediate superior is a member of the upper unit. The liaison between prime and upper unit is maintained at the politico-politico's superior synapse, where the information about the upper unit's view of specific decision alternatives can be exchanged in its various forms. These forms include specific directives, discussions in other contexts which allow for translation, or repeated exposure to upper-unit communication generally, which facilitates a reading of mood or a comparatively educated guess about likely reactions based on behavior in related situations. More precisely, what is facilitated is maintenance of the *appearance* (justified or not) that an individual has access to information in these forms.

As long as prime-unit participants perceive the structure of the organization accurately, we may expect them to perceive the advantage of the politico in this regard. That is, they would perceive his advantage in superior information about the character of likely upper-unit responses to the outcomes associated with various prime-unit options under consideration. We will call this the *politico's edge in the means-ends chain,* to emphasize that it is rooted in organizational perspectives on values (ends) as means to further ends.

To reiterate, this edge becomes an advantage insofar as organizational conditions introduce an empirical dimension to the ordering of outcome values. This empirical dimension concerns questions of fit between participants' preferences and those of their superiors. It concerns the extent to which prime-unit decisions might be acceptable to upper units and, by implication, the extent to which individuals whose interests are associated with the standing of the prime unit would be harmed by failure to win such upper-unit acceptance.

The questions raised in this regard are thus questions of feasibility in terms extraneous to options merits in the narrow sense. They concern the art of the possible, we might say, and are thus "political" questions as that term is used in the popular sense. They concern values and the merits of pushing them in the face of opposition from those with power to affect the pushers and the problem they are involved with. In a sense, then, the politico advantage in the means-ends chain is understandable as a sort of advantage in perceived *expertise*.[20] The expertise pertains to certain empirical matters where the empirical matters specifically concern politics itself. The politico's advantage in the means-ends chain is thus the organizational-level equivalent of the expert's (empirical) persuasive edge, and it arises as organizational conditions make the advisability of pursuing given goals a partly political issue.

Like the senior's advantage described earlier, the politico's edge in the means-ends chain is a function of certain properties which may characterize the organizational setting. In principle, the notion of the means-ends edge can apply to experts as well, if it is the expert who in fact holds the senior position within the prime unit. Ascribing the advantage to the politico reflects our guess about the locus of de jure authority in the type of group of interest to us. The *senior's advantage* is linked to the nature of the collegiality-differentiation balance in what we are now calling the prime unit. In a sense, the means-ends edge is linked to the inter-unit equivalent of the collegiality-differentiation balance, which we described earlier as the degree of autonomy characterizing a given decision unit. That is, where the collegiality-differentiation balance reflects the extent to which individuals are formally accountable to others within the decision group, the degree of autonomy enjoyed by a given decision group reflects the extent to which that group is accountable to other groups within the organization.

Focusing on the politico's edge in the means-ends chain, the politico's edge in this case concerned preeminence with respect to calculations about the merits of options as decisions. This is in contrast to the superior's advantage which concerns the merits of options for their personal attractiveness to individuals concerned with side-payment issues. If the means-ends edge is an advantage in discussions of the value component of options in particular, it is possible to extract some notions about the ability of politicos to persuade in terms of the "psychic space" described in Chapter 4. Recall Table 4.1.

Politico Persuasiveness in the Psychic Space of Option-Component Perception

The point was made in Chapter 4 that the expert's persuasive edge stemmed from preeminence on the empirical dimension associated with probability-of-success judgments. This followed the assumption that where the presence of experts was relevant, probability judgments concerning the causal relationship between strategies and associated outcomes would involve questions within the realm of expertise. This translated as an advantage in inducing movement on the *horizontal* plane of Table 4.1.

The politico's means-ends edge would translate as an ability to induce movement on the *vertical* plane of Table 4.1. Here, because of organizational considerations, the politico who is in the senior group position can best argue the desirability of outcomes associated with given options. Desirability, as indicated, is understood as the desirability of the outcome as the upper unit would perceive it. This becomes a component in judgments about desirability within the prime unit as long as that unit is concerned with avoiding upper-unit wrath or securing upper-unit approval. As indicated earlier, the politico's advantage in this regard should be understood as a kind of expertise in an aspect of value-related matters. This expertise would fall within the category of expertise justified by having superior information and/or experience.

The strategic possibilities that flow from this notion of an advantage in persuasion on the vertical dimension follow the pattern indicated for experts on the horizontal plane. For example, experts seeking to induce a third party to re-evaluate, where re-evaluation involves some vertical adjustment, would do well to align themselves with sympathetic politicos. Politicos can resist persuasion on the vertical plane without appearing unreasonable more easily than experts can. Where a third party who is the object of persuasion is pressed to cross either his upper or lower utility limit, the active lobbying of politicos is absolutely essential, and so on.

Politicos more so than experts can induce a third party to re-evaluate perceived suicidal options as being relatively attractive options. Politicos have a comparative advantage in urging that components initially perceived by target individuals to be unattractive in excess of their actual shortcomings (as the target's usual evaluation pattern would indicate) should be viewed objectively. That is, politicos can best urge that such options be viewed in a more detached manner where bargaining about them becomes possible. Politicos enjoying the means-ends advantage can best succeed in having nightmarish options reassessed on second inspection as being unrealistic, and so on.

. The means-ends advantage is not one that can be exercised by all politicos with equal facility. Rather it would most likely be the province of those politicos who occupy relatively senior positions in the intragroup hierarchy—where such hierarchies obtain, of course. As for lesser politicos in such a setting, it becomes an empirical question as to whether they can invoke anything like a means-ends-based advantage in persuasion concerning the value component of options before the group. Having earlier defined the politico as the participant whose ware is acknowledged to be strategic behavior, it is reasonable to consider that some pretension toward insight concerning upper-unit behavior would be granted any politico worth his role in dealing with nonpoliticos. But where the claim to upper-unit understanding is not supported by organizational liaison with that unit, and must therefore rest solely on claims to mastering the art of the possible, no confident judgment, even in comparative terms, can be made a priori. If we assume that skill in "political" matters is not perceived to involve a hard technology comparable to substantive expertise in empirical matters, then claims to anticipate upper-unit reaction patterns which are not reinforced by formal access to upper units would seem relatively weak. At least, we would suppose, they should seem weak enough to rise and fall with purely situational factors which we cannot anticipate on the level of generalization we are striving for.

Thus, while we may note that an edge in feasibility discussions traceable to politico status alone is a possibility in the real world, it is a consideration best excluded from a list of "basic trump cards" such as we are trying to construct. The eventual discovery of any such politico per se advantage in discussions of feasibility would not confound the formulations so far. They would merely serve as an additional source of politico advantage. Parenthetically we may expect that, were such an advantage to be uncovered, it would probably be an advantage traceable to considerations on the role dimension which operates in turn on the task dimension.

Returning to the strategic implications of the means-ends edge ascribed to relatively senior politicos, those suggested up to this point are concerned with effecting changes in counterparts' option-component perceptions. There are, however, other strategic issues associated with the means-ends edge. They concern participant perceptions of the conditions necessary for maximizing that advantage.

We would expect in this regard that politicos will have the fullest benefit of their potential for in-group influence on option deliberations the more that participants are aware of the relevant organizational constraints that operate on the group. Other things being equal, politicos would do well to stress the closeness of their relations with upper units, the significance of formal hierarchy distinctions in the organizational ideology, the obligation of participants to adhere to that ideology, the power of upper units to affect the prime unit, the purely instrumental view that upper units take of prime-unit ends, and so on. It behooves the expert who opposes the politico making such a case to minimize the relationship between action on the problem at hand and those other organizational considerations. One would expect here, for example, the stressing of uncommitted experts' obligation to wider professional norms that exclude reaction to "political" pressures.

So far we have identified two "trump cards" which politicos would be expected to wield under specified organizational conditions. The two factors whose variation can lead to the availability of these trump cards have been termed the degree of decision-unit autonomy, and the direction of the collegiality-differentiation balance. These factors concern the rigor of authority relationships between decision groups and within decision groups respectively.

A Third Organizational Factor

The next factor on the organizational level which affects expert-politico interaction may be called the *degree of departure from the unanimity rule* in arriving at decisions. Riker's work bears on this concept in another context, concerning the size of the minimum winning coalition.[21] Chapter 1 noted that one of the important assumptions associated with the group context of concern to us had to do with the rule by which options could be authoritatively selected as a decision. The need for negotiating in the decision process was seen partly as a consequence of the need to join forces so that a large enough majority could be secured on behalf of a given option. The option could then become the group's decision. It was assumed that decision rules in somewhat collegial settings usually tended toward unanimity and certainly majority.

The degree to which a decision group departs from the unanimity rule is a factor in expert-politico interaction. This is because the ratio of supporters to dissenters which must obtain before an option can become the group decision determines the extent to which participants can manipulate interpersonal frictions without endangering the size of the necessary majority. Chapter 2 noted that interpersonal compatibility would vary with task effectiveness. Also, where undesirable task influences were anticipated, members might move to distract potential detractors with interpersonal preoccupations.

Where the decision rule chosen approaches unanimity, coalitions within the expert-politico group can far less afford to vent interpersonal hostilities without jeopardizing the chances for the option's being carried before the group. We assume interpersonal compatibility to be a relatively inflexible component of participant relationships. It follows that while frictions within a group may be de-emphasized for the sake of harmony, a certain minimum of unavoidable friction is present in every group. In groups where a given amount of interpersonal friction obtains then, other things being equal, the larger the winning coalition required by the group decision rule, the more exacerbated will be intracoalition haggling, and the less efficient will be intracoalition deliberations.

The assumption here is that participants must cast a larger net to reach minimum winning size when the decision rule approaches unanimity. Where larger coalitions become the norm, then, more and more combinations of strange bedfellows become the norm. As this occurs (keep in mind the constant minimum of friction in all groups) intracoalition frictions are likely to increase on the average.

It is important to raise the interpersonal issue in this discussion of organizational factors, then, because the decision rule (implicit or explicit) governing needed pluralities will determine (other things being equal) the likely cohesion of factions and the extent to which individuals may be free to attempt isolating others interpersonally. This factor is of interest in expert-politico groups because of our expectation that certain postures arise which have specific interpersonal profiles. This means that where interpersonal machinations do arise they will follow broadly predictable patterns in expert-politico groups. (See Chapter 3).

If one wishes to invoke the assumption once again that politicos will man the senior positions in the case of stratified groups, a second possibility arises concerning the effect that such organizational conditions would have on the strategic opportunities associated with the interpersonal dimension. Consider the effect of politico sovereignty on the relationship between interpersonal compatibility and the staffing of intragroup work teams.[22]

Occasionally the established norms of decision-group work patterns and the perceived problem properties are such that it becomes appropriate to fashion ad hoc work groups within the decision group. In cases where the politico wields organizational influence appropriate to senior authority status, he has an advantage in reducing adversary task effectiveness. This can be done by placing the adversary in a work group where interpersonal frictions and an initial polarization of problem views predominate. In work groups of this character, distraction from task and reduced task effectiveness will predominate, other things being equal. The limits on the use of this tactic as well as on all other opportunities for interpersonal machinations, are defined in part by the degree of unanimity (let us say, the size of the winning coalition) required according to the decision rule.

Our third factor, then, the degree of departure from the unanimity rule, should be seen as the organizational determinant of the number of adversaries that politicos, or any member for that matter, can hope to neutralize on the interpersonal level. The factor also determines the degree of difference that coalition members must tolerate among themselves and therefore the amount of concession that will be necessary if intracoalition negotiation is to be productive.

As indicated earlier, this factor also has an effect on the average task effectiveness that can be expected from coalitions where there is no tampering. The latter effect can be anticipated even if one prefers not to assume that senior politicos may influence the organization of ad hoc work groups within the decision group proper. Thus the latter factor is admittedly not a consideration appropriate to expert-politico groups alone. Its inclusion here is still warranted, however. For the factor may be seen as an organization-level constraint on the play that may be given to interpersonal frictions stemming from considerations raised in Chapter 3.

Summary

This chapter cited three factors on the organizational level which, it was suggested, can influence the character of expert-politico interaction. The factors were described as the direction of the collegiality-differentiation balance, the degree of decision-unit autonomy, and the degree of departure from the unanimity rule in arriving at authoritative decisions.

Various "trump cards," as we have been calling them, were linked to the operation of these factors. The trump cards, or edges and advantages in negotiation, include facility in dispensing patronage, playing on identification with the organization, facilitating counterpart re-evaluation of options' value components, and playing upon interpersonal frictions through organizational manipulation.

The crucial assumption underlying a number of arguments presented in this chapter is that, other things being equal, politicos tend to occupy the senior (de jure) authority positions in organizations of the type described above. The point was made that, for the most part, the advantages thus ceded to politicos *can* accrue to nonpoliticos if they occupy the right organizational positions. However, we contend that this is unlikely.

It appears from the ideas presented here that organizational influences on expert-politico interaction generally work to the advantage of the politico. Conversely, the expectation is that experts will fare best in the haggling process of decision-making when organizational constraints on interaction are minimal.

We cannot resist the observation that this notion has strong intuitive appeal, particularly when one considers the usual view that experts operate as intruders on the organizational scene. This is not at all to deny the pervasiveness of their influence; the image merely suggests that when issues take a turn in the direction of organizational matters, the expert is on the politico's turf. If this is true, perhaps there is a kind of poetic justice at work (or if one prefers, a meta-level tendency toward equilibrium) regarding the competitive element of interaction. As discussion on the task dimension suggested, the expert has his own area of persuasive primacy. This chapter has suggested that on the organizational level the expert's task-level primacy can be counterbalanced (albeit to a degree unknown at this time).

In the chapter that follows, we will turn our attention to broader societal trends which seem to exert an overarching influence on the role that experts play in the technological society, and on what individuals have come to expect of experts qua experts, justified or not.

NOTES

1. See F. G. Bailey, "Decisions by Consensus in Councils and Committees: With special Reference to Village and Local Government in India," in *Political Systems*

and the Distribution of Power, Association of Social Anthropologists of the Commonwealth Monographs 2 (New York: Praeger, 1965) pp. 1-21.

2. On the pervasiveness and significance of informal arrangements, see Melville Dalton, *Men Who Manage* (New York: Wiley, 1959); Michael J. Hill, *The Sociology of Public Administration* (New York: Crane, Russak, 1972) chapter 3; Peter M. Blau, *The Dynamics of Bureaucracy* (Chicago: University of Chicago Press, 1963).

3. See Fred H. Goldner, "The Division of Labor: Process and Power," in Mayer N. Zald (ed.), *Power in Organizations* Nashville: Vanderbilt University Press, 1970). On the matter of legitimacy in this vein, see Chester I. Barnard, *The Functions of the Executive* (Cambridge: Harvard University Press, 1968) regarding the theory of authority.

4. See Barnard, op. cit., on status. Also consider Presthus's upward mobile and his view of the organization and his superiors. Robert V. Presthus, *The Organizational Society* (New York: Vintage, 1965).

5. We will develop this issue through the concept of side payments in bargaining and exchange generally. Any of the basic-game theory works employ the concept, though exchange theorists tend to minimize the distinction between side payments and general play rewards, since for the latter theorists the net balance of cost-benefit calculation determines the rational act. As such, the source of benefits is of less intrinsic interest. As an illustration of this trend in exchange theory, see R. L. Curry, Jr., and L. L. Wade, *A Theory of Political Exchange* (Englewood Cliffs, New Jersey: Prentice Hall, 1968).

6. For some discussion of persuasive power and its relation to group identification, see Allport's summary of early theories of social influence: G. W. Allport, "The Historical Background of Modern Social Psychology," G. Lindzey (ed.), *Handbook of Social Psychology* (Cambridge: Addison-Wesley, 1954) pp. 3-55.

7. The implication here is that some modeling accounts for subordinate behavior patterns. For a basic description of the modeling concept, see A. Bandura, *Principles of Behavior Modification* (New York: Holt, Rinehart & Winston, 1969).

8. These alternatives summarize the notions of positive and negative reinforcement, and punishment. See G. S. Reynolds, *A Primer of Operant Conditioning* (Glenview, Illinois: Scott, Foresman, 1968).

9. If these conditions were not applicable some strongly coercive environment would be implied. For the view of such an environment as an organization, see D. R. Cressey, "Prison Organizations," in J. March (ed.), *Handbook of Organizations* (Chicago: Rand McNally, 1965) chapter 24.

10. This is also consistent with standard social psychology maxims concerning the relation between group cohesiveness, member conformity, and participation in other groups. See P. Secord and C. Backman, *Social Psychology* (New York: McGraw-Hill, 1964) chapter 10.

11. Regarding politics and career expectations see J. Schlesinger, *Ambition and Politics* (Chicago: Rand McNally, 1966).

12. See Weber's distinction between politics as vocation and as avocation. H. Gerth and C. Mills, *From Max Weber: Essays in Sociology* (New York: Oxford University Press, 1958).

13. On fact and value generally and the limits of the distinction, see W. Quine, *From a Logical Point of View* (New York: Harper & Row, 1963).

14. H. Simon, *Administrative Behavior* (New York: Free Press, 1965) chapter 4.

15. See H. Simon, D. Smithburg, and V. Thompson, "Relationships of Planning Units." in *Public Administration*. The authors imply this notion in citing the conflicting pressures on long-range planning units and units facing the workaday problems of the organization. This can also be seen as a particular instance of the general problem of intra-organizational (inter-unit) communication. See K. Deutsch, "Communication Models and Decision Systems," in J. Charlesworth (ed.), *Contemporary Political Analysis* (New York: Free Press, 1967).

16. Consider internal TVA problems with general policy upsetting local accommodations. Philip Selznick, *TVA and the Grass Roots* (New York: Harper and Row, 1966).

17. The problem of such natural interference, as it were, would presumably vary directly with the appropriateness of functional differentiation for dealing with the properties of the referent to be administered. This is often treated as a problem in the organization of management. In this vein see C. Habersroth, "Organization Design and Systems Analysis," in March, *Handbook of Organizations*, op. cit.

18. This is the question of morale. The argument here is that morale considerations concerning lower-unit attitudes will generally not override day-to-day pressures to get a particular job done within the prime unit—especially if the prime unit is middle-level itself. Most of the morale literature so phrased comes, not surprisingly, from study of the military. See for example S. Adams, "Social climate and productivity in small military groups," *American Sociological Review*, 1954, 19, pp. 421-5.

19. This discussion is consistent with those placing great store in by-passing mechanisms in bureaucratic systems. See A. Downs, *Inside Bureaucracy* (Boston: Little, Brown, 1968) pp. 123-26.

20. See Ellul on politics as technique. J. Ellul, *The Technological Society* (New York: Vintage, 1964).

21. W. Riker, *The Theory of Political Coalitions* (New Haven, Connecticut: Yale University Press, 1962).

22. This kind of manipulation is often associated with Franklin Delano Roosevelt. Neustadt touches on this issue and FDR in a discussion relevant here for its concern with the relation between subordinate manipulation through work assignment overlap and means of securing and insuring leader power. See R. E. Neustadt, *Presidential Power* (New York: Wiley, 1964).

Chapter 6

SOCIETAL FACTORS INFLUENCING THE EXPERT-POLITICO RELATIONSHIP: INSTITUTIONAL TRENDS AND THE ORIGINS OF ROLE STEREOTYPES

This chapter, concerned with societal-level factors in the expert-politico relationship, examines our chosen problem on the last remaining dimension of analysis. In one way it bridges the gap between our micro and the more usual macro treatments of expert-politico relations. In another way it takes us back to the point of origin—the individual and his orientation to interpersonal dealings in the decision-making setting. The macro perspective is characterized by the search on the societal level for system-wide forces that represent the action-through-negotiation metaphor on the grandest scale. The micro perspective is characterized by the search on the societal level for the origins of those cultural cues that can lead the expert to perceive himself as the kind of interpersonal actor he appears to be.

In the search for factors in this chapter we will maintain this distinction between societal factors as sources of role cues to individuals and societal factors as influences on the direction of institutional development. It will be best to consider societal-level influences on the development of individual role expectations first, but before doing so it is necessary to disclaim any pretension to comprehensiveness in a discussion undertaken on this, the broadest of all our dimensions.

Eclecticism at Its Most Obvious

The notion of a conceptual framework implies a treatment of sufficient scope to encompass the full range of factors that determine the character of all relationships of interest in a given problem sphere. Given the state of the art concerning the study of expert-politico interaction, the offering of factors on all the preceding levels was necessarily eclectic in the sense that, while the factors were indeed offered with an eye to the full range of activity associated with a particular perspective (level), the arguments for choosing certain concepts to be elevated to the status of factors was of necessity idiosyncratic.

On the societal level, the arguments made are again idiosyncratic in origin; that is, our starting points are unabashedly arbitrary, as must always be so with first cuts. But also on this level, the assertion that the range of significant relationships can be satisfactorily accounted for must remain comparatively tenuous. The issues to be discussed here were chosen because they seemed to touch upon the most oustanding dynamics at work. But because the shortcomings of working in bold strokes are most keenly felt at this level, it seems wisest to stress at the outset that the factors are suggested with the knowledge that a lot must go unexplained.

Societal Values and Individuals' Perceptions of Expertise

Chapter 3 raised the issues of role postures and the interpersonal orientation of individuals. The point was made that the constant element in expert postures—and the line of cleavage between laboratory test and control groups—concerned the display of controlling (i.e., pivotal, high-profile) behavior. The postures anticipated for career experts held in common this tendency toward assertion. The distinction between these so-called careerist patterns for experts and the other patterns displayed by laboratory experts turned on the display or avoidance of what we took to be assertive behavior.

Thus the difference between experts and laymen in the laboratory could best be summarized as a difference in the exaggeration of reactions to the control element in interpersonal dealings. We hypothesized that the effect of internalizing expertise was to exaggerate the display of controlling behavior.

Dealing now on the societal level, we are led to ask *why* conferring the title of expert might be perceived as a charge to display controlling behavior in the deliberative setting. What forces operate in our society to create the expectation that properly performing experts must strive to display some form of controlling behavior in excess of that felt to be necessary for nonexperts in the identical intragroup setting?

We are portraying this issue as one of two separable aspects of societal factors bearing on the manifestation of expertise. We will continue to maintain that the latter micro manifestations of values associated with expertise can be distinguished from institutional-level consequences of the expertise-related values of society. It must be realized at the same time, however, that factors broadly defined on this level can have effects on both the macro (institutional trend) and micro (individual cueing) dimensions simultaneously. So we are acknowledging that factors we will describe on the micro dimension (the interpersonal, individual cueing dimension) are *ultimately* linked to counterpart factors on the macro (institutional behavior) dimension of this societal-level discussion. However, it will be easier to appreciate the subtlety of these social factors by stressing the differences between effects on individuals and effects on institutions at first, reserving a discussion of their consubstantiality for later. Consider the *individual*-societal nexus first.

Social Cueing and Experts' Pivotal Behavior

Regarding the social dynamics at work to portray expertise as a responsibility to be pivotal in the individual's field of relationships, one factor in the mass, technological society looms largest in our minds. This strongest of all signals to the individual from society concerning expertise pertains to the value of pretensions to knowledge as a legitimating agent for the self in face-to-face interaction.

Many social critics surveying the technological society have suggested that much of today's modern dilemma stems from the fact that people's capabilities for environmental control have outpaced the capacity to judge how such control should best be utilized.[1] In the technological society, means are always available for ends that have yet to be evaluated.

In politically oriented theses, this becomes a focus on problems created by seemingly unlimited production and consumption capabilities that are not geared to a larger ethic independent of such material matters.[2] Indeed the usual observation in this vein is that unlimited production and consumption have become ends in themselves. According to this view, consumption, at first associated with the satisfaction of some basis needs independent of the production cycle, has itself become the by-product of production systems which at this point generate their own raison d'etre.[3]

The image often is one of a society whose whole system of divided labor is organized solely to maximize the acceleration of the production/consumption cycle. The cycle is seen as self-perpetuating, self-contained, ever-escalating, and by implication commensurate with a never-satisfying social system.[4] The system is self-contained (i.e., closed) in the sense that it is not (or at least no longer) anchored in any value system whose premises might be independent of it. This critique is often associated with bemoaning the loss of the positive aspects of traditional society.

According to this view, the technological society's culture is without an ontological argument; there are no first causes, no essences—only essential processes which are in turn defined tautologically by their own metaphoric representations. The technological society is propelled through time and space by the whirring of its own repeating cycle. It is plugged into itself, a perpetual acceleration machine.[5]

The prime ethic becomes more supply for more demand for more supply, and the prime organizational rule becomes coordinated effort for greater capacity to produce in order to consume in order to necessitate further production. Social critics of this persuasion are led to ask how such a system remains able to absorb individual energies if satisfaction in some end state—or even conceptualization of some end state—is impossible.

The response to this question varies. Some contend that the system must inevitably wither because individuals forever deprived of enduring satisfaction will one day not show up for work.[6] Others contend that whether the drones show up or not, the system's demands will outpace the capacity of even the most willing workers who may then just fade away at their stations.[7] Still others argue that the system is far more perverted and can endure beyond others' imaginings, because it has a capacity to fool (there is no other word) individuals into believing that their unhappy state is really happiness. This slight of unseen hand produces severe social strains but prolongs the agony almost indefinitely.[8]

Putney and Putney are among those who take the latter approach; they emphasize dislocated sources of satisfaction and invoke the notion of "indirect self-acceptance." The idea is simply that being deprived of primary sources of satisfaction, the individual in the technological society seeks acceptance (legitimization of the self) by adopting behavior patterns and aspirations which are compatible with the rootlessness, mindless technology, and spiraling need creation that such a society fosters. Indeed, their point seems well-taken. I believe that the common denominator of such an "artificial" aspiration system is the striving for the appearance of what we may take as "system indispensability."

While it is presumed that all viable social systems must somehow satisfy needs at some level, the technological society is seen to be an unhealthy arrangement because artificially created needs are ultimately poor replacements for more basic human values. The nature of these particular values deemed basic for humans is not important of itself. Freud implied one particular set of descriptions for such values, Maslow offered a hierarchy in somewhat different terms; Skinner operates with another emphasis. Among critics of the technological society, the shared view is that whatever basic needs are, modern ersatz facsimiles simply will not do in the long run.

Whether the long run is near its final form or extremely far into the future, the point of near universal agreement is that the technological society's value system, by its artificial character, produces severe dislocations for individuals.[9]

Mass Dislocation; Individual Dislocation

This dislocation is manifest in an instrumental view of the worth of an individual—both of others and of oneself. Values are rooted in perpetuation of the accelerating production-consumption spiral. Because the cycle is indeed self-perpetuating, all products of the system—including goods, social conditions, attitudes, and people—are valued for *their* value in turn, as means to further fueling the cycle itself. People, as a part of the society notwithstanding, then, are evaluated for their essentiality to this system which is in perpetual overgrowth.

For the moment, consider the technological society as an organization. In this context it is trapped by a means-ends chain that never ends. Everything it produces (including personalities it shapes) is viewed instrumentally, and every goal it aspires to is defined instrumentally. There is no meta-system of values shaped apart from the frenzy. There are no fixed points in the value scheme except perpetuation of it. Individuals as part of the system evaluate themselves and others in terms of successful participation in the system. This means securing an esteemable position in the consumption-production network.

Thus the system, by its nature requires maximum input of individuals in both their consumption and production roles. Satisfactions from the cyclical system—though they may only be poor and perverted substitutes for approval denied from other sources—stem from providing maximum consumption/production input. Thus the culture and so the peer influence of socialized individuals serve to encourage people to inflate their contributions to the cycle.[10]

Inflating the Self in the Instrumental Environment

In a system where the watchword is instrumentality, an individual's importance looms largest when he provides some system input that others cannot. In the technological society, as in most societies, scarcity tends to be associated with value.[11] In the technological society, where the division of labor is so extreme, individuals can inflate their social worth by asserting the indispensable character of their role in the production system.[12] This entails exaggerating the skills necessary to execute the role, exaggerating the uniqueness of the task associated with it, and maximizing identification with that role.

The latter phenomenon would also be predicted from the assumption that the main source of individual satisfaction lies in system identification where the system, owing to its pervasiveness, is all there is. Thus all roles are institutionalized and all task performers tend to identify by role and—as far as the culture cooperates—by role mystique. Perhaps the single most familiar manifestation of this tendency is the career and professionalism syndrome. This contemporary issue needs no belaboring here beyond the point that individuals tend to exaggerate the uniqueness of any occupations that require some specialized skill. *People crave expertise and capitalize on any skill which can be parlayed into such an expert image;* they do so because they perceive that expertise is indispensable, indispensability implies uniqueness and thus importance, and importance is proof of success in a society operating on an ethic of instrumentality.

The guiding rationale, we are suggesting, is that where people are measured by the part they play in the system, they will appear more important—and more unique—if their work appears to be more important and more unique. Where the system of displaced satisfactions teaches that people with important positions must be happy, the people who can view their work as such *will* be happy. Because the system absorbs all energies, this becomes the only realm for securing happiness. Proponents of this view describe the popular definition of happiness as a misnomer for self-acceptance which the masses measure in the reflection of peer evaluation.[13]

Expertise and High-Profile Behavior

With the system anchored in no larger system—plugged into itself as it were—the definition of individual worth through system affiliation is always defined contextually. One assesses one's worth by comparison with others in face-to-face contact and by comparison with stereotyped images of phenotype role occupants in the larger environment. The tendency is always to exaggerate individual importance. This means exaggerating the essentiality of one's input in the larger system and the face-to-face work setting. To exaggerate essentiality is to insure that others feel the weight of one's presence and so, by implication, the undesirability of one's absence.

Where the expert is in a group whose task appears susceptible to expert input (recall the curvilinear notion of expert input on perceived technological issues) the expert justifies his presence and legitimates the self by expanding his intragroup position as much as possible. This includes drawing as much deference as possible and so leads to a perceived need to display high-profile behavior.

In this context, our laboratory findings suggest that the perceived need to play a commanding role will vary to a degree with the individual's interpersonal orientation as a personality. Laymen whose perceptions of their proper role (contrasted with co-member roles) provide no kernel of essentiality to build upon fall into follower patterns. The variations thereof might prove traceable to the degree to which personality needs to control allow for adaptation to secondary positions.

From this line of reasoning it follows that politicos, whose real-world status is linked to organizational-level networks, maintain the claim to self-perceived importance by stressing the relationship between task and organizational concerns.[14] This indeed would tend to corroborate our notion, developed independently in earlier chapters, that the politico's strategic interests lie in stressing the organizational context while the expert would do well to stress task considerations proper. What discussion on the societal level indicates is that while task and organizational considerations make undertaking the latter strategies advisable, societal factors make undertaking them a likely occurrence in real-world interaction. This follows from the contention that societal forces are at work to socialize the individual in the technological society in such a way that personal satisfaction is linked to the appearance of indispensability. Indispensability is best portrayed by redefining issues to emphasize their relation to the individual's prime area of competence.

Interestingly, Schattschneider predicts behavior along these lines in another context.[15] What we are suggesting here can be seen as an impetus on the psychological dimension for his predicted definition and redefinition of issues commensurate with redrawn coalition patterns. Redrawing coalition patterns provides an advantage to those who can control the redrawing. Individuals negotiating serious issues from different sources of contextually defined role strength should tend to push for a redefinition of those issues along lines that would suggest their presumed preeminence in resolving them.

The contention is that societal forces operate to make controlling behavior appear commensurate with expert status. It is suggested here that these forces stem from:

(1) The large-scale absorption of individuals in the production/consumption scheme with its associated emphasis on the instrumental view of *all* things, including individuals, and

(2) From the related deprivation of other sources of approval.

The technological society emphasizes technique and operates with a self-justifying ethic which is manifest in the paradox of preoccupation with instrumentality for its own sake. This can be seen as a contradiction stemming from a system in perpetual acceleration. Summarizing this notion in phrasing appropriate to the conceptualization of factors, we can describe the factor in this vein as a socially created pressure to appear indispensable according to an ethic of instrumentality. It is the technological society's answer to the categorical imperative. This societal factor serves to elicit striving for pivotal status as a means of self-legitimization. For convenience we can name it the *instrumental imperative*.[16]

The Instrumental Imperative and Institutional Trends; Macro Dynamics

So far we have discussed, albeit in general terms, the relationship between the societal ethic of instrumentality and the cues individuals take for interpersonal conduct in a technological society. The discussion in this regard was designed to indicate how societal values lead individuals to interpret the expert mantle as we presume they do. Undertaking a discussion in this vein was described as taking the micro view of societal forces influencing expert-politico interaction. The latter terminology was chosen to indicate that social forces were being analyzed for their impact on attitudes about person-to-person dealings. In distinguishing between micro and macro conceptions of social factors influencing expert-politico relations, the macro view was associated with the search for factors influencing institutional trends that affect expert-politico interaction. Discussion in this vein would isolate patterns in institutional behavior that serve in turn to shape the character of expert-politico interaction.

We should state at the outset that a single factor on the societal level seems to explain all the pertinent institutional trends we can conceptualize in this regard. Again, it is the *emphasis on instrumentality.* Suggesting that the prime force governing expert-related issues on the macro societal level is the same force shaping expert behavior on the micro societal level does not deny the utility of separating these two emphases. More will indeed be said eventually about the consubstantiality of factors discussed in this chapter.

It is appropriate to distinguish the effect of this instrumental imperative on expert socialization from its effect on institutional trends; doing so helps to conceptualize the trends themselves in a way that can stress both their dynamic character and common roots. It is tempting to reserve the term "factor" for the institutional trends themselves that characterize the societal setting of expert-politico interaction. But to describe institutional trends as factors is to confuse the symptoms with their cause. The *ethic of instrumentality* (or "norm") is our factor on the macro societal level. It encourages certain institutional trends which may be taken as its system-level manifestations.

The discussion here will be concerned with isolating these manifestations, because grasping them will provide insight into the institutional milieu of contemporary expert-politico dealings. Conceptual rigor, however, requires that the notion of a societal-level factor be reserved for the common source. Hopefully our judgment on the common source will be justified in the course of what we shall have to say in discussing its manifestations. In what follows, then, several trends characteristic of the institutional environment of expert-politico encounter are suggested. The contention is that they influence all expert-politico interaction insofar as environment can shape behavior.

Programmed Innovation

One of the most awesome aspects of the technological society is its routinization of the discovery process. The individual inventor as entrepreneur is replaced by the Research and Development community. On a system-wide scale, the technological society has institutionalized the discovery process. Traditionally, quantum leaps in knowledge were an unforeseen consequence of the amoeba-like progress of relatively small scientific communities. "Breakthroughs," which were before part of the mystery of life in the modern era, are now problematic functions of resource investment calculated in cost-benefit terms. An investment of X dollars can—indeed the phrasing is *will*—produce a given innovation in a particular time frame; an investment of X + Y will reduce the time lag by a roughly specifiable amount.[17]

The unknown is to the technological age what a new market was in the heydey of capitalism. Now, once the profit goals are established, once the costs of the new investment are computed, once the lead time for tolerable return is calculated, securing the expected yield becomes a mechanical process. The double-or-nothing roll has been replaced by the actuarial table.

The trend towards programmed innovation may be interpreted as a consequence of the technological society's uncommon need to reduce uncertainty in the environment.[18] With the huge investment of resources required by the mass-production and consumption system, the need for predictability approaches almost intolerable proportions. The production machinery of the society is like a fairy-tale giant, slow to react and incapable of reaction without a large investment of energy. False steps are costly; minor miscalculations result in greatly magnified errors. Operating with uncertainty becomes especially risky in these circumstances, and so this argument goes, great energies are devoted to methodically—predictably—reducing uncertainty by reducing the unknown. The effort, moreover, is collective and must necessarily be so, for several reasons.

First, the complexity of issues increases because the demands for predictability (knowledge) are so stringent, given the low tolerance of error. Increasingly complex issues requiring solution in predictable and compressed time frames, at generally specifiable costs, are beyond the capacities of uncoordinated individual effort.[19]

Second, control of the discovery process to insure its proper direction requires an elaborate organizational superstructure. If industry requires data communication by satellite, for instance, but invention is entrepreneurial and undirected, the result might be a better mousetrap.

Third, if the technological society is in a state of perpetual acceleration, it has a capacity to absorb innovation, translate it into new production and consumption, thereby produce a still greater demand for innovation, and so find only temporary satisfaction at best with even a greater innovation effort. This requisite magnitude of effort alone necessitates organization.

Programmed Innovation, Experts, and Politicos

Organized, programmed innovation on an ever-widening scale to serve an ever-increasing societal demand for reducing uncertainty about the environment means that experts will multiply. Moreover, they will have an increasing impact on resource allocation in all the system's major institutions. Where predictability of the environment is an important condition of system stability, predictors become important participants. Where prediction is routinized, erstwhile value judgments as we have described earlier become empirical questions. Judgments of a category formerly relegated to synaptic, arbitrary (creative) processes yield to technique. Thus the trend is toward reliance on expertise to execute the process.

In sum, various pressures in the technological society lead to a strong need for environmental control. This in turn necessitates programming the discovery process which thereby places a premium on technique. The consequence in terms of our focus is to raise the expert to a crucial social actor.

Every important social issue in an instrumentally oriented society has a technique associated with it. With varying degrees of sophistication, every important problem in the technological society is perceived to be amenable to expertise. Whenever the need for solutions is great enough to warrant the resource investment, then, expertise will be introduced. Indeed, depending on situational factors, it may be *institutionalized* in particular organizational schema, so that experts become an integral part of the formal decision body.[20]

We have suggested that various side effects on the system level are associated with the trend toward programmed innovation. Among them is the need to mobilize substantial resources and collectivize efforts. It seems fair to say in this regard that a concomitant development is the increasing involvement of government in the programmed innovation process. Theoretical issues aside, this is already a frequently observed fact of contemporary life.

Government and Programmed Innovation;
Enter the Politico

Pressures in this direction can be traced to at least two sources. First, the cost of institutionalizing large-scale innovation programs will not be born by the so-called private sector unless it can be assured of government assistance in the event of failure, subsidy to the point of insuring profit in research, or a guaranteed market for the results of research—its actual merit notwithstanding. The government has become, in large part, an underwriter.

Second, the technology of government operation itself is perceived to have become so complex as to require that the government buy innovative talent both through absorption of expertise in its own organization and through contract arrangement with private corporations. Additional impetus in this regard is provided by the tendency in certain quarters to associate national prestige with R & D prowess and thereby instigate governmental sponsorship of the expertise community as a means of insuring national security in an era of perceived global competition.[21] The result appears to be that government is deeply involved in the programmed innovation business, and is there to stay.

Certainly this is to be expected as programmed innovation continues to absorb so large a portion of society's resources and energies. It would be surprising if government circles failed to perceive a relation between their sphere of interests and the possible effect of such a large-scale social trend in resource allocation. From the nongovernmental side, it would also be surprising if corporate management could continue to make a commitment to the R & D pattern of resource investment without clear expectations about likely government behavior in all related matters.[22]

The upshot from our perspective is that the institutional trend toward programmed innovation in an instrumental society has not only been to enlarge the numbers and role of experts, but also to ensure that politicos will come in contact with them with increasing frequency, on a wider range of issues, for periods of extended interaction. In summary, the institutional trend toward programmed innovation in the technological society makes the expert-politico relationship more and more a core component of sociopolitical activity in the system.

The relationship is played out by ever-increasing numbers of individuals; it is characteristic of increasing varieties of interpersonal relationships on the institutional plane, and hence is more and more the relationship format for decision-making on matters of public policy.[23] Notice too that the forces working to make matters so also facilitate a trend toward absorbing a wider variety—and greater number—of policy issues in the public (government-related) sphere.

On the latter point, consider that public-policy-making today includes issues such as the development of energy sources, care of the poor, adjusting the economic growth rate, structuring education, facilitating racial integration, underwriting explorers, financing "pure" research, ecological management, ensuring equality of the sexes, adjusting housing patterns, influencing marketing and pricing behavior, altering migration patterns, altering habits of travel, manipulating sanctions on sexual behavior—of course, the list is endless.

The point here is not the trite contention that government does many things it once did not do. Rather, the important issue is that the government operates in each of these areas, and all that might be added, by *soliciting the input of experts* and by *developing organizational (administrative) structures to program the now expert-politico-produced response as a matter of public policy.* This suggests that the expert-politico relationship will continue to gravitate to the core of our social habits having to do with collective choice-making.

Thus the effect of the system-wide instrumental ethic in this case is an emphasis on programmed innovation, the perception of a technological component (albeit with varying degrees of sophistication) in every public issue, and consequently, the elevation of the expert *qua expert* to the role of a central political actor in the so-called public-policy process.

Divergent Recruitment Patterns and Socialization Differences

If experts are appearing on the political scene in ever-increasing numbers, obviously they must be coming from somewhere. In settings comprised of political networks related to government or government-associated institutions, expertise usually involves technologies that are at least moderately sophisticated. Thus they involve special training and peer-group identifications, loyalties, and perspectives, marking out distinct subgroups somewhat like tribes. Expert-politico units (or clusters of units) dealing with such government or government-related matters are populated in part by members whose career patterns may follow distinctly different lines.

Regarding expert-politico groups that are part of government agencies proper, politicos come to their positions generally as a result of upward movement through a career sequence that may include increasingly pivotal party involvement, appointments to increasingly coveted administrative posts, election to a series of increasingly powerful offices, upward progress through a hierarchy of civil-service positions, and so on, until the politico rises to whatever post we find him in at the time he is observed.[24]

In the expert-politico setting, it often seems to be the case that the expert counterparts of given politicos come to their posts through a distinctly different career sequence. In decision circles involved with relatively sophisticated technological issues, experts often make entre by lateral jumps from their respective professional spheres to expert-politico decision units involved with government.

Thus while an ambassador or a mayor may attain his position by completing a sequence of political tutelage, the expert he may now find himself involved with may have most likely come to the country team or city hall on an express train straight from academia—or at least after only an abbreviated experience with public service. When parties arguing options in the White House have gained access almost directly from MIT on the one hand, or through twenty years of political service on the other, the differences in orientation to the task situation, and to the setting of in-group strategizing should be substantial.

Of course, in undertaking a general discussion of this issue as part of the search for a larger conceptual orientation, we must be content with a discussion in terms of pure types. The assumption is that a kernel of truth can still be extracted from such an overview when eventually moving to the consideration of individual cases. Thus we can pursue this question of how differential recruitment patterns for experts and politicos lead to certain differences in problem approach without undue fear of distortion.

It is also true that, in a sense, consideration of these issues may seem appropriate to the previous discussions of organizational and role considerations rather than to the present discussion of social factors. However, the contention here is that the phenomenon of differential recruitment is a product of the system-level push toward en masse absorption of experts in politics. This is indeed what justifies raising it to prime importance in expert-politico interaction.

The alternative of treating the differential recruitment phenomenon and its attendant problems under the organizational or role rubrics is to portray it more as a contingency than a constant. The implication in the former scheme would be that the differential recruitment phenomenon has only a problematic impact as issues associated with role conflict and organizational peculiarities take a turn one way or the other. Instead, by emphasizing that the problems associated with differential recruitment have systemic roots—and that some force in their effects is therefore more that probabilistic—we will treat the problem as a system-level characteristic, one that is a virtual constant in expert-politico dealings.

Socialization

The crux of the problem we suggest in this regard concerns the nature of expert-politico differences in career patterns, and expert-politico differences in attitudes about dealing with matters defined in political terms. The problem can best be understood by focusing on the expert. The politico in this context is dealing with political problems. Politics for good or ill is precisely what politicos do. Thus it seems wise to assume that, by definition, the politico is socialized professionally to perform his duties as a deliberator of political issues associated with the conduct of political organization.

As we have proposed in other contexts, when the problem at hand surfaces as part of the work routine of a formal, political (government) institution, it is the expert who is out of water. We do not mean here that the expert cannot function effectively; the point is simply that in approaching the question of who is not socialized for performance in the political (government-related) environment per se, the integral connection between the concept of a politico and politics requires that we take the expert as our starting point in searching for relationship peculiarities that stem from diverse recruitment patterns.

In sketching the pure-type politico in this regard, and also to affirm in passing that proper socialization is a separate question from the *quality* of contribution to the political process, consider Nicolson's remarks about a frequent pitfall in the development of the career diplomat (an acceptable instance of our politico):

> Nor am I unaware of the functional defects which the professional diplomatist tends to develop. He has seen human folly or egoism operating in so many different circumstances that he may identify serious passions with transitory feelings. . . . He is so inured to the contrast between those who know the facts and those who do not know the facts, that he forgets that the latter constitute the vast majority. . . . He may have deduced from experience that time alone is the conciliator . . . and he may thus incline to the fallacy that on the whole it is wiser, in all circumstances, to do nothing at all. . . .

And he often becomes denationalised, internationalised, and therefore dehydrated, an elegant empty husk.[25]

In a similar vein, a number of works seem to suggest that a major
behavioral component of the professional politico is a disposition to
bargain—to eschew the assumption that there is a "right" decision in
conflict situations in favor of the assumption that there is what we may
call a "feasible" decision.[26]

Conventional academic wisdom can be translated here as the view that
successful politicians *in their daily unpublic dealings* are often governed by
contextual, pragmatic considerations as part of go-along/get-along environments. The thrust of this view is basically that the socialization of the
experienced, successful politico—in the pluralistic setting at any rate—
works to inhibit doctrinaire postures in deliberation. The pressures at work
in politics as a profession militate against extreme reactions in problem-
solving interaction. Mastering the art of the possible requires staking out
the middle ground.

The politico career pattern associated with the development of these
norms is upward movement through the hierarchy of coveted positions
with movement fueled by ambition. Regardless of whether the politico
acquires his facility in perceiving bargainable situation components *before*
he enters the system, or enters the system *because* he has such an intuitive
skill to begin with, it is a common point of agreement that the career
experience sharpens his touch.[27] In doing so the career experience presumably dulls his taste for extreme, ideological (better "cerebral") problem approaches as well.

This notion of professional politico socialization and its inverse relation
to extreme, primarily cerebral (idealistic) approaches to the group haggling
setting takes on special importance in a discussion of the expert-politico
relationship. Our earlier discussion of trends in expert recruitment posited
the ever-increasing frequency of expert entrée by synaptic leaps from
nongovernmental breeding grounds to the government-related setting. This
suggests that forces at work in the technological society serve in this case
to fashion deliberative groups where politicos deal with experts who are
not likely, other things being equal, to share the politicos' taste for
moderation or their sensitivity to the need for ranking political feasibility
above intrinsic merit in option evaluation.[28] Societal forces may work, in
short, to make the expert more idealistic (if not more ideological) than the
politico; to make the expert's involvement cerebral rather than visceral. If
by definition experts are less appropriately socialized to politics than

politicos, and their behavior is therefore more extreme, cerebral involvement eschewing the middle ground suggests two patterns in the approach that experts take to governmental involvement. Again, each pattern represents an extreme compared to the relatively pragmatic approach posited for politicos.

The first pattern involves what may be called *experts as mechanics*. Especially when they occupy an adjunct position in the formal organization, experts often become preoccupied with the technology of their subject matter and indifferent—indeed oblivious—to the value or implications of larger political issues associated with their work. They are immersed in the technological aspects of their work and perceive it as an intellectual abstraction—a chess game sponsored by government or corporation. The involvement is cerebral in the sense that the expert is numb to political problems associated with the work of his unit. The image is one of cerebral involvement as disinterested mechanic.[29]

Second, in contrast, consider what may be called the zealot syndrome. The pattern here is that of cerebral involvement as *idealism* untempered by the political cynicism or pragmatism that would otherwise inhibit extreme behavior as it presumably does in the career politico, other things being equal.

The expert as idealist may see every aspect of his work, however dry and technical, as directly contributing to the promulgation of a particular political philosophy or the vested interests of a particular political clique on high. The flexible, pragmatic, bargaining approach to intragroup matters is eschewed. This is not because the immediate problem before the group is not susceptible to negotiation. Rather it is because the perceived philosophical connection between intragroup matters and larger (perhaps even stale) political controversies is so preoccupying for the expert that he translates all acts on the intragroup scale into metaphors of death-grip struggle between abstractions of political good and evil.

We may speculate that in perceiving his move from his nongovernmental home ground to government-related work as a deliberate entrance into public matters, the philosophical overtones of the transition could loom large in the expert-as-zealot's mind. They would loom larger, we expect, than the day-to-day issues of his new intragroup setting. Furthermore, such intragroup matters would likely be new to his experience and hence not the primary interaction setting that reflects his life experiences the way it does for the politico. This makes it easier for the expert-as-zealot to take the long view too seriously—to the exclusion of interest in the problems that are the province of his immediate work unit. Moreover, the "zealot" expert may be further prone to extreme and unpredictable shifts in attitude toward the group.[30]

Where the group is seen to be furthering the cause of Right in imagined titanic battles, the expert-as-zealot will burn the midnight oil on its behalf. (Such dedication might still be associated with uncompromising behavior in day-to-day dealings as the zealot refuses to deal with the devil's agents.) But should the zealot ever conclude that the group now works against the Right—either because the character of the titanic struggle has changed, the group has been subverted, or its titan sold out—the zealot expert will have the capacity to turn on the group with frightening effectiveness and in all sincerity. If the expert-as-mechanic is rigid in his indifference, the expert-as-zealot should be dangerous in his volatility. We are suggesting that both patterns, as idealizations, could be developed from the presumption of the lack of moderating experience through having to live and let live as a profession in the world of politics.

The cerebral involvement of experts, for lack of socialization in the day-to-day world of career politicos, would seem to foster expert orientations of two extremes regarding attitudes toward coveting the middle ground. The expert as mechanic or zealot represents behavior patterns which are inconceivable coming from politicos. We are tracing this to differential patterns of recruitment and socialization for participation in the governmental, expert-politico setting. In these instances, in short, the expert will lack the tempering to which career politicos are exposed in this regard.

Parenthetically, the perennial debate concerning the responsibilities of scientists in political matters related to their work would seem to be one more instance that bears this out. The issues raised are often framed as ethical ones where academic detachment is contrasted with humanitarian obligations. To the extent that the debate continues to attract participants, it seems unresolvable if only because its normative cast precludes a pragmatic vocabulary.[31]

The significance of this discussion of diverse recruitment and socialization patterns for politicos and for experts grafted onto government is that, while intragroup politics are inevitable from our bias, they will be viewed differently by expert and politico participants. Specifically, they will be more or less susceptible to solution by horsetrading.

Moreover, aside from attitudes toward the intragroup politics of option selection, this discussion suggests that intergroup (i.e., organizational level) politics will also be viewed differently by experts and by politicos. As we have inferred from other lines of reasoning in previous chapters, the politico is more likely than the expert to urge consideration of the organizational-level consequences of intragroup decision. Specifically, the politico would be expected to stress questions of organizational-level politics—of feasibility—prompted by a pragmatic view of inter-unit politics. The expert, in contrast, is more likely to react to these issues according to either of two extremes.

The expert as mechanic would be comparatively oblivious to them; the expert as idealist would be obsessed, not with the practical politics of organizational life, but rather with organizational doctrine. He would be obsessed with organizational ideology that practitioners and idealogues themselves would take far less seriously.

The contention is that this distinction in approaches to political participation is traceable to differential patterns of recruitment and differential patterns of socialization. If the difference were to be summarized in a phrase, it might be described as a difference between cerebral and visceral orientations.

Of course, these are no more than abstractions as pure types. But the institutional trend in broad terms seems to justify such a summary considered as a general tendency. The force behind such an institutional trend, again, would seem to be the general tendency toward instrumentality. The instrumentality mania ensures the absorption of experts in the society's policy centers. It fosters, in turn, the tendency to phrase problems so that they involve a technological component. With problems so phrased, it is easy to be persuaded in turn that the technology of the problems necessitates expert input.

The Division of Labor and Fragmented Images

The last institutional trend to be discussed in this chapter has been alluded to previously in passing, but bears some notice in its own right. This particular trend can be understood as a force in institutional development which serves partially to reinforce pressures on the individual to adapt to the instrumental ethic. In a sense this particular trend in institutional development acts as a "loop" by creating an institutional environment for individuals which encourages their perception of interpersonal relationships in instrumental terms. While all the institutional trends we have discussed work at least in part to influence the individual in society, the link between institutional trends (macro-level developments) and individual orientation (micro-level considerations) is strongest here. What we have in mind is the trend toward *increasing division of labor*.

A truism of social science is that the evolution from relatively primitive to modern forms of society is accompanied by increasing functional specificity—by the differentiation of social institutions by function—by an increasingly intricate division of labor.[32] The point concerning the technological society is that the division of labor may be carried to such an extreme that serious negative effects can develop.

In the technological society the complexities of empirical components of decision-making tend toward awesome proportions at times. Moreover, various forces we have described work to exaggerate both preoccupation with empirical components and ascription of empirical character to problem elements generally. The drive to distinguish oneself by task uniqueness reinforces the career/professionalism syndrome. The end result is a system where the complexity of issues and the desire to exaggerate complexity work together to reduce confidence in any problem-solving institution that is not perceived to be organized around a complex network of appropriately expert units.

Several undesirable consequences for the mobilization of social energies flow from such a setting. The most frequently noted problem is that the managerial function becomes crucial in such a system and tends to tap energies which might better be at least partially directed to the task function itself. Also, the location of first sources of error is increasingly more difficult to determine as the distribution of responsibility associated with the distribution of labor increases correspondingly in complexity. Error control becomes a major undertaking in itself.

Additionally, the elaborate compartmentalization of function and hence task definition as it is perceived by the individual participant or unit leads to an insensitivity toward the larger problem in favor of a preoccupation with narrow organizational responsibility. As individual units confuse specified goals appropriate to their task level with the larger system-level problems, the monitoring of true problem progress becomes an awesome problem. Definition of the original problem itself is no longer universal.

Elaborate (functionally "over-differentiated") structures also reduce the chances for successful problem-solving on the system level by reducing adaptive abilities vis-à-vis unforeseen turns in the development of problems being attacked. That is, in overly differentiated organizations where problem parameters are not perfectly understood or perfectly predictable, too many problem facets otherwise susceptible to treatment can fall between the spaces as it were.[33] Truly creative innovation—i.e., improvisation—is programmed out of the organizational repertoire. This occurs when operating orders for particular units are overly circumscribed. Rigid operating rules have the effect of reducing the unit's capacity to pursue unforeseen opportunities for novel action, or to fulfill the demands of unforeseen crises.

The effect of this situation on expert-politico interaction is that defining the problems that arise in ongoing organizations can become more difficult than the complexity of the problems alone would suggest, if they could be viewed without the fractured lenses of over-elegantized (bureaucratized, differentiated, elaborate) organizational schema. This difficulty in problem description that is thus introduced leads in turn to a further difficulty which we have touched on. This is error isolation (let alone correction), which takes on special meaning in expert-politico dealings.

Experts, Politicos, and Identifying Error

Consider error identification to entail the judgment that particular participants are performing improperly. This can include incorrectly defining the problem in the immediate setting, consistently choosing poor strategies, carrying out chosen strategies poorly, and so on. With the empirical components of options exaggerated, and with expertise a prerequisite to action in each sphere, it is difficult for those who would criticize malfunctioning units to make an effective case. This is because each issue area tends to a degree to be absorbed within the perceived sovereign area of given experts. It is thus difficult to criticize effectively, because the critic is easily portrayed as an outsider or novice. Performance evaluation is further impeded by the cloak of professional privilege that surrounds experts of a particular stripe. Though the cloak can be lifted, doing so is an added cost in error-monitoring.

Such costs may be expressed in terms of ego-bruising with secondary interpersonal and hence further task-effectiveness implications. Also the costs can take the form of having to suffer organizational sabotage, distracting inter-unit competitiveness, or further avoidance of real responsibility on the part of criticized units or individuals. The costs may also appear as side-tracking confrontations with professional organizations at large which are mobilized by presumably abused experts within the organization proper. Costs of error-monitoring in this environment may also take the form of management's future avoidance of incorporating expert input on related issues where it may in fact be necessary.

In sum, the trend in the technological society toward division of labor in the extreme can have a number of undesirable consequences on the system level. It can lead to undue emphasis on the technological aspect of problem-solving, a corresponding tendency to seek solutions through technology where it may not be appropriate, the excessive absorption of energy and resources in the management (coordinating) function, the compounding of error, the magnification of error where there is an in-line patterning of work units, general difficulty in isolating error, difficulty in tracing personnel responsibility for error, and the creation of barriers to error correction. These barriers can take the form of professional immunities circumventing debate as well as various secondary costs associated with attempting to alter behavior patterns in such a setting generally.

The Micro/Macro Cycle; Fragmented Functions and Self-Legitimization

The extreme division-of-labor characteristic of problem-solving institutions in the technological society also works to reinforce the instrumental imperative that cues individuals in their interpersonal relationships. The identification of individual contributions to society with the performance of highly specialized tasks can lead to a kind of reductionism whereby the whole person is socially defined by a sharply circumscribed description of his/her task responsibility.

The difficulty arises as descriptions are narrowly defined. What we have called the instrumental imperative leads to equating the individual *in toto* with the now fragmented description of his societal input.

The obvious dislocations lead to a cycle whereby the unsatisfying reduction of the self to a career (occupationally defined) stereotype leads to a striving for esteem through greater task identification—which further emphasizes the dislocation—and so on. Institutional developments on the system level thus serve ultimately to reinforce the instrumental ethic that fuels the system. In the attempt to create a societal niche for themselves, individuals define themselves by their task functions. They are professionals—with a job to do, a single purpose and hence an identity derived from merger with the purpose. The purpose, as we have suggested, is cruelly the ever more efficient performance of the task itself.

One of the most intriguing manifestations of this syndrome is the depersonalization of even those endeavors that have traditionally represented the epitome of individualism. The technological society in the interpersonal realm routinizes the personality component of human endeavor the way it programs innovation.

Astronauts, as perhaps the most ambitious explorers of all time, are faceless. Bomber pilots who personalized their machines a generation ago now operate with rotated planes that are identified only by number, and with crews that are regrouped for each mission. Corporate heads and union negotiators crave anonymity for the most part, and brief-case-carrying cadres from academia have now replaced on both sides the cigar-chompers who once lent a distinct individual touch to the issues and commanded public attention. With the normal need for identification repeatedly frustrated through channeling on the instrumental dimension exclusively, Sisyphus pushes harder; the cycle is completed, and its repetition accelerated.

Caveat and Summary

Lest anyone excuse himself to slit his throat, let us stress again the excesses traceable to dealing in pure types. Our technological society is, at this point in time at least, an analytical abstraction and not a summary statement of reality. It is an idealized statement of what modern society could come to *if* various trends we (and myriad others) have pointed out were to continue unchecked development.

I believe the elements of accurate description rest in indicating that various trends are developing which could ultimately push society to such a state, but obviously we are not there yet. The effects of each of these trends that we have pointed to, and their relationship to an underlying obsession with instrumentality—both on the interpersonal level and the system level—are indeed forces to be reckoned with. But at this juncture in time and space their evolution is imperfect and we do not pretend to see any inexorable outcome. Marcuse looks to the university as the weak link in this chain of social distortion and Galbraith in an afterthought to the *New Industrial State* notes an increasingly popular challenge to the military-industrial complex—a sign perhaps that remission is in the offing. One cannot know.[34]

Whether these trends toward the technological society are evolving inexorably or are about to be arrested in partial form, we can here and now consider them as societal-level influences on the specific problem of expert-politico relations. The factor we have cited in this vein is the underlying instrumental imperative in interpersonal dealings and the general pressure of instrumentality on the system level.

The institutional trends associated with the latter, and which have a direct bearing on the expert-politico encounter, were described as the trends toward programmed innovation, the consequent role of government as underwriter, the operation of divergent recruitment and socialization patterns, and the extreme division of labor. The latter, it was suggested, leads to social perceptions which ultimately reinforce pressures to sustain the instrumental orientation to interpersonal dealings. The aim in identifying these trends, of course, was to indicate how they influence the expert-politico encounter, and hopefully this has been demonstrated.

With this chapter we have completed examination of the expert-politico relationship, mostly by peeking over the expert's shoulder. Our goal was to develop a conceptual framework of factors influencing the relationship on the abstracted dimensions of role cues, personality predilections, task properties, organizational constraints, and societal pressures. In the next and concluding section, some effort will be made to take stock of where we are now.

NOTES

1. This seems to be a fair statement of the underlying assumption of almost all the environmental politics literature that approaches its subject on the system level. It is also a key assumption of the critics concerned with formulating goals for the use of nuclear technology, and seems generally to be the kind of assumption that instructs most reports by presidential commissions, given the types of problems with which they are charged. See, respectively, R. A. Falk, *This Endangered Planet* (New York: Vintage Books, 1971), B. M. Baruch, "U.S. Atomic Energy Proposals, Statement of U.S. Policy on Control of Atomic Energy as presented by Bernard M. Baruch to the United Nation Atomic Energy Commission, June, 1946. (Washington, D.C.: U.S. Government Printing Office, 1946); C. M. Marcy, *Presidential Commissions* (New York: King's Crown Press, 1945).
   Szent-Gyorgyi approaches the problem explicitly and in broadest terms. Albert Szent-Gyorgyi, *The Crazy Ape* (New York: Grosset and Dunlap, 1971).

2. This is of course characteristic of most anti-capitalist polemics, but can be found as well in cogent works. For a by now near-classic presentation of this view, see J. K. Galbraith, *The Affluent Society* (New York: Mentor, 1958).

3. Galbraith pursues this point in *The New Industrial State;* J. K. Galbraith, *The New Industrial State* (Boston: Houghton Mifflin, 1967).

4. At this point, where the conventional critique of the technological society moves to a discussion of dislocations it produces in the patterns of social interaction, the literature turns to a discussion of what may perhaps be called "modern social pathology." See for example S. & G. Putney, *The Adjusted American* (New York: Harper & Row, 1966).

5. Here one enters into the literature implying an almost diabolical force concerning the technological society. See C. Reich, *The Greening of America* (New York: Random House, 1970).

6. Reich, ibid.

7. See Alvin Toffler, *Future Shock* (New York: Bantam, 1971).

8. See Putney & Putney, op. cit. The Marcuse school offers a description of the mechanism with the notion of "repressive tolerance."

9. Ellul comes back to this point over and over again in various contexts. Jacques Ellul, *The Technological Society* (New York: Vintage, 1964).

Thayer suggests a redesign of basic organizational schema as a result of taking such a perspective. (He builds on the less socially based, more management-based work of Likert.) Frederick C. Thayer, *An End to Hierarchy! An End to Competition!* (New York: New Viewpoints, 1973); Rensis Likert, *New Patterns of Management* (New York: McGraw-Hill, 1961). Thayer's work in this context, might be described as somewhat a "Greening of America" for public administration.

10. Lieberman seems to miss this point, but has written a book about expertise-mania which, if correct, seems to presume such a notion. J. K. Lieberman, *The Tyranny of the Experts* (New York: Walker, 1970).

11. Slater sees the notion of scarcity as a functional myth necessary to convince the mass goat that the carrot is still out of reach and that the goat ought to therefore keep running. Whether the scarcity is real or contrived, most agree that it is perceived by the goat. See P. Slater, *The Pursuit of Loneliness* (Boston: Beacon Press, 1971).

12. This does not mean part of the identity problem is not also taken out in conspicuous consumption. We are suggesting a conspicuous production tendency as well. One interesting line of speculation is that the latter may tend to overshadow the former if the consumer role at certain levels of affluence becomes a plateau for the bulk of the population and is so perceived, and the consumer role enacted at the given level of luxury becomes too widely shared to lend a feeling of uniqueness. There are also implications here of the individual emphasizing the producer role partly as a result of being psychologically "hooked" on organizational life. This appears now and then with varying tinges of alleged neuroticism. See James Glass, "Consciousness and organization; the disintegration of Joseph K and Bob Slocum," *Administration and Society,* 7; 3, November 1975, pp. 366-384. Less ominously, see Harry Levinson, "Reciprocation: The relationship between man and organization," *Administrative Science Quarterly,* 9, 4, March 1965, pp. 370-390.

13. The organization-man genre of social criticism of the 1950s seems to have operated from this perspective though it lacked the implication of a sinister component in the system. It is interesting to note the 1960s sequels to this literature which stress, in contrast, a more disturbing element in the pressure of striving to maximize what the society values. Contrast W. H. Whyte, Jr., *The Organization Man* (New York: Anchor, 1957) and F. W. Howton, *Functionaries* (Chicago: Quadrangle, 1969).

Skinner on the other hand seems prepared to turn the system on its head, arguing that the definition of "up' is arbitrary anyway. B. F. Skinner, *Beyond Freedom and Dignity* (New York: Knopf, 1971).

14. Support for this view can be found in Ellul, in his discussion of politics as technique. Ellul, *The Technological Society,* op. cit. Also see Presthus on the multiple bases of authority. Robert V. Presthus, "Authority in organization," *Public Administration Review,* 20, 1960, pp. 86-91.

15. See E. E. Schattschneider *The Semi-Sovereign People* (New York: Holt, Rinehart & Winston, 1960).

16. This view is consistent with survey data reporting the near-worship of education as a key to social advancement, and is consistent generally with the

frequently bemoaned condition of degree-mania in American Education. See C. Jencks, *Inequality* (New York: Basic Books, 1972).

17. The multinational involvement with R & D is a commonly described aspect of contemporary international relations study. For a recent discussion of R & D investment patterns, see K. Pavitt, "Technology, international competition, and economic growth," *World Politics*, XXV, 2, January 1973, pp. 183-205. As far as the tone of such thinking is concerned, popular literature on the "can-do" mentality of government specialists hits the mark well. Such discussions are a frequent component of the Vietnam post-mortems and exposés. Toffler deals with this as well; *Future Shock*, op. cit. In the Viet Nam vein, see D. Halberstam, *The Best and the Brightest* (New York: Random House, 1972).

Innovation less programmatic in its execution may still thrust experts forward (as we are about to suggest with programmed innovation) and they may appear even more explicitly as actors to be reckoned with in a "politicized" decision-making process within the organization. See Thompson on the introduction of "corrosive pluralism" by the "truly innovative R and D Unit." Victor A. Thompson, *Bureaucracy and Innovation* (University, Ala.: University of Alabama Press, 1969). Also, Thompson and Tuden on computational decision-making. James D. Thompson and Arthur Tuden, "Strategies, Structures, and Processes of Organizational Decision," in James D. Thompson, et al. (eds.), *Comparative Studies in Administration* (Pittsburgh: University of Pittsburgh Press, 1959).

18. See Galbraith, *Industrial State*, op. cit., on the corporate need for environmental control.

19. Most of the literature relating to PPBS made this point in a somewhat narrower context, and with varying degrees of explicitness. See for instance Freemont, Lyden, and Miller (eds.), *Planning Programming Budgeting* (Chicago: Markham, 1972), especially chapter 8: M. J. White, "Criticisms and Prospects."

20. Freidin and Bailey deal with this "infiltration" in matters related to foreign affairs. See S. Freidin and G. Bailey, *The Experts* (New York: Macmillan, 1968). Related to the factors affecting the modes such an institutionalization could take, see Amitai Etzioni, "Authority structure and organization effectiveness," *Administrative Science Quarterly*, 4, 1960, pp. 43-67. Also for an interesting suggestion of a specific organizing scheme, Robert T. Golembiewski, *Organizing Men and Power: Patterns of Behavior and Line-Staff Models* (Chicago: Rand McNally, 1967).

21. Pavitt, "Technology, Competition, Growth," op. cit.

22. We must not forget the government impact on universities training the researchers either. Philip H. Abelson, "A Critique of Federal Support of Research," in Paul J. Piccard (ed.), *Science and Policy Issues: Lectures in Government and Science* (Itasca, Illinois: F. E. Peacock, 1969).

23. This is especially true in the defense establishment. See U.S. Congress, *Administration of National Security*, Subcommittee on National Security Staffing and Operations, Eighty-Eighth Congress (Washington, D.C.: U.S. Government Printing Office, 1965), especially pp. 413-420, "Memorandum on the Department of State's Politico-Military Organization and Staffing." Of special interest here is the description of the duties and purpose of the office of Deputy Under-Secretary of State for Politico-Military Affairs.

24. See J. A. Schlesinger, *Ambition and Politics* (Chicago: Rand McNally, 1966). Also Gordon Tullock, *The Politics of Bureaucracy*, (Washington, D.C.: Public Affairs Press, 1965).

25. H. Nicolson, *The Evolution of Diplomatic Method* (London: Constable, 1954) pp. 78-79.

26. G. S. Black, "A theory of professionalization in politics," *American Political Science Review,* LXIV, 3, September 1970) pp. 865-878. Also John W. Soule and James W. Clarke, "Amateurs and professionals: A study of delegates to the 1968 Democratic National Convention," ibid., pp. 888-898.

27. The intuitive-skill argument seems to appear with less frequency as behaviorist perspectives predominate, but for an example of the intuitive conception, see C. Thayer, *Diplomat* (New York: Harper, 1959) pp. 233-234, concerning the notion of *Fingerspitzengefuehl.*

28. See Brewer's discussion of academics. Gary D. Brewer, *Politicians, Bureaucrats, and the Consultant* (New York: Basic Books, 1973) especially pp. 84, 210-212.

29. Insofar as idealism may be associated with the mechanic extreme, it should be understood as fidelity to professional norms of conduct defined by peers through professional associations, traditions, and the like. For an excellent study discussing the relation between the character of professional affiliations and impact on policy, see Robert Friedman, *Professionalism: Expertise and Policy Making* (New York: General Learning Press, 1971).

30. Media accounts of the career of Daniel Ellsberg, if accurate, would tend to support this view by way of illustration. We have in mind accounts describing Ellsberg's early hawkish position while in Viet Nam and the contrast with later activity related to the Pentagon Papers.

31. See J. Haberer, *Politics and the Community of Science* (New York: Van Nostrand Reinhold, 1969) especially chapters 9 and 12. Strickland notes the political process frequently at the heart of things. If his conclusions do not lean toward our kind of emphasis, his excerpt from the remarks of "one of the older Chicago activists" is reinforcing. Donald A. Strickland, *Scientists in Politics* (Lafayette, Indiana: Purdue University Studies, 1968) p. 141. Also see Price on the difficulty of training scientists in "anonymous discretion"; Don K. Price, "The Diffusion of Sovereignty," in Robert T. Golembiewski, et al. (eds.), *Public Administration* (Chicago: Rand McNally, 1976) p. 500.

32. David Easton, "Political Anthropology," in B. J. Seigel (ed.), *Biennial Review of Anthropology* (Stanford: Stanford University Press, 1959) pp. 237-45.

33. Landau notes one of the possible negative effects; Martin Landau, "Redundancy, rationality, and the problem of duplication and overlap," *Public Administration Review,* 29, 1969, pp. 346-358.

34. John Kenneth Galbraith, *How to Control the Military* (New York, Doubleday, 1969).

Chapter 7

SOME CONCLUDING COMMENTS

We have tried to comprehend the dynamics of expert-politico interaction by approaching the subject on a number of different levels. More precisely, we have tried to gain some understanding of the problem by positing that a *part* of the problem occurs on *each* of several levels. Each level reveals not so much a different image of the problem in toto, but rather, each level reveals a single facet of the multifaceted problem.

Insofar as the previous pages have indicated this, we have succeeded in a first cut at developing a conceptual framework of expert-politico interaction. The task of a theory, which is certainly not attempted here, would be to specify the linkages between factors and across levels; factors which might then be better described as variables would be weighted, and the logic of their complex interaction would be specified systematically and in detail. The theory could then be applied to predict (or explain in the sense of retrodicting) how it is that empirical instances of expert-politico interaction would lead (had led) to whatever outcomes were associated with them.

What is offered here in contrast is more a basic conceptual tool kit than a blueprint. But the notion of a basic conceptual tool kit implies some judgment about the analytical properties of the task at hand. Our implied judgment about the character of any eventual theory in this regard, then, is that its basic components could all be culled from the basic components of our conceptual framework.

A summary statement of this framework's components is difficult to make because the internal logic of each of the preceding chapters involves a number of inferential turns based on a variety of contentions super-imposed on one another. However, we can touch on some of the central issues examined on each level. The point is to suggest in broad terms where the linkages would be most crucial that theory must provide. It bears stressing that the presumed context of all these ideas is the kind of intragroup deliberative milieu of decision-making which was developed at length in Chapter 1.

Insofar as expert-politico interaction is affected by role-related influences, theory must consider the distortion in behavior that is produced by internalizing the expert image. Ultimately some hard (but comprehensive) empirical study must be undertaken to identify what it means to *behave* like a professional politician on a face-to-face basis. The findings of the laboratory study reported here are far from conclusive, not only because the data reported concern a single study. The laboratory participants were "instant" experts which is far from the real thing, their "skill" did not allow for the display of sophisticated technology, the problem they worked on was not only nonsensical but also simple and nonsensical. The interaction period was brief, the communication medium was limited, the rewards were in dollars rather than career advancement, certain methodological subtleties which were abandoned for the sake of manageability could have been introduced if the work were undertaken on a larger scale, and in short, the study had at least all the limitations that laboratory investigation always has.

Yet we can draw some understanding of the role influences on expert-politico interaction from this experimental work if its larger purpose is kept in mind. We have seen that accepting identification as an expert, and awareness of being *perceived* as an expert on substantive issues involved in negotiation, can change one's behavior.

We have not made much of individual behaviors significantly altered by internalizing expertise because of the interest in focusing on behaviors likely for careerists. The single behaviors isolated in the laboratory included behavioral input of individuals later assumed to be unlikely career types. But as factor analysis indicated regarding the total orchestration of behaviors for bogus experts (when compared to that computed for the control group) behavior *patterns* may indeed change. Moreover, they may be clearly distinguished not only by their components but by their relation to a concept of pivotal, high-profile behavior.

Expertise does something to a person's interpersonal approach to the haggling setting (involving perceived politicos, at any rate). It makes a person behave differently—and predictably so—within generally defined limits. The clear distinction between expert patterns and nonexpert patterns is of great importance in pursuing the expert-politico relationship. The political arena, the person, problem, organizational environment, and societal milieu all aside, being an expert per se appears to change a person's action pattern.

In trying to reconstruct the whole person, we suggested that theoretical work involving diagnostic inferences about interpersonal behavior offers valuable insights. This question was raised as departure from the role dimension led to the question of why roles are stylized in different ways by different individuals. The attempt was made to capture the nature of a personal touch in role portrayal by invoking the notion of role postures. Consider that postures with distinct differences are sought out by individuals who are not coerced in their selection. At the same time, for all the differences between them, postures associated with a larger role are limited in their actual number.

This suggests that there is some pattern in the choice sets that individuals implicitly consider when structuring their approaches to dealing with others. From the available knowledge on interpersonal diagnosis, and from our uncovering of the components of the postures we were led to posit, it was possible to suggest a broader interpersonal profile for each of the expert patterns predicted for careerists. Of course, these suggestions are highly speculative.

From what social psychology has uncovered about interpersonal compatibility and group performance, we were able to suggest what the group consequences might be if particular experts of a particular interpersonal stripe were combined in a deliberative setting with politicos who had given interpersonal profiles of their own, defined on the same dimension. Thus it was possible to develop some perspective on how role perceptions and interpersonal orientations might combine to affect expert-politico interaction. At the same time it was possible to maintain some distinction between the relationship inputs traceable to individual personality predilections as opposed to role orientations. This made it possible to distinguish conceptually between those relationship difficulties stemming from role conflicts and those stemming from idiosyncratic differences between particular participants.

Most important of all, these distinctions were grounded in a workable and easily testable vocabulary. Certainly, this is of value, if only for its usefulness in ordering the all-too-often cross-purposes discussions about how individuals have historically made a difference in the course of given policy deliberations.

Discussion on the so-called task dimension—on the matter of how debate about the merits of a situation alone can have an independent effect on the outcome of intragroup processes—was again aimed at providing a vocabulary. The sought-after vocabulary was one that could facilitate maintenance of a distinction between what was and was not relevant to politicking about issues on their merits alone.

This raises the subject of one of the underlying convictions of this book: That discussion of a complex relationship is impeded not only by the complexity of the relationship itself but by the tendency to see competing strategies purely as responses to previous actions in kind. It was indicated here that responses to competitions invoked by others are often made on relationship dimensions that are different from those associated with the initial challenge.

As our analysis has suggested, for example, the politico vying with experts for the support of third parties is at his most effective, *not* when taking the expert on his own terms, but when introducing organizational considerations, patronage issues and the like, which transform the locus of contention.

The advantage of this view is to persuade the analyst to see that haggling competition, when it occurs, is not solely decided by the superior persuader, but by the context in which he chooses to make his case and the context in which adversaries choose to respond. This is more than the truism that defining the alternatives is prejudicing the outcome in policy-making. It is a further alert that the confrontation is played out in many contexts simultaneously and that the participants may have good strategic reasons for consistently defining the dimensions of conflict differently. In the latter regard, the usual view that failure to similarly define conflict often impedes resolution may be too sweeping a judgment.

For if conflict resolution where differing definitions obtain may not involve reaching mutually satisfactory solutions, it can involve reaching solutions that are satisfying to a sufficient majority of the participants to carry the day. For good or ill, this is what the persuasive/deliberative setting is often about.

Only theory can calculate the net balance of advantages in the multi-context setting that accrue to experts or politicos. However, a conceptual framework can reveal the various contexts involved and can underscore in doing so the point that a multicontext view is crucial to cogent analysis.

The discussion of expert-politico interaction on the task dimension alone led to the view that the expert has his strongest footing here. It also suggested, among other things however, that the politico's best recourse is to pursue as far as possible the persuasive struggle on the organizational dimension. The chapter devoted to this issue suggested additionally that the politico's advantage on this dimension is itself multifaceted. The manipulation of patronage, organizational identification, images of inter-unit politics, and informal work associations, all these are part of the astute politico's arsenal.

With the simultaneous perception of the expert-politico relationship as an action setting framed by role, personality, task perceptions, and organizational considerations, the larger societal milieu loomed as a fifth dimension of relationship determinants. In this regard, the primary interest was in considering the grand social design in which was grounded expert-politico interaction. Various institutional trends were pointed to in this regard. The underlying interest was in showing how the direction of societal development in relevant areas:

(1) Reinforced particular individual perceptions noted earlier;
(2) Provided an institutional setting with specific properties relevant to the relationship;
(3) Assured the continuation of a partial divergence of interests and perceptions on the part of the players; and
(4) Assured an increasing frequency in their encounters.

If the conceptual framework stresses such an overview, it also allows for guarded summary statements about the strategic balance of the expert-politico relationship. By dealing in pure types and confining generalizations to issues involving the manifestation of extremes, some general maxims can be provided. Of course the preceding chapters are replete with many such remarks in the guarded "other things being equal" vein—which is a product of operating in a multifaceted setting of simultaneous interaction. To generalize about the strategic aspects of the relationship by way of grand overview, by peeking over the expert's shoulder the following can be said:

Other things being equal, the career expert will work most efficiently with politicos whose needs for inclusion, control, and affection can be reconciled with those need patterns associated with the corresponding expert posture. Such reconciling where initial frictions obtain can be facilitated by mutual recognition of differing areas of sovereignty concerning organizational prerogatives for the politico and task preeminence for the expert.

The career expert will be most effective where his contribution is not in a purely adjunct capacity perhaps encouraging the expert-as-mechanic pitfall, and where ideological aspects of involvement are minimal; the latter condition reduces the likelihood of expert-as-zealot orientations. Strategically the expert will be most effective where the relevant technology is perceived to be not excessively sophisticated, where organization tends to collegial, where decision-unit autonomy is greatest, where work-group composition is flexible, where participants have independent sources of career and material satisfaction, where identification with organizational values is perceived not to be implicitly at issue, where professional affiliations can be mobilized if necessary, where the option preferences of participants to be influenced are different from the expert's in regard to the empirical component primarily, where target individuals chosen to be persuaded by the politico adversary perceive options within the prohibited areas of value assessment defined by their "psychic space" limits, where the implied or explicitly required size of the minimum winning coalition does not require excessive bargaining efforts or middle-ground mastery, where allied politicos are available when target third parties differ from the expert on value judgments, and so on. The permutations on all the maxims we have developed in each of the preceding chapters are numerous; there is no need to belabor the issue.

The point is that while a conceptual framework is not a theory, it does allow for all these sorts of hypotheses as useful starting points in empirical investigation. Thus the conceptual framework not only facilitates further progress toward theory proper, but also toward improved conceptual frameworks. Moreover, each of these sample hypotheses is grounded in a larger systematic discussion which provides a set of related concepts in each case. Sensitivity to these larger conceptual relationships can help to reduce confoundings in initial formulations yet to be proposed by others.

Most of the available work on expert-politico interaction is confined to what we have called the societal dimension and, to a lesser degree, the organizational dimension. The properties of face-to-face cooperation and competitiveness, the strategems of task-related sparring, and the role dimension are often neglected by comparison.

Most material on the organizational dimension as well is primarily concerned with life in the organizational environment, broadly construed. While this is important, of course, taken alone it gives little if any attention to how the organizational context displays predictable features which offer different *strategic advantages* to the expert and politico players. One of the additional dividends in struggling for a conceptual framework can be the development of a tool for sorting out the implied scope and level of problem conception that available works bring to their subject.

Further Research

One of the disadvantages in undertaking a conceptual framework is that it is difficult to conclude with the usual disclaimer that the answers to questions raised in closing lie far beyond the scope of the present undertaking. If a proposed conceptual framework is worth attention, treatment of issues germaine to its subject should be anything but beyond its scope. One feels obligated in this situation, then, to indicate not only how future work might proceed in general terms, but also to indicate the relation the present framework should be able to maintain with such future research, broadly defined.

With regard to possible foci of further research related to what we have called the role and individual personality dimensions, further laboratory studies are important. Aside from the obvious need to corroborate the findings reported here, some variations in task, expert/politico ratio, manner of communication, feedback on performance, and so on—would be most appropriate even on first inspection.

The pretesting of subjects to establish individual subject scores on assertiveness and other dimensions of interpersonal orientation is an important consideration. The corroboration of laboratory findings through archival investigation would also seem an appropriate next step.

In the latter regard, systematic investigation of memoir material involving several persons' recollections of what it meant to work with a given expert could be especially useful. One could indeed reconstruct through memoirs or establish through interviews the scores that historically significant experts would rate on standard diagnostic tests of interpersonal orientation.

Certainly all these forms of investigation appropriate for testing and refining our notions about experts should eventually be applied to the study of politico behavior in the same context. We need a behavioral, operations-level definition of a politico, as well as a close study of where the hack, the statesman, and the bureaucrat overlap, appear distinct within the larger politico category, or are indistinguishable.

Aside from behaviorists' perennial desire to administer paper-and-pencil tests to public figures, future case studies might include some consideration of the patterns that govern individual reactions to options portrayed in given ways. Too often the one-shot case study fails to consider, not the history of a given issue, but the history of given participants' reactions to categories of options that are associated with particular options open at the time.

Ideally, in addition to identifying real-world decision-makers' idiosyncratic limits on detached analysis, it may be possible to identify individuals' "pockets" or "islands" of irrationality within their psychic space of option evaluation, as it were, which they bring to particular problems. This would seem to be a feasible and useful line of investigation for those dealing with historical figures. Social—but even more, clinical—psychology can offer much by way of theory and technique in this regard. Political science has shown the great use to which economic theories of decision-making behavior can be applied. Some investigation of possibilities for theories of abnormal decision-making—idiosyncratic, "nonrational" individuals—may be worth the effort.

With regard to the organization, our presentation was in the spirit of viewing the organization as an arena of conflict with special properties of its own. Continued effort at understanding how the organizational setting can be manipulated by members is of unquestionable value. On the societal level, cross-national study comparing task (expert) and political elites (politicos) for differences in behavior within their respective countries, while further distinguishing by comparable stages of development, would surely be a tremendous advance in understanding the effects of social factors in expert-politico interaction.

I offer these suggestions for further expert-politico research with great timidity. Others have already shown that there is much to be learned about modern politics by investigating the role that so-called experts play in it. But the utility of conducting that investigation from the particular perspective offered here is, of course, another question. In any event, the perspective sketched in these pages will have proven useful if even in its discarding it precipitates some novel dialogue on so important an aspect of contemporary political life.

Appendix:

THE LOGIC OF FACTOR LABELING

Table 2.13 presents the rotated factor matrix of thirty-six variables for laymen. Table 2.14 presents the rotated factor matrix for experts. The matrices suggest that both the array of layman and expert scores can each be interpreted according to a four-factor structure. Tables 2.3, 2.4, 2.5, and 2.6 list the principle variables for each layman factor. Principle variables loading negatively are not rephrased to reflect the direction of loading. Such rephrasing is employed in Chapter 2. Combinations of variables connected by arrows reflect conceptual similarities among variables. The arrows are offered as aids in identifying the behavior pattern a factor seems to represent.

In Table 2.3 the first layman factor is described as tromped-on follower behavior. The label is based on an interpretation of the total context of principle loading variables. Variables 5, 8, and 26 are connected by arrows to indicate a conceptual similarity. In this factor, little positive references to one's own role and little negative references to politicos' role would indicate an elevation of politicos over the subject. This is reinforced by the co-occurrence of little positive references to subjects' own ability. Together these three behaviors share the implication of deference to counterparts. Little reference to group progress or politico tactics indicates

Table 2.13 Rotated Factor Matrix for Laymen

			Factor	
Variable*	1	2	3	4
1	0.10957	-0.06723	0.30674	0.58550
2	-0.17252	0.02678	0.43329	0.78615
3	-0.42459	-0.42977	0.24634	-0.03951
4	0.06872	0.69003	0.11664	-0.18661
5	-0.95049	-0.10429	-0.01353	0.08900
6	-0.05882	0.26543	0.30328	-0.31425
8	-0.95049	-0.10429	-0.01353	0.08900
9	0.11237	0.12798	-0.00185	0.58508
10	0.00620	-0.13786	0.53551	-0.00873
11	-0.06808	0.21679	0.58271	0.20637
12	-0.23371	0.61437	-0.30881	0.22486
13	-0.64638	-0.24253	0.42958	-0.02657
14	-0.85554	0.05007	0.12429	0.04699
15	-0.31678	-0.49306	0.03233	-0.06704
16	0.07264	0.47033	-0.09829	0.10621
19	0.12759	0.18253	-0.23074	0.68013
20	-0.66509	0.01589	0.15744	-0.24993
21	-0.41250	0.12161	-0.05081	-0.48027
22	-0.76735	0.09624	-0.21690	-0.14823
23	0.03363	0.14726	0.03153	-0.36021
24	-0.67678	-0.20837	-0.13944	0.00796
25	-0.65888	0.25553	-0.27897	-0.21409
26	-0.87932	0.12317	-0.10454	-0.11712
27	0.00060	0.66430	0.34052	-0.09001
29	-0.00535	-0.09657	-0.66874	-0.17996
31	0.11219	-0.15970	0.59241	-0.09741
32	0.35982	-0.45370	-0.16799	0.07073
33	0.13917	0.25162	0.36846	-0.26587
34	0.00509	0.68353	0.22806	0.05740
36	-0.71646	-0.14838	-0.37823	-0.03029
37	0.10806	0.59392	-0.13267	0.62935
38	-0.00336	-0.17610	0.28642	0.18132
39	0.08239	-0.50750	0.19207	0.18378
40	0.21308	-0.14622	-0.28584	0.04942
41	0.33998	0.13943	0.75130	-0.12790
42	0.25588	-0.22892	0.27810	-0.01320
	Cumulative Proportion of Total Variance			
	0.20478	0.31368	0.41571	0.49944

* Note that variables 7, 17, 18, 28, 30, and 35 are deleted from the factor analysis because of zero means for either or both groups.

Table 2.14 Rotated Factor Matrix for Experts

Variable*	Factor			
	1	2	3	4
1	-0.02485	-0.12402	0.02960	0.72455
2	0.41330	0.21284	0.07903	0.62511
3	-0.53055	0.20268	-0.51567	-0.00355
4	0.34004	-0.21552	-0.44759	-0.13322
5	-0.21281	0.30009	-0.54703	0.45699
6	-0.07145	-0.25207	0.02990	0.02726
8	0.09330	-0.07488	0.09078	-0.39032
9	-0.11866	-0.08254	0.41854	0.67625
10	-0.28259	-0.21974	0.16328	0.34375
11	0.30516	0.24472	0.35067	0.47907
12	0.05167	0.38627	-0.69268	0.13105
13	-0.03625	0.63078	0.25482	-0.42822
14	-0.22302	0.83004	0.03824	-0.04511
15	-0.31965	-0.02652	-0.27426	-0.01467
16	0.60946	0.44306	0.11713	0.00117
19	-0.10553	-0.05308	-0.63759	-0.00829
20	-0.15060	0.50323	0.05376	0.41149
21	0.29841	0.36382	0.02710	0.20506
22	0.00591	0.65702	-0.19491	-0.06821
23	0.72282	0.02287	-0.15289	-0.15370
24	-0.24670	0.73546	0.17161	0.03007
25	0.43830	0.15904	0.09848	-0.27377
26	0.17185	0.25464	-0.19222	0.03944
27	-0.49775	0.04909	-0.05395	-0.15286
29	-0.45569	0.08481	-0.00514	0.09964
31	-0.26881	0.06855	-0.06092	-0.35820
32	0.54582	-0.08330	-0.11149	-0.04074
33	-0.03226	0.06866	0.28187	-0.49015
34	0.25728	-0.24797	-0.65975	0.04145
36	-0.28190	0.01155	0.22707	-0.19544
37	0.00885	0.65247	0.30613	-0.02277
38	0.54641	0.22112	0.12902	0.36221
39	0.55170	0.54409	-0.13456	0.09161
40	-0.14751	0.25618	0.53152	0.22879
41	0.23769	-0.08096	0.48229	0.39963
42	0.50585	-0.16214	-0.24985	0.22315
	Cumulative Proportion of Total Variance			
	0.13034	0.24565	0.34481	0.43027

*Note that variables 7, 17, 18, 28, 30, and 35 are excluded from the factor analysis because of zero means for one or both groups.

absence of the meta-perspective which may be expressed as avoiding overview.

In little challenging response to personal attack (in the context of variables 5, 8, and 26) this pattern appears to involve taking abuse. The negative loading on variable 36 here appears best interpreted as aversion to questioning purpose. The most consistent interpretation of the remaining components is that they together represent an aversion to locking horns, or plotting, against others. The generally deferential tone, reluctance to question purpose, willingness to take abuse, avoidance of overview, and reluctance to lock horns—especially in light of insult behavior—suggest being at the mercy of others. The pattern seems to reflect clearly subordinate behavior. These notions seem best reflected in the label "tromped-on follower."

In Table 2.4 the second layman factor is marked company-man behavior. The co-occurrence of variables 4 and 34 suggest consensus-making. The variables can be interpreted as encouragement for sticking together on the basis of the need for agreement (consensus) because the grand coalition in this game cannot be rationally argued unless there is substantive agreement. Notice however that no behaviors are indicated which would actually involve movement toward solution agreement in substantive terms.

Similarly, while agreement as a principle is encouraged, variables 37 and 39 suggest that comments in favor of action are not followed up. There is a characteristic lack of follow-through. Variable 27 indicates at the same time that there is self-effacement in this pattern. The image is one of arid and lofty (overview) commentary on the merits of agreement and the team perspective, coupled with a low self-opinion and no follow-up. The pattern also distinctly excludes substantive problem action. The company-man label is designed to reflect these features on the assumption that the phrase involves images of vapid yes-men.

The third layman factor is presented in Table 2.5. It is labeled cooperative, contributing-follower behavior. Variables 10 and 11 suggest an anxiousness to invite and offer proposals for problem solution. However the absence of any monitoring in terms of structuring counterpart consideration of proposals, combined with the co-occurrence of variable 41, shows no pressuring associated with the interest in proposed solutions. Variable 29 seems especially significant (conceptually) in this regard. Note variable 31. In this context it indicates that the solution interest is not frivolous. It is also consistent with variable 41 in the implication of a conciliating, nonrigid posture. However, there is no indication of any leadership pattern. This combination of components suggests the cooperative, contributing-follower label. It reflects constructive participation without any authoritative element.

Table 2.6 presents the fourth layman factor. In this factor, variables 1 and 2 indicate communicativeness. Variable 9 suggests a disposition to deal with the problem in substantive terms and a willingness to pressure others for their solution views. (Note that the co-occurrence of these variables is interpreted differently for the fourth expert factor because the context of remaining variables is different.) The display of positive responses to offers of secret coalition indicate in context, a readiness to follow in intrigue. This implies preparedness to alienate a third party. In context, variable 37 suggests a readiness to make demands.

The behaviors associated with this pattern seem to contribute to a general tone of active participation. There does not seem to be any pretension to leadership here; coalitions are not initiated. Monitoring or structuring counterparts seems minimal in this context. There is, however, a clear preparedness to alienate under certain circumstances as well as a preparedness to exert pressure (but not leadership) in a sense. The image here seems to be of one who does not lead, but whose following is at the same time conditional on his interests being attended to insofar as they may be specified. To reflect the nonleadership description and at the same time the absence of any unconditional cooperativeness, the label conditional-follower behavior was applied.

Table 2.7 presents the first expert factor. The negative loading of variable 3 suggests an aversion to opting out which may be stated positively as a commitment to the group format. The co-occurrence of variable 16 may be interpreted in this context as an interest in building consensus. For, unlike secret coalitions, open coalitions (though for two) may be interpreted as steps toward unanimity. They lack the calculating tone of secret coalitions because they are by definition announced to the third member.

Similarly in this vein, variable 42 indicates a willingness to compromise for the sake of unanimity. Unanimity is involved here because, unlike variable 41 concerned with the number of concessions made throughout interaction, variable 42 measures the concession value of the final offer. It is the subject's best judgment of the offer that he can make that would be most attractive to counterparts while still preferable to no agreement for him. This offer may represent, in a sense, the value of maintaining the triad.

Variable 23 indicates that the subject will avoid confrontation. Defusing might be more appropriate since the subjects' behavior here involves low-key responses rather than, for example, a negative loading on insults initiated. Variable 32 suggests a solution orientation. It is not viewed as a flaunting of expertise because variable 27 (negative references to own ability) loads at .497.

Variables 38 and 39 suggest structuring and subsequent monitoring of counterpart behavior. Sending identical messages indicates coordination and a concern with clarifying positions perhaps, and generally seeking greater coherence in exchange. Requests for reports on other dyads in this context may be interpreted as patterned follow-up behavior.

The co-occurrence of tendencies to structure, clarify, and monitor with tendencies to build consensus, compromise for unanimity, sidestep confrontation, and a solution orientation suggest, in toto, brokerage. Because the broker here would necessarily be a participant with his own interest in the proceedings, the factor is labeled participating-broker behavior.

Table 2.8 presents the second expert factor. In this factor, references to group progress and politico tactics indicate a sensitivity to overview. Rejection of all forms of two-person coalition suggests aloofness. References to progress (variable 13), to counterpart behavior (variable 14), giving instructions (variable 37), and requesting feedback on others' interactions (variable 39) all suggest extensive monitoring and evaluation when viewed as a group.

Variables 22 and 24 indicate fighter-like behavior for obvious reasons. In the larger context, variables 37 and 39 together suggest order-giving and follow-up as well as contributing to the notion of monitoring and evaluation generally. The image in sum is one of taking the long view, aloofness, fighter behavior, and order-giving with follow-up expectations. The leader label seems to capture this combination of implications best. The leader behavior implied is dictatorial, aggressive leadership, especially given the emphasis on close monitoring, belligerency, order-giving, all in the context of presumably informal interaction.

Table 2.9 presents the third expert factor. Variable 40 suggests independent-mindedness for obvious reasons. The co-occurrence of variables, 3, 19, and 34—all with negative loadings—suggests a commitment to format but an aversion to alignment. In this regard, both the secret (variable 19) and the grand (variable 34) coalition are aversive. However, the format (variable 3) is valued. This suggests that the primary element in variable 34 is the grand coalition and not the object of the game. The negative loading on variable 21 in the context of variable 34 and variable 5 suggests that abstraction (here role, unanimity, and the group dilemma) is alien to this pattern. This is described as no overview. In sum, the co-occurrence of a lack of overview, commitment to format but aversion to alignment, and independent-mindedness (in the absence of hostility) suggests a pattern best described as nonhostile, independent behavior. The image is one of detachment and suppressed overview, but without personal friction.

Table 2.10 presents the fourth expert factor. This table includes variables 11 and 33 to provide more clues in arriving at a label. The variables score .479 and − .490 respectively.

In this factor, variables 1 and 2 together indicate much communication. Variable 9 is interpreted as testing and direction-seeking in the absence of any monitoring or otherwise assertive or controlling behavior. In this context, variables 11 and 33 seem to indicate a preoccupation with task (note variable 11 occurs with variable 9 in this pattern). The indication is also an aversion to triad dynamics, or abstractions. The judgment regarding variable 33 stems from there being no other anti-coalition behaviors or belligerent behaviors in this factor. This suggests that variable 33 does not here involve an anti-alignment posture.

This seems especially true since such an anti-alignment posture would seem more closely related to two-person behaviors, given that grand coalition issues may be associated more with reaching the group's goal than with strategic combination. Furthermore the presence of variables 1 and 2 in this factor suggest that variable 33 should not be interpreted as withdrawal of any sort. It seems that viewing this pattern as insecure behavior allows for a consistent and integrated view of all the components. There is testing and direction-seeking, task concern, aversion to discussing triad dynamics, and much communication. The latter would be consistent with an anxiousness to clarify or a general groping which, we may speculate, captures the tone here. Notice the absence of any monitoring, which seems consistent with the label.

This concludes the discussion of the logic factor labeling.

BIBLIOGRAPHY

Adams, S. "Social climate and productivity in small military groups," *American Sociological Review*, 1954, 19, pp. 421-5.

Allison, G. *Essence of Decision: Explaining the Cuban Missile Crisis* (Boston: Little Brown, 1971).

Allport, G. "The Historical Background of Modern Social Psychology." In G. Lindzey (ed.) *Handbook of Social Psychology* (Cambridge: Addison-Wesley, 1954) pp. 3-55.

Backman, C. and P. Secord. *Social Psychology* (New York: McGraw-Hill, 1964).

Bailey, F. G. "Decisions by Consensus in Councils and Committees: With Special Reference to Village and Local Government in India," *Political Systems and the Distribution of Power*, Association of Social Anthropologists of the Commonwealth, Monographs 2 (New York: Praeger, 1965).

Bales, R. F. *Interaction Process Analysis* (New York: Addison-Wesley, 1950).

Bandura, A. *Principles of Behavior Modification* (New York: Holt, Rinehart & Winston, 1969).

Banfield, Edward. *Political Influence* (New York: The Free Press, 1961).

Barnard, C. I. *The Functions of the Executive* (Cambridge: Harvard University Press, 1968).

Baruch, B. M. *U.S. Atomic Energy Proposals* (Washington, D.C.: U.S. Government Printing Office, 1946).

Berrien, F. K. "A General Systems Approach to Human Groups." M. D. Rubin (ed.). *Man in Systems* (New York: Gordon and Breach, 1971).

Bijou, S. W. and D. M. Baer. *Child Development I: A Systematic and Empirical Theory* (New York: Appleton-Century-Crofts, 1961).

Black, G. S. "A Theory of Professionalization in Politics," *American Political Science Review*, LXIV, 3, September 1970, pp. 865-78.

Blau, P. M. *The Dynamics of Bureaucracy* (Chicago: University of Chicago Press, 1963).

———. *Exchange and Power in Social Life* (New York: Wiley, 1964).

Brewer, G. D. *Politicians, Bureaucrats, and the Consultant* (New York: Basic Books, 1973).

Campbell, Donald and Julian Stanley. *Experimental and Quasi-Experimental Designs for Research* (Chicago: Rand McNally, 1963).

Cartwright, D. "Risk-taking by individuals and groups," *Journal of Personality and Social Psychology*, XX, 3, 1971, pp. 361-78.

Chertkoff, J. M. and M. Conley. "Opening offer and frequency of concession as bargaining and strategies," *Journal of Personality and Social Psychology*, 7, pp. 181-85.

Cole, D. " 'Rational argument' and 'prestige-suggestion' as factors influencing judgment," *Sociometry*, 17, 1954, pp. 350-54.

Cressey, D. R. "Prison Organizations." In J. March (ed.). *Handbook of Organizations* (Chicago: Rand McNally, 1965).

Curry, R. L., Jr., and L. L. Wade. *A Theory of Political Exchange* (Englewood Cliffs, N.J.: Prentice-Hall, 1968).

Dalton, Melville. *Men Who Manage* (New York: Wiley, 1959).

Deutsch, Karl. *The Nerves of Government* (New York: Free Press, 1966).

———. "Communication Models and Decision Systems." In J. Charlesworth (ed.). *Contemporary Political Analysis* (New York: Free Press, 1967).

Dorsey, J. T., Jr. "A communication model for administration," *Administrative Science Quarterly*, 2, 1957, pp. 307-24.

Downs, A. *An Economic Theory of Democracy* (New York: Harper, 1957).

———. *Inside Bureaucracy* (Boston: Little, Brown, 1968).

Dreikurs, Rudolph. *Children: The Challenge* (New York: Hawthorn, 1964).

Easton, D. "Political anthropology," *Biennial Review of Anthropology*, B.J. Seigel (ed.) *Stanford University Press, 1959)* pp. 237-45.

Easton, David. *The Political System* (New York: Knopf, 1967).

Ellul, J. *The Technological Society* (New York: Vintage, 1964).

Etzioni, A. "Authority structure and organizational effectiveness," *Administrative Science Quarterly*, 4, 1960, pp. 43-47.

———. *Modern Organizations* (Englewood Cliffs, N.J.: Prentice-Hall, 1964).

Falk, R. A. *This Endangered Planet* (New York: Vintage, 1971).

Festinger, L. *A Theory of Cognitive Dissonance* (New York: Harper, 1957).

Freemont, Lyden and Miller (eds.). *Planning Programming Budgeting* (Chicago: Markham, 1972).

Freidin, S. and G. Bailey. *The Experts* (New York: Macmillan, 1968).

Freud, S. *Civilization and Its Discontents* (New York: Norton, 1962).

———. "Infantile Sexuality." In S. Freud. *Three Essays on the Theory of Sexuality* (New York: Avon, 1962).

Friedman, R. *Professionalism: Expertise and Policy Making* (New York: General Learning Press, 1971).

Galbraith, J. K. *The Affluent Society* (New York: Mentor, 1958).

———. *How to Control the Military* (New York: Doubleday, 1969).

———. *The New Industrial State* (Boston: Houghton Mifflin, 1967).

Garson, G. D. "On the origins of interest-group theory: A critique of a process," *American Political Science Review*, 68, 4, December 1974, pp. 1505-19.

George, A. L. "The case for multiple advocacy in making foreign policy," *American Political Science Review*, LXVI, 3, September 1972, pp. 751-85.

Gerth, H. and C. Mills. From Max Weber. *Essays in Sociology* (New York: Oxford University Press, 1958).

Gilpin, Robert. *American Scientists and Nuclear Weapons Policy* (Princeton, New Jersey: Princeton University Press, 1962).

Glass, J. "Consciousness and organization; the disintegration of Joseph K and Bob Slocum," *Administration and Society*, 7, 3, November 1975, pp. 366-84.

Goldner, F. H. "The Division of Labor: Process and Power," M. N. Zald (ed.). *Power in Organizations* (Nashville: Vanderbilt University Press, 1970).

Golembiewski, R. T. *Organizing Men and Power: Patterns of Behavior and Line-Staff Models* (Chicago: Rand McNally, 1967).

———. "Small Groups and Large Organizations," J. G. March (ed.). *Handbook of Organizations* (Chicago: Rand McNally, 1965).

Gulick, L. H. and L. Urwick (eds.). *Papers on the Science of Administration* (New York: Institute of Public Administration, 1937).

Haberer, J. *Politics and the Community of Science* (New York: Van Nostrand, Reinhold, 1969).

Halberstam, D. *The Best and the Brightest* (New York: Random House, 1972).

Halperin, Morton. "The Gaither Committee and the policy process," *World Politics*, XIII, no. 3, pp. 360-84.

Hare, Paul. *Handbook of Small Group Research* (New York: Free Press, 1962).

Hill, M. J. *The Sociology of Public Administration* (New York: Crane, Russak, 1972).

Holst, Johan. 'Strategic Arms Control and Stability: A Retrospective Look." In J. Holst and William Schneider, Jr. (eds.). *Why ABM: Policy Issues in the Missile Defense Controversy* (New York: Pergamon, 1969).

Hoops, Townsend. *The Limits of Intervention* (New York: McKay, 1969).

Howton, F. W. *Functionaries* (Chicago: Quadrangle, 1969).

Ikle, Fred. *How Nations Negotiate* (New York: Harper, 1964).

Inkeles, A. "Sociology and Psychology." In S. Kotch (ed.). *Psychology: A Study of a Science*, VI (New York: McGraw-Hill, 1963).

Janis, I. L. *Victims of Groupthink* (Boston: Houghton Mifflin, 1972).

Jencks, C. *Inequality* (New York: Basic, 1972).

Kahn, D. *The Codebreakers* (New York: Macmillan, 1967).

Kaplan, Abraham. *The Conduct of Inquiry* (San Francisco: Chandler, 1964).

Kaufman, Johan. *Conference Diplomacy* (New York: Oceana Press, 1968).

Kelly, H. and T. W. Lamb. "Certainty of judgment and resistance to social influence," *Journal of Abnormal and Social Psychology*, 1957, 50, pp. 137-39.

Kluckholn, Clyde. *Mirror for Man* (Greenwich, Connecticut: Fawcett, 1963).

Lall, A. *Modern International Negotiation* (New York: Columbia University Press, 1966).

Landau, Martin. "Decision theory and comparative public administration," *Comparative Political Studies*, I, 2, July 1968).

———. *Political Science and Political Theory* (New York: Macmillan, 1972).

———. "Redundancy, rationality, and the problem of duplication and overlap," *Public Administration Review*, vol. XXIX, no. 4, July/August 1969.

Lasswell, H.D. *Power and Personality* (New York: Viking, 1962).

Leary, Timothy. *Interpersonal Diagnosis of Personality* (New York: Ronald Press, 1957).

Lerner, Abba. "Consumer's surplus and micro-macro," *Journal of Political Economy*, vol. 71, 1963, pp. 76-81.

Lerner, Allan W. " 'Experts' and 'Politicos' in Negotiating Situations: An Experimental Analog to a Critical Class of Encounter." In R. T. Golembiewski (ed.).

Two Decades of Small Group Research in Political Science (Athens, Georgia: University of Georgia Press, 1976).

    Experts, Politicians, and Decisionmaking in the Technological Society (Morristown, New Jersey: General Learning Press, 1976).

Levinson, H. "Reciprocation: The relationship between man and organization," *Administrative Science Quarterly,* 9, 4, March 1965, pp. 370-90.

Lieber, R. M. et al. "The effects of initial offer on interpersonal negotiation," *Journal of Experimental Social Psychology,* 1968, 4, pp. 431-41.

Lieberman, J. K. *The Tyranny of the Experts* (New York: Walker, 1970).

Liebert, R. M. et al. "The effects of information and magnitude of initial offer on interpersonal negotiation," *Journal of Experimental Social Psychology,* 1968, 4, pp. 431-41.

Likert, R. *New Patterns of Management* (New York: McGraw-Hill, 1961).

Lindblom, C. E. "The science of 'muddling through,'" *Public Administration Review,* XIX, 1959.

Lindblom, C.E. and D. Braybrooke. *A Strategy of Decision: Policy Evaluation as a Social Process* (New York: Free Press, 1963).

March, J. G. and H. Simon with H. Guetzkow. *Organizations* (New York: Wiley, 1958).

Marcy, C. M. *Presidential Commissions* (New York: King's Crown Press, 1945).

Mausner, B. "The effect of one partner's success in a relevant task on the interaction of observer pairs," *Journal of Abnormal and Social Psychology,* 1954, 49, pp. 557-60.

Merton, Robert. *Social Theory and Social Structure* (New York: Free Press, 1968).

Mitchell, W. C. "The Shape of Political Theory to Come: From Political Sociology to Political Economy." Paper presented at the meeting of the American Political Science Association, Chicago, 1967.

Moos, R. H. and J. C. Speisman. "Group compatibility and productivity," *Journal of Abnormal and Social Psychology,* LXV, 3, pp. 190-196.

Morgenthau, Hans. *Politics Among Nations* (New York: Knopf, 1965).

Mouzelis, Nicos P. *Organization and Bureaucracy: An Analysis of Modern Theories* (Chicago: Aldine, 1968).

Neustadt, R. E. *Presidential Power* (New York: Wiley, 1964).

New York State Legislative Annual, 1971, pp. 226-27.

The New York Times. August 19, 1970: 1:7; August 26, 1970: 82:1; November 14, 1970: 1:2; November 19, 1970: 94:4.

Nicolson, H. *The Evolution of Diplomatic Method* (London: Constable, 1954).

Parsons, Talcott. *Structure and Process in Modern Societies* (Glencoe, Illinois: Free Press, 1960).

Pavitt, K. "Technology, International Competition and Economic Growth." *World Politics,* XXV, 2, January 1973, pp. 183-205.

Piccard, P. J. (ed.). *Science and Policy Issues: Lectures in Government and Science* (Itasca, Illinois: F. E. Peacock, 1969).

Presthus, R. V. *The Organizational Society* (New York: Vintage, 1965).

Price, D. K. "The Diffusion of Sovereignty." In R. T. Golembiewski et al. (eds.). *Public Administration* (Chicago: Rand McNally, 1976).

Pruitt, D. and J. L. Drews. "The effect of time pressure, time elapsed, and the opponent's concession rate on behavior in negotiation," *Journal of Experimental Social Psychology*, 1969, 5, pp. 43-60.

Pruitt, D. and D. F. Johnson. "Mediation as an aid to face-saving in negotiation," *Journal of Personality and Social Psychology*, 1970, 14.

Putney, G. and S. Putney. *The Adjusted American* (New York: Harper, 1966).

Quine, W. *From a Logical Point of View* (New York: Harper, 1963).

Raven, B. H. and J. I. Shaw. Interdependence and group problem-solving in the triad," *Journal of Personality and Social Psychology*, 1970, 14, pp. 157-65.

Reich, C. *The Greening of America* (New York: Random, 1970).

Reynolds, G. S. *A Primer of Operant Conditioning* (Glenview, Illinois: Scott, Foresman, 1968).

Riker, William. *A Theory of Political Coalitions* (New Haven: Yale University Press, 1962).

Rosenthal, R. and Rosnon. *Artifact in Behavioral Research* (New York: Academic Press, 1964).

Rummel, R. "Understanding factor analysis," *Journal of Conflict Resolution*, II, 4, pp. 444-80.

Schattschneider, E. E. *The Semi-Sovereign People* (New York: Holt, Rinehart & Winston, 1960).

Schelling, Thomas. *The Strategy of Conflict* (Cambridge: Harvard University Press, 1960).

Schlesinger, Arthur M., Jr. *A Thousand Days* (Greenwich, Connecticut: Fawcett Publications, 1967).

Schlesinger, J. A. *Ambition and Politics* (Chicago: Rand McNally, 1966).

Schlossberger, J. A. "The Individual as a Complex Open System." In M. D. Rubin (ed.). *Man in Systems* (New York: Gordon and Breach, 1971).

Schutz, W. *The Interpersonal Underworld* (Palo Alto, California: Science and Behavior Books, 1970).

Selznick, P. *TVA and the Grass Roots* (New York: Harper and Row, 1966).

Simon, H. *Administrative Behavior* (New York: Free Press, 1965).

. *Models of Man* (New York: Wiley, 1957).

Simon, H., D. Smithburg and V. Thompson. *Public Administration* (New York: Knopf, 1964).

Skinner, B. F. *Beyond Freedom and Dignity* (New York: Knopf, 1971).

Slater, P. *The Pursuit of Loneliness* (Boston: Beacon Press, 1971).

Smesler, William. "Dominance as a factor in achievement and perception in cooperative problem-solving interactions," *Journal of Abnormal and Social Psychology*, LXII, 3, 1961, pp. 535-42.

Snow, C. P. *Science and Government* (Cambridge: Harvard University Press, 1961).

Soule, J. W. and J. W. Clarke. "Amateurs and professionals: A study of delegates to the 1968 Democratic National Convention," *American Political Science Review*, LXIV, 3, September 1970, pp. 865-78.

Spielberger, C. "The Effects of Anxiety on Complex Learning and Academic Achievement." In C. Spielberger (ed.). *Anxiety and Behavior* (New York: Academic, 1966).

Starbuck, W. H. and D. F. Grant. "Bargaining strategies with asymmetric initiation and termination," *Applied Social Psychology*, 1971, I, pp. 344-63.

Stein, E. and E. Jacobson. *Diplomats, Scientists and Politicians: The United States and the Nuclear Test-Ban Negotiations* (Ann Arbor, Michigan: University of Michigan Press, 1964).

Strauss, A. "The Hospital and its Negotiated Order." In E. Freidson (ed.). *The Hospital in Modern Society* (New York: Free Press, 1963).

Strickland, D. R. *Scientists in Politics* (Lafayette, Indiana: Purdue University Studies, 1968).

Szent-Györgyi, A. *The Crazy Ape* (New York: Grosset and Dunlap, 1971).

Taylor, D. "Decision-Making and Problem-Solving." In J. March (ed.) *Handbook of Organizations* (Chicago: Rand McNally, 1965).

Thayer, Charles, *Diplomat,* (New York: Harper, 1959).

Thayer, F. C. *An End to Hierarchy! An End to Competition!* (New York: New Viewpoints, 1973).

Thibaut, J. W. and H. H. Kelley. *The Social Psychology of Groups* (New York: Wiley, 1959).

Thompson, J. D. and A. Tuden. "Strategies, Structures and Processes of Organizational Decision." In J. D. Thompson et al. (eds.). *Comparative Studies in Administration* (Pittsburgh: University of Pittsburgh Press, 1959).

Thompson, V. A. *Bureaucracy and Innovation* (University, Alabama: University of Alabama Press, 1969).

. *Bureaucracy and the Modern World* (Morristown, New Jersey: General Learning Press, 1976).

. *Modern Organization* (New York: Knopf, 1961).

Toffler, A. *Future Shock* (New York: Bantam, 1971).

Truman, David. *The Governmental Process: Political Interests and Public Opinion* (New York: Knopf, 1951).

Tullock, G. *The Politics of Bureaucracy* (Washington, D.C.: Public Affairs Press, 1965).

Turner, C. *How Communists Negotiate* (New York: Macmillan, 1955).

U.S. Congress. *Administration of National Security,* Subcommittee on National Security Staffing and Operations, Eighty-Eighth Congress. (Washington, D.C.: U.S. Government Printing Office, 1965).

Vinokur, A. "Cognitive and affective processes influencing risk-taking in groups: An expected utility approach," *Journal of Personality and Social Psychology,* XX, 3, 1971, pp. 472-86.

Voss, E. H. *Nuclear Ambush: The Test-Ban Trap* (Chicago: Regenery, 1963).

Walton, C. C. and F. W. Cleveland, Jr. *Corporations on Trial: The Electric Cases* (Belmont, California: Wadsworth, 1964).

Weiss, Robert L. "Negotiating Therapy in Marriage." Paper presented at meeting of Western Psychological Association, San Francisco, 1971.

. Unpublished research on outside reinforcers and the dyad. Department of Psychology, University of Oregon.

Whyte, W. H., Jr. *The Organization Man* (New York: Anchor, 1957).

Winch, R. 'The theory of complementary needs in mate selection: A test of one kind of complementariness," *American Sociological Review,* XX, 1955, pp. 52-56.

York, H. F. *Race to Oblivion: A Participant's View of the Arms Race* (New York: Simon and Schuster, 1970).

Young, O. R. *The Intermediaries* (Princeton: Princeton University Press, 1967).

Zaleznik, Abraham. Paper presented at the meeting of the American Psychoanalytic Association, New York, 1971.

Ziller, R. C. "Scales of judgment: A determinant of the accuracy of group decisions," *Human Relations,* 1955, 8, pp. 153-64.

ABOUT THE AUTHOR

ALLAN W. LERNER took his B.A. at Brooklyn College, CUNY, and his M.A. and Ph.D. at the University of Oregon. His main areas of interest are Bureaucratic Politics, Public Administration, and International Relations. Dr. Lerner is the author of "Experts, Politicians, and Decisionmaking in the Technological Society" (General Learning Press module) and other articles. He is currently working on the problem of ambiguity and its effect on organizations. His present position is with the Department of Political Science, Herbert H. Lehman College, CUNY.